W9-BWD-527

Beyond Burnham:

An Illustrated History of Planning for the Chicago Region

This drawing, labeled "An Interurban Roadway: Parallel Team, Trolley, and Pleasure Ways," was created in 1908 by the Commercial Club of Chicago's interurban roadways sub-committee in support of the *Plan of Chicago*. Although automobiles were still in their infancy, some saw a future in having trams and road vehicles sharing the byways. *(Special Collections, Lake Forest College library)*

Beyond Burnham:

An Illustrated History of Planning
for the Chicago Region

LAKE
FOREST
COLLEGE
PRESS

HT
168
.C5
S39
2009

First published 2009 Lake Forest College Press

Box A-16
Lake Forest College
555 N. Sheridan Road
Lake Forest, IL 60045

lakeforest.edu/lfcpress

Copyright © Lake Forest College Press 2009

All rights reserved

Lake Forest College Press, based at Chicago's National Liberal Arts College, publishes in the broad spaces of Chicago studies. Our imprint, &NOW Books, publishes innovative and conceptual literature, and serves as the publishing arm of the &NOW writers' conference and organization.

ISBN-13: 978-0-9823156-1-3
ISBN 10: 0-9823156-1-9

Book design by Omar Garcia
Pastels featured on cover by Nancie King Mertz (far left) and Mitch Markovich (far right).

Printed in the United States

LAKE
FOREST
COLLEGE
PRESS

ACKNOWLEDGEMENTS

This volume would not have been possible without the extensive editorial and research contributions of John A. Shuler and Jim Bowman. We are also indebted to John Allen, Lawrence Christmas, and Andrew Plummer for their assistance.

We would like to acknowledge the following individuals who provided interviews or shared information: Susan Aaron, Lorenz Aggens, John Baird, Frank H. Beal, David Boyce, Robert Bruegmann, MarySue Barrett, Norm Carlson, Michael Davidson, Joseph DiJohn, Robert Ducharme, Michael H. Ebner, Norman Elkin, Robert Fishman, Reuben Hedlund, Doris Holeb, George Hemmens, Charles Hoch, Ellen Rockwell Galland, Jacques Gourguechon, Daniel Lauber, Ann Lousin, Larry Lund, Laurie Marston, R. Eden Martin, Scott McFarland, Dennis McClendon, Judith McBrien, Corrine Proctor, George A. Ranney, Jr., Eugene Schlickman, Kristen Schaffer, Lisa Schrenk, Adele Simmons, Marshall Suloway, Jack Siegal, Deborah Stone, Rachel Weber, Mary Woolever, and David Young. We also thank the descendants and relatives of Daniel H. Burnham, Jr., especially Lyn Burnham Messner and Liza Otis.

Many individuals at DePaul University also lent a hand, including Hugh Bartling, Lauren Fischer, Kathryn DeGraff, Gloria Simo, Joseph Kearney, and Liz Wilp, as well as recent graduates of the School of Public Service, especially Sara Smith.

Finally, we also recognize Robert Boylan and the Chaddick Foundation for their assistance and support as well as staff at Lake Forest College, including Omar Garcia, Art Miller, Sarah Spoto, Edward Brown, Emily Snowberg, and Davis Schneiderman, Director of Lake Forest College Press.

University Libraries
Carnegie Mellon University
Pittsburgh, PA 15213-3890

TABLE OF CONTENTS

LIST OF ACRONYMS

CATS – Chicago Area Transportation Study

CMAP – Chicago Metropolitan Agency for Planning

IDOT – Illinois Department of Transportation

ISTHA – Illinois State Toll Highway Authority

MWRD – Metropolitan Water Reclamation District

MPC – Metropolitan Planning Council (formerly MHPC)

MHPC – Metropolitan Housing and Planning Council

NIPC – Northeastern Illinois Planning Commission and
Northeastern Illinois Metropolitan Area Planning Commission *(prior to 1967)*

RPA – Chicago Regional Planning Association

RTA – Regional Transportation Authority

A group gathers at City Hall on December 18, 1959 to commemorate the 50th anniversary of the Chicago Plan Commission. Pictured *(l-r)* are commission member Ira Bach; Daniel H. Burnham, Jr.; Mrs. Ella T. Wacker, widow of the advisory body's first chairman Charles Wacker; James C. Downs, Jr.,; Mayor Richard J. Daley; and commission chairman Clair Roddewig. *(Chicago Tribune)*

At a late 1959 event, Mayor Richard J. Daley, standing with Daniel Burnham, Jr., Edward Bennett, Jr., and Mrs. Charles Wacker, praised the 1909 *Plan of Chicago* and its authors, Daniel Burnham and Edward Bennett. Fifty years after that landmark plan was published, Chicago's powerful mayor and the famous planners' descendents stood side by side to honor its legacy. Daley used the occasion to highlight his own efforts to "achieve the renewal of cities," revealing not only the plan's living legacy, but its continuing power to inspire, even in an era vastly different from that of Burnham and Bennett's.[1]

INTRODUCTION:
THE STORY OF THE CENTURY

That moment fifty years ago occurred during a great urban transformation, with the metropolitan region reinventing itself once again in dramatic ways. Superhighways were spreading out from the heart of the region, while more than 100 miles of new "tollways" opened in a single year. A magnificent new international airport connected travelers to cities around the world. To remain competitive, commuter railroads poured millions of dollars into modernization. Suburban communities on the region's periphery prepared for an explosion of housing subdivisions, shopping centers, and industrial parks.

Regional planners, meanwhile, imagined the *distant* future, looking to Burnham and Bennett's plan as the gold standard by which to measure their efforts. Transportation planners devised an enormous, technically sophisticated analysis to determine how people should move through the region. Land-use planners also began to prepare the metropolitan region for its seemingly ceaseless expansion, proposing the best arrangement of land and people. Daley moved forward with his ambitious 1958 Central Area Plan, considering it a sequel to the portions of the 1909 *Plan* that focused on downtown Chicago.

Today, fifty years after his father, and 100 years after Burnham, Mayor Richard M. Daley still invokes the *Plan of Chicago* in his efforts to propel the city into a new global age. Occasionally, suburban leaders also turn to it, mining the plan for ideas that lend support to their own initiatives. The 2009 centennial celebrations for the "Burnham Plan" strengthened its legacy, giving impetus to improve and expand regional "greenways," while cultivating public support for yet another comprehensive plan for the metropolitan area.

A Compelling Story of Regional Planning

This book, *Beyond Burnham: An Illustrated History of Planning for the Chicago Region*, describes a century of public and civic initiatives to transform the Chicago region. We attempt to demonstrate how the vision for the region, as conveyed in planning initiatives, has changed over time. We tell this story through the experiences of people—the generations of professional and citizen planners coming after Burnham and Bennett—who believed that change could be achieved through the creation of great plans.

From the beginning to the end of the story, the *Plan of Chicago* remains an inspiration, even while gradually losing much of its direct relevance. Like all plans, it was a creature of its time. Some of its ideas fell into obsolescence as the region became more complex, transitioning from a city of railroads and streetcar lines to a huge metropolitan area served by a dynamic mix of trains, planes, buses, and automobiles. Small suburbs around train stations became large population centers supported by busy arterial roads connecting subdivisions, malls and office parks. As the region changed, so did the visions and values of planners.

Prevalent themes appear and reappear throughout this history. Nevertheless, in writing this book, we were impressed not so much by the plans but by the people. Their energy and their confidence in their ability to shape the future helped to prepare metropolitan Chicago for its role as a global city. For the region's leaders, the *Plan of Chicago* remains of timeless value, offering a bold demonstration of how to create a compelling vision of a better region, which is to say a better home, through planning.

Nevertheless, planners coming after Burnham and Bennett have found encore performances to be no easy tasks. They assumed an increasingly technical apparatus, with their plans looking more and more like technical documents—even while they tried to infuse these with the human substance that inspires change. Still, as new generations of professional and citizen planners pushed for new plans for the region, they found much to learn from the past. That learning process continues today.

A Story of Consensus and Conflict

Readers will see that conflict is a major part of our story. Big plans collide with fierce political opposition, as strong-willed citizens confront official planning organizations. Opponents of coordinated planning see its recomendations as a harbinger of socialism or, at least, of unwanted intrusion into local affairs. While the city of Chicago often looked to regional planning with indifference, or for its own gain, the suburbs often viewed planning with resentment and suspicion. From these tales of confrontation and cooperation, regional vision and rivalry, a compelling story emerges. Our chapters show that creating and implementing plans for a region as complex as metropolitan Chicago is profoundly difficult.

Even the most seasoned, reasonable advocates of regional planning, like prominent real estate executive John Baird, despaired over the prospect of ever gaining real regional consensus. "We have to come face-to-face with the hard reality that . . . the legal structure within which our society operates has clearly NOT accepted planning as an important, much less an essential activity," he wrote almost forty years ago, in his letter of resignation from the Northeastern Illinois Planning Commission (NIPC).[2] Readers of this book will come to understand why Baird and others sometimes despaired yet carried on, and why their work in some ways succeeded.

This cycle of planning hope and frustration plays out in a distinctly local way, as the labyrinth of local government structures confounds decision making. An almost Byzantine arrangement of municipalities, townships, counties, park districts, school districts, water districts, and even cemetery districts, leaves regional planners with little choice but to paint on a canvas that always seems to fray. The fractured governance prevents the Chicago region from achieving the sort of civic consensus that sometimes appears in other, smaller metropolitan areas. Yet, in spite of all of this, a vibrant "global city" emerges.

We do not provide more than brief summaries of the histories of planning institutions; nor do we discuss in detail many planning achievements that are specific to the city of Chicago. Instead, we attempt to tell a regional story focusing on the people and organizations who promoted various visions for the metropolitan area's future. We describe critical events that frame this history, starting with the build up to the heavily publicized moment when the *Plan of Chicago* was presented to the world—on July 4, 1909.

This image, created using extended time-exposure photography, offers an artistic perspective of the People's Gas Building *(center)*, designed by Daniel Burnham & Co., and other properties in the South Michigan Avenue Historic District. The income Burnham earned from such projects allowed him to create many of his city plans on a pro bono basis. This view faces northwest from the Art Institute of Chicago. *(Ben Toews and Kelsie Kliner Collection)*

The story, of course, is interwoven into a broader American saga about enormous urban change over the last century. Ultimately, we want readers to see the progression of ideas and initiatives in response to changing times. Readers will understand that, while some planning efforts succeeded and others failed, they together become part of a tapestry of urban and suburban development, one inadequately documented in previous works.

Structure of the Book

Chapters 1 through 5 span the period from the *Plan of Chicago* to the dawn of the Interstate Highway era in the mid-1950s. These chapters show the significant progress that civic institutions made in promoting and implementing the 1909 *Plan*, starting with Charles Wacker's Chicago Plan Commission. Daniel Burnham, Jr., also comes to the fore, working to advance the agenda of the Chicago Regional Planning Association across a growing suburbia. After World War II, dynamic civic organizations, such as the Metropolitan Housing and Planning Council, push for new and more powerful state-sponsored planning organizations.

Chapters 6 through 11 follow the second half of the century from the late 1950s to the early 2000s, when state-sponsored public agencies take leading roles. We divide the story into separate, but related, narratives. The first three chapters discuss transportation planning, while the next three focus primarily on land-use planning. These chapters describe the work of generations of planners who struggled to bring transportation plans into more comprehensive schemes, ones that were understood and accepted by the public. We see, for example, how NIPC's "Finger Plan" of the late 1960s—the first comprehensive plan since Burnham and Bennett's—offers a new vision for the future derived from a methodology quite different from that of the 1909 *Plan*.

In Chapter 12, we describe the civic forces the finally brought transportation and land-use planning together. Near the close of the book, in Chapter 13, we describe the vexing political circumstances surrounding efforts to expand the region's airports. The chapter provides a kind of case study of the "realpolitik" of regional planning and decision making. In the appendices, we highlight research that complements ours, particularly that prepared by planning practitioners, including works on the history of NIPC and the Chicago Area Transportation Study.

An interesting dynamic occurs throughout this story as institutions rise in prominence, while others recede or disappear. The Chicago Regional Planning Association disappears in the 1950s, while the Chicago Plan Commission eventually surrenders its independence to become an arm of Chicago's government. At the same time, new organizations, such as Chicago Metropolis 2020 and the Chicago Metropolitan Agency for Planning arrive on the scene. Despite all this dizzying change, the will to create a "consensus vision" never subsides.

The Civic Sector in Regional Planning

Readers should be aware that our main concern is not with regional issues *per se*. Our chapters do not provide thorough treatments of the debate over race and class, poverty and inequality, housing and jobs, wealth and its distribution. Much has been written on these topics, as our appendices and citations suggest. We focus on the people, groups, and institutions striving to create and implement comprehensive regional plans.

If we were to direct readers to a major theme, it would be the continuing presence of Chicago's remarkably dynamic civic sector. Private citizens concerned with the metropolitan area have time and again formed regional associations and sponsored regional initiatives. They have planned, pleaded, pushed, schemed, and otherwise compelled public officials and agencies to pursue ambitious planning efforts.

Regional planning requires interplay between private and public bodies. It cannot be effectively led by any one official or community but instead must involve many constituencies and transcend municipal boundaries. Its essence is a care for the "commons." As we show, this care by the civic sector enjoys an especially rich history in the metropolitan area featured in this book.

Mayo Fesler of the City Club, evoking the words of Daniel Burnham, observed in the 1920s that "Chicago has always been noted for her willingness to undertake big tasks where small ones have made no appeal to the imagination."[3] Our history indicates that such ambition—fueled by civic leaders— will surely continue as we enter the next "Burnham Century."

ENVISIONING CHICAGO
AS A REGION

View north from the Colonnade at the 1893 World's Columbian Exposition, including the Obelisk. Daniel Burnham guided the fair's Beaux-Arts architectural program while serving as its director of works. *(Chaddick Collection)*

1

IN THIS CHAPTER

Planning for the region takes root with Daniel H. Burnham and Edward H. Bennett's *Plan of Chicago*, commissioned by the Commercial Club of Chicago. The celebrated plan sets in motion the creation of the Chicago Plan Commission, whose first chairman, Charles Wacker, promotes a vast public-works program in the city. Efforts to create a large forest preserve system move forward. By the early 1920s, however, there is need for new strategies—and institutions—to deal with rapid suburban development.

CREATING THE *PLAN OF CHICAGO*:

1900 – 1922

In the early Twentieth Century, Daniel Hudson Burnham was perhaps America's best known architect. His reputation and fame grew from his leadership in organizing the World's Columbian Exposition of 1893 and his carefully considered plans to reshape entire cities along beautiful symmetrical lines. "Make no little plans. They have no magic to stir men's blood and probably themselves will not be realized," he is reputed to have proclaimed.[1]

Burnham conducted his work during a time of growing optimism about the future of cities. The Progressive Era was in full bloom as civic leaders called for improvement, enlightenment, and reform. Technological advancements—including electric power, new construction techniques, and rapid transit systems—were transforming urban life. Through a remarkable feat of engineering, the flow of the Chicago River was reversed in 1900. Extensions to the city's streetcar system made urban travel faster and more efficient.

The family of Daniel Hudson Burnham poses next to a globe, circa 1894. Standing in the front row *(from left)* are Daniel, Jr., Hubert and Ethel B. Behind them are John, Margaret, Daniel, and Roland Woodyatt. *(Daniel H. Burnham Collection, Ryerson and Burnham Archives, The Art Institute of Chicago. Digital file © The Art Institute of Chicago)*

Sensing the time was right, prominent businessmen-turned-civic leaders promoted bold planning and investments to rid Chicago of its gritty image and start it on the way to greatness. Meatpacker George Armour, retailer Marshall Field, industrialist Cyrus McCormick, and others used money and influence to push the city to create amenities and new public works. Meanwhile, social scientists reported on ways to reorganize public and private institutions along more rational lines.

Burnham was closely linked to such Progressivist themes, having organized the World's Columbian Exposition in the city's Jackson Park in 1893. Working with Frederick Law Olmstead, he brought together celebrated architects, planners, and sculptors to create exhibit grounds showcasing architecture in the Neoclassical Beaux-Arts. An awe-inspiring "White City" emerged from their work, encompassing almost 700 acres of land roughly bounded by Cottage Grove Avenue, Lake Michigan, and 56th and 67th Streets. Hundreds of thousands visited the fair.

The exposition's legacy, however, was far different than its promoters anticipated. The fair's buildings and grounds, meant to highlight Chicago's progress in planning and design, instead offered a stark contrast to the actual city, with its industrial grime and neighborhood blight. To many Chicagoans, the city's ugliness was an embarrassment that could no longer be tolerated. People began to question why Chicago could not transform itself into an attractive and orderly place as appealing as the fair's White City.

Out of such sentiment emerged the City Beautiful Movement, which drew upon the themes of Progressivism to chart a new destiny for America's poorly planned and crime-ridden cities. As one of its guiding stars, Burnham looked beyond typical Progressive goals for improved sanitation and living standards, helping to inspire a national discourse on the importance of public space, grand public works, more efficient transportation, and managed land use.

Burnham's Rise

His success in designing urban spaces notwithstanding, Burnham never formally studied architecture. Born in upstate New York and raised in Chicago, he failed entrance exams to both Harvard and Yale. He worked various jobs in Chicago, including an apprenticeship in the office of famed architect William Le Barron Jenney.

Burnham became intrigued by architecture and admired Jenney, but he remained restless. Uncertain about his future, he accepted a friend's offer in 1869 to travel west to Nevada to try mining.

Burnham soon gave up on mining and resumed his search for an occupation. After returning to Chicago in 1871, he ran unsuccessfully for a seat in the Illinois state senate. His restlessness receding, he returned to architecture, met John Root, and with him founded the firm of Burnham & Root. After rocky beginnings, the new partnership successfully secured its first major contract in 1874, designing a house for stockyards magnate John B. Sherman. It was through this relationship that he met his future wife, Sherman's daughter, Margaret. The match proved invaluable for Burnham, professionally and socially. The Shermans introduced him to wealthy clients who, admiring his work on the Sherman house, hired Burnham & Root to design their own homes. His career took off.

Daniel H. Burnham works on a sketch while accompanied by an unidentified man in the early 1890s. This photograph appears to have been taken on the beach. *(Daniel H. Burnham Collection, Ryerson and Burnham Archives, The Art Institute of Chicago. Digital file © The Art Institute of Chicago)*

Burnham devoted a good amount of energy to seeing after the wellbeing of friends and family. He hired a personal trainer for himself and his son, Daniel, Jr., and organized several wilderness trips to restore ailing friends to health. All the while, he continued to partake in the finer things, traveling overseas on several occasions, buying expensive cigars, and cultivating his interest in gadgets and various kinds of automobiles.

Burnham's civic involvement was no doubt shaped by his devotion to Swedenborgian Christianity. Swedenborgian teachings follow the general tenets of Christianity but place particular emphasis on the importance of "doing good," encouraging believers to improve society and even take stances on controversial social issues, such as the abolition of slavery. Burnham led informal religious services with his family, in his library on Sundays, where he quoted passages from Swedenborgian texts and led family discussions about life's mysteries.[2]

After the World's Columbian Exposition of 1893, Burnham earned a considerable fortune as an architect while honing his skills in city planning, combining these disciplines in a way that set him apart from most of his contemporaries. He developed a scheme to improve Lake (later Grant) Park and the south lakeshore of Chicago, linking a formal garden and museum area to a six-mile long, picturesque parkway. Later, in 1901, he played a lead role on the Senate Park Commission that reshaped the Capitol and mall grounds in Washington and created a park plan for the federal district.

These efforts supported the expanding movement to preserve open lands and natural areas in rapidly growing metropolitan areas. In 1901, the city of Chicago established the Special Park Commission, chaired by noted landscape architect Dwight Perkins, a friend and professional associate of Burnham. Two years later, Cook County established the Outer Belt Park Commission, which advised the speedy creation of a county-wide forest preserve district.[3]

Daniel Burnham *(second from left)* and other Chicago Plan Commission members gather for a luncheon in the architect's offices in the Railway Exchange Building. This photo, appearing in Charles Moore's 1921 biography of Burnham, is believed to have been taken on September 7, 1910. *(Daniel H. Burnham: Architect, Planner of Cities, by Charles Moore)*

Believing the time was right for planning on an even larger scale, Chicago's civic elite looked to Burnham to lead a major initiative. The Commercial Club of Chicago welcomed him as a member in 1901 and asked him to take charge of its planning agenda. But while Burnham's commercial architecture practice blossomed, he concentrated his ambitious civic pursuits elsewhere. The city's Merchants Club tried to persuade him to undertake a plan for Chicago. In 1903, two of its members, railroad executive Frederic Delano, uncle of future president Franklin Delano Roosevelt, and insurance executive Charles Norton, the club's president, honored him for his work in Washington. But Burnham still had qualms about accepting.

Burnham completed city plans for Cleveland in 1903, San Francisco in 1905, and Manila in 1906. These plans emphasized the *physical* city, with grand boulevards and parkways, beautiful fountains, majestic buildings, and inviting public spaces. Burnham devised compelling arrangements of avenues and buildings that could sustain economic growth and social progress while promoting a sense of order and harmony. For the most part, he performed this work pro bono, continuing to earn a comfortable living from his firm's work on commercial buildings.

Burnham's reputation as a planner and architect grew not only from his compelling vision for cities but also from his power of persuasion and his capacity to anticipate his clients' needs. By 1906, he was such a towering figure in his field that Chicago's civic boosters again felt compelled to recruit him for a major planning effort. This time one of them succeeded—Merchants Club member and Chicago Tribune publisher Joseph Medill McCormick. Hearing of Burnham's willingness, Delano and Norton re-extended an offer of financial support.

Before a deal was struck, however, Burnham reputedly told Norton that he'd been informed by his doctor that deteriorating health left him just three years to live. Norton, at first stunned, recovered quickly, adding that the job would take *only* three years. Burnham accepted the assignment (he went on to live six more years).[4] The Merchants Club membership eagerly consummated the deal, approving initial funding in late 1906.

The persistence of these civic-minded businessmen showed the sense of responsibility that civic groups felt for their city. Private associations, claiming to speak for the common good, constantly monitored and critiqued public authorities, pushing them to make plans to benefit both commerce and communities. It was within this rich civic context that work on the Chicago plan began.

The challenge facing Burnham was certainly daunting. Chicago's metropolitan population at the time exceeded two million, substantially larger than other cities for which he had planned. Many city neighborhoods were notorious hodge-podges of land use, while the suburbs were rapidly expanding, engulfing marshes, farmland, woods, and prairie. Between 1900 and 1906, twenty new suburban communities were incorporated. The middle class, once largely confined to crowded urban neighborhoods, was spreading out, settling on the edge of the city as well as Cicero, Maywood, Melrose Park, Wilmette, and other blossoming suburbs.

Burnham selected Edward H. Bennett, a Beaux-Arts designer and architect twenty-eight years his junior, to help organize and draft the plan. He had relied heavily on Bennett for a comparable—but much smaller—comprehensive plan for San Francisco the previous year. Indeed, he had asked that Bennett be given complete control over that project, saying, "No one can take Bennett's place in this work, not even I."[5] For the Chicago plan, labor was divided similarly, with Bennett managing day-to-day affairs, while his mentor Burnham provided broad oversight by soliciting critical input, cultivating key relationships, and drawing upon his lifetime of experience.

Edward H. Bennett *(right)* with artist Fernand Janin in the studio atop the Railway Exchange Building, circa 1890. This photo may have been taken by Pierce Anderson, who introduced Bennett to Burnham. *(Marcia O. and Edward H. Bennett III Collection, Special Collections, Lake Forest College library)*

The two enjoyed remarkable chemistry, despite their difference in age. Bennett, born in England, had finished his architecture and design studies at Ecole des Beaux-Artes in Paris only a few years before. He worked briefly under famous New York architect George B. Post, who, fatefully, agreed to "loan" him to Burnham to help with a 1903 competition entry for the U.S. Army's West Point campus. Although Burnham failed to get that commission, he became so impressed with the young architect's talent and demeanor that he invited Bennett to join his firm, and sought his assistance on the San Francisco plan.

A Test of Talent

The talents of the planner-architects would be put to the test, as Burnham insisted upon a thoroughly researched and well-conceived plan, illustrated with color renderings. Merchants Club members also wanted no corners cut. Consequently, costs began to spiral, rising from an initial estimate of $25,000 to nearly $80,000.

To help rectify the budgetary shortfall, Merchants Club members secured a list of "subscribers"—consisting primarily of Chicago's business and cultural elite, to support the *Plan* at various contribution levels. Merchants Club members themselves antied up at critical moments. Shortly after work began, the Merchants Club merged with the Commercial Club, which assumed responsibility for guiding the project to completion.

Burnham and Bennett's draftsmen conducted their work in a special "studio"—a shed atop the Railway Exchange building on South Michigan Avenue. "Being up there we can constantly see the city and everything else and this will be of great value to us," Burnham noted.[6] From the start, Burnham placed emphasis on promotion and public relations, sending out letters to people across the country to gather input, while identifying groups and individuals who might resist the plan. He and his Commercial Club associates devised strategies to enlist widespread support. They carefully staged the plan's promotion to sway public opinion long before its release.

Commercial Club members worked behind the scenes to garner the support of influential civic leaders. Burnham reached out to prominent politicians, including governor Charles Deneen, mayor Fred Busse, even the city's sometimes unsavory aldermen. Burnham sought advice from business leaders, asked railroad executives about the wisdom of consolidating passenger terminals, and queried Michigan Avenue merchants about a "double-decker" bridge over the river. He sounded out such diverse voices as social reformer Jane Addams, architect Frank Lloyd Wright, the Army Corps of Engineers, and the Chicago Harbor Commission.

Committees organized by the Commercial Club joined Burnham, Bennett, and Charles Moore, the plan's editor, to continually refine and improve the plan. In the process, however, lengthy descriptions about the relationship between social ills, government action and urban development were removed, eliminating much of what the authors had to say about the responsibility of city government to protect the common man.[7] Recommendations to put schools in closer proximity to students' homes, to create day care centers for working parents, to have police departments conduct their business in full public view, were among the more progressive ideas stricken from the text.

What emerged, consequently, was a plan that focused on the physical city, emphasizing architecture, transportation, and the spatial arrangement of private and public institutions—themes consistent with the

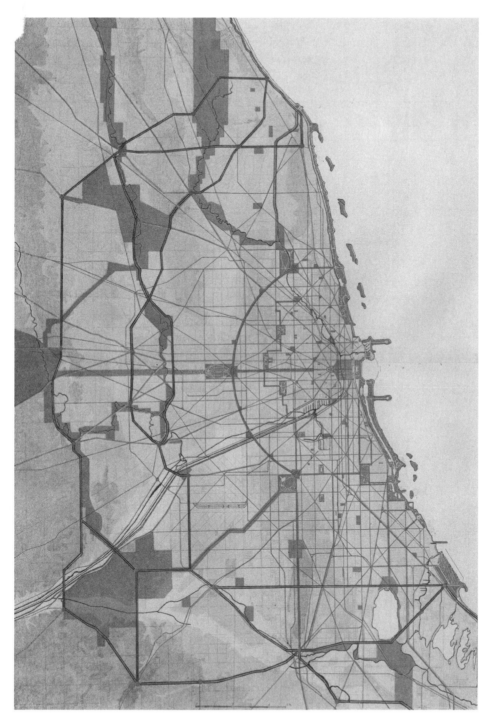

A map from the *Plan of Chicago* conveys an attractive balance of city and nature, with a symmetrical road pattern leading to greenways and parklands. On the periphery, the plan envisions generous amounts of land in forest preserves. By 1922, the Forest Preserve District of Cook County was the largest county district in the United States, having grown to more than 32 square miles. *(Chicago History Museum)*

original intent of the Commercial Club. The club's general committee approved the final text in March 1909 and turned to club member Thomas Donnelley's Lakeside Press for printing. Lakeside prepared a specially bound leather copy for Burnham and printed 1,650 hardbound copies for general distribution, all with the serene illustrations of artists Jules Guerin and Fernand Janin.

The *Plan of Chicago* was released on July 4, 1909, with great fanfare and with strong support from the city's elite. It was "a document which all good Americans will read," proclaimed the *Chicago Tribune*, which ran a front-page story featuring extensive quotes from the plan itself. Guerin's illustrations appeared in a special four-page section of the newspaper, filled with optimistic accounts of the city's future. Yet the Tribune's editorialists remained skeptical, for the "base, sordid reason," they stated, that the city would be "too poor, in this generation at least" to implement the plan.[8]

The *Tribune's* skepticism aside, the *Plan of Chicago* was ambitious and eloquent, depicting a gritty industrial city transformed into a shining neoclassical metropolis. Colorful images prepared by Guerin,

The 1909 *Plan of Chicago*

The metropolitan area that Burnham and Bennett envision in the *Plan of Chicago* extends from southern Wisconsin to northwestern Indiana and is colorfully depicted in the plan's first graphic—a beautiful bird's eye view showing a vast expanse of land spreading out 60 miles or more from Chicago to Kenosha, Wisconsin; DeKalb, Illinois; and Michigan City, Indiana. An "outer belt highway" arcs through the countryside, connecting farm town to farm town, while a series of circumferential roads lace through the countryside, forming successive rings of roads separated by parks and preserves.

While comprehensive in nature, the plan focuses heavily on the urban core, the heart of the industrial city in and around downtown Chicago. An integrated system of transit lines—subways, elevated trains, and trolley lines—provides mobility within the central city, while the city's streets are made more efficient by new diagonals carved through the grid. These diagonals or "circuits" surround the central area and reach into it, forming a web pattern. Railroad freight yards are removed to outlying parts, while the six downtown passenger terminals are consolidated into two union stations—one to the south on 12th Street (Roosevelt Road) and another along the river just west of the Loop.

Grand boulevards provide critical axes of movement through the heart of the city. A northward extension of Michigan Avenue, made possible by an elegant bridge over the Chicago River, enhances north-south movement. The proposed Congress Parkway, an east-west axis, is anchored by museums in Grant Park and a magnificent complex of civic buildings just west of the central business district.

The central area opens to a fine harbor east of Grant Park. From there, a serene lakefront is sculpted along the south shore, with woods and a long lagoon, while an "outer drive" leads to Jackson Park. By such means, the plan deftly ties the city to the great body of water along its eastern edge and promises to open the entire lakefront to the people. As Frank Lloyd Wright commented several years later to a European audience, "Thanks to … Dan Burnham, Chicago seems to be the only great city in our states to have discovered its own waterfront."[9]

intended to inspire and generate enthusiasm for the plan, exuded confidence in peop.
their environment. The sheer beauty of the book impressed the public and won over man.

A Lasting Legacy

Only a few months after its release—on November 4, 1909—Chicago's mayor and aldermen agreed to create a new public agency, the Chicago Plan Commission, and give it responsibility to make recommendations for the plan's implementation. Mayor Fred Busse appointed 328 men to the commission, many of them Commercial Club members, including Charles Wacker, who was appointed chairman. An executive committee, comprising a somewhat more wieldy twenty-six members, would shape the agenda with help from Walter Moody, a publicist hired by Wacker to be managing director. Although the commission had a "bully pulpit," implementation of the plan would require forging relationships with city departments, other governing bodies, and the state government. And although

The plan's perspective on the future is less clearly articulated on the city's western periphery, where a new suburbia was already emerging. Burnham and Bennett acknowledge that the city would inevitably spill out beyond its boundaries, as it had throughout its history. Yet the qualities and characteristics of this periphery are not strongly conceptualized. Beyond the city limits, the plan is vague. The premonitions are there, and the authors discuss the suburbs and the rising use of the private auto in their narrative, but the future look of these outer areas is not as clearly articulated as the city center.

In sum, the plan is less a new proposal than a thoughtful combination of existing ideas that Burnham and his associates had been discussing for well over a decade. Indeed, parts of the plan, including the south lakefront and the regional open space system, originated in proposals that Burnham and others created in the years after the 1893 exposition.[10] But the plan's skillful combination of ideas, its demonstration of the region's potential, and its thoughtful arrangement of transportation and land-use improvements across a huge area, made it extraordinary. Burnham and Bennett's talent as architects—their innate ability to arrange mass and form into something both aesthetically pleasing and functional— are amply demonstrated.

Plan of Chicago (Special Collections, Lake Forest College library)

An advertisement prepared by Rapid Transit Lines, operator of the "L," shows the new, elegant bi-level Wacker Drive before the ornate Jewelers Building, circa 1928. *(Chicago History Museum)*

the plan discussed the potential power of zoning, it would be another decade before local governments in the Chicago region used this tool.

Despite legal and financial shortcomings, the Plan Commission made good progress under Wacker's leadership, especially in maintaining an ambitious agenda that argued for physical improvements in the city while cultivating public support through educational programs. In addition to sponsoring public meetings and presentations, the commission published stories in newspapers, magazines and trade journals and, later, took part in radio broadcasts. *Wacker's Manual of the Plan of Chicago*, a lively 137-page textbook by publicist Moody, was published in 1912 and used in city schools as eighth-grade reading material, teaching a generation of students about the plan's principles and its precedents in the history of city planning.

Burnham did not live to see many of these achievements, dying suddenly in 1912 while travelling in Europe. Frank Lloyd Wright eulogized him, saying "...there was no man in the professional life of the United States who has given more of his life to the public, without having filled public office, than Daniel Burnham."[11] At the time of his death, his firm D.H. Burnham & Co., was the largest architectural firm in the world. And the Burnham family would remain prominent in the region's affairs for another forty years. Burnham's oldest son, Hubert, and second son, Daniel, Jr., continued the architectural business, eventually taking the name Burnham Brothers. As discussed in Chapter 2, Daniel, Jr., spent much of his life trying to advance the principles of the *Plan of Chicago*.

The two brothers, together with noted Prairie School architects Dwight Perkins and Thomas Tallmadge (both formerly of D. Burnham & Co.), continued to advance the City Beautiful tradition, producing, for example, the Plan of Evanston in 1916. Their vision for the lakeside community, the region's second largest city, echoed the *Plan of Chicago* with its magnificent civic spaces, although it placed heavier emphasis on mitigating congestion and improving vehicular flow.[12] Edward H. Bennett, meanwhile, continued to spread his talent throughout the region, preparing plans for Elgin, Highland Park, Joliet, Lake Forest, and Winnetka in Illinois, as well as Gary, Indiana.

But the *Plan of Chicago* stood alone in its eloquence, grandeur, and ability to capture the public's imagination. Beyond the Chicago Plan Commission, the *Plan* helped spur the creation of public institutions devoted to preserving natural areas. In 1915, Cook County voters gave one of the nation's first forest preserve districts the power to levy taxes. Voters in DuPage County approved a similar agency the following year. Soon after a 1916 court ruling resolved questions about whether these districts could acquire property, Cook County took ownership of its first property, Deer Grove in west suburban River Forest. The DuPage district acquired the seventy-nine-acre York Woods in Oak Brook in 1917.

Metropolitan Chicago was on its way to assembling one of the most extensive forest preserve systems in the country. By 1922, the Forest Preserve District of Cook County was the largest county district in the United States, having grown to more than 21,000 acres (more than thirty-two square miles).[13] By the mid-1920s, the "greenbelt" envisioned by Burnham and Bennett was largely achieved.

The city never built the long lagoon and "necklace of islands" along the south lakefront, as rendered in the 1909 *Plan*. As recommended in the plan, however, it did build Northerly Island, later the site of The Century of Progress Exhibition and Meigs Field airport, and beautified the south lakefront as far as Jackson Park, assembling a continuous band of green space.

Charles H. Wacker, chairman of the Chicago Plan Commission, with his wife Ella and their grandson, Charles Wacker Zimmerman, 1929. *(Photo by Charles H. Keller, Chicago Evening American, Chicago History Museum Collection)*

By the early 1920s, Chicago was, as one historian noted, in the midst of a "golden age of comprehensively planned civic improvement."[14] Major bond issues, ushered in by Wacker's Plan Commission, helped pay for many enhancements. In 1920, Michigan Avenue was widened and raised, and equipped with a double-decker bridge, allowing motorists to travel in grand fashion to points north of the Chicago River. Wacker Drive, another centerpiece of the plan, gave the city a curved bi-level boulevard that beautified the riverfront while diverting commercial traffic around the Loop. Union Station, for which Burnham prepared the original design, was another legacy, although that terminal did not see its first trains until 1925.

Changes Unforeseen

The 1909 *Plan*'s great emphasis on the central area suggests that its authors were planning for a monocentric industrial city. The plan envisions the Loop district

A depiction of the riverfront along the new Wacker Drive showcases progress in implementing the *Plan of Chicago*. This Chicago Plan Commission illustration faces southward down Wabash Avenue *(left center)*, 1926. *(Chicago History Museum)*

surrounded by dense worker neighborhoods and huge factory districts. Burnham and Bennett did not anticipate how the region's rural townships and small villages would develop into suburbs, or how open spaces would come to serve suburban residents. The forest preserves, as envisioned in the plan, provide a kind of recreational release for people coming out to them from the city. Their actual role, however, was more heavily oriented toward a burgeoning suburban population, one growing much faster than the city's population soon after the plan was written. The "outer belt highway" concept, meant to connect farm towns, would eventually be replaced with sophisticated plans for superhighways.

Criticism has been directed at the plan for its relative silence on issues important to the working class population.[15] The plan focused on the arrangement of buildings and public spaces while having relatively little to say on education, health care, and social justice—omissions partially due to the removal of sections that dealt with these issues in earlier drafts. Scholar Kristen Schaffer, in her foreword to a 1993 reprint of the *Plan of Chicago*, contends that the document might have found a far different place in history had these "unpublished" sections been included.[16] Without attention to critical social issues in the plan, it was perhaps inevitable that the finished product would be seen by some as exclusively devoted to the goals of the civic elite.[17]

For its part, the Plan Commission established itself as an effective actor in the city, but showed an inability to embark on suburban projects. This left a vacuum that could not be easily filled. As described in the following chapter, Daniel Burnham, Jr., the late architect's youngest son, spent much of his life trying to fill that gap. He came to see the limitations of the Plan Commission and promoted a more regionally-focused civic association.

Legacy

Edward H. Bennett remained in Chicago, maintaining his practice and promoting a civic agenda. He led the effort to draft Chicago's first zoning ordinance in 1923, served on the Chicago Plan Commission in various capacities into the 1930s, and was a board member of the Chicago Regional Planning Association. He designed Buckingham Fountain and the Michigan Avenue Bridge as well as structures for the Century of Progress Exposition of 1933–34.

Portrait, Edward H. Bennett, circa 1930. *(Marcia O. and Edward H. Bennett III papers, Special Collections, Lake Forest College library)*

Bennett's influence as a planner spanned the continent. By 1922, he had prepared plans for Buffalo, Brooklyn, Detroit, Minneapolis, Phoenix, Portland, St. Paul, and other U.S. cities as well as for Ottawa, Canada. He used the *Plan of Chicago* as a prototype for transportation planning, the location of government and civic structures, zoning, and the creation of parks and public spaces.

None of his later efforts, however, achieved the fame of the *Plan of Chicago*. Other cities made significant plans, but few—for issues of timing and politics, as well as the persuasive abilities of their creators—would leave so deep an imprint on an entire metropolitan region. For subsequent generations, the 1909 *Plan* would be the gold standard by which others plans were judged.

Onlookers examine a model of a proposed subway station on display at the Palmer House in the mid-1920s. The model depicts an elaborate multi-level design, with one level for utilities and another serving as a passenger concourse, both above the tracks. Groundbreaking for the city's first below-ground transit route, the State Street subway, would not occur until 1938. *(CTA Collection)*

2

IN THIS CHAPTER

Daniel Burnham, Jr., who shares his father's passion for ambitious plan making, pushes for the creation of the Chicago Regional Planning Association. Unlike the Chicago Plan Commission, which promoted the *Plan of Chicago* principally within the city, the new organization conducts its business across a growing metropolitan area. The RPA— with Burnham, Jr., as president—becomes a catalyst of intergovernmental collaboration but is hindered by the Great Depression and struggles with the awkward division of responsibilities between itself and the Plan Commission.

DANIEL BURNHAM, JR., AND THE CHICAGO REGIONAL PLANNING ASSOCIATION:

1923 – 1935

Daniel Burnham, Jr., had a style of problem-solving that was more measured and consensual than his father's. What he lacked in fervor and persuasive ability, he compensated for with meticulous preparation and a talent for building relationships. But he and his father had similar aspirations, with the younger Burnham seeking nothing less than to "apply the Chicago Plan principals to the vast tracts of vacant land in the regional plan area outside of the city, and not wait until traffic and congestion force drastic action."[1]

The Chicago Plan Commission had been created with such lofty goals in mind. By early 1923, however, the younger Burnham and other civic leaders were convinced that the advisory body was not properly designed to take the actions necessary to achieve them. While created to implement his father's plan, it was oriented toward and financed by the city—and prevented from expending much effort to promote new policies for areas beyond city limits.[2] Any plans it had for suburban areas were prepared primarily to support its work within the city of Chicago.

Daniel H. Burnham, Jr., circa 1933. This photo appeared in the 1933 *Official Guide Book of the Fair* with foreword by Rufus C. Dawes. *(American Planning Association)*

The senior Burnham along with Bennett had envisioned a variety of organizations advocating for planning throughout the region. Now, many civic leaders—Burnham, Jr., included—felt that the region needed one dominant organization to steer the city and suburbs toward this goal. Enthusiasm for this idea ran deep, especially at the City Club of Chicago, which already convened a committee to discuss this idea. The club had recently hired executive director Mayo Fesler, who brought experience from Cleveland and New York, where similar ideas were being explored.

Regional Planning Takes Root Nationwide

Chicago's efforts were part of a budding regional planning movement spreading across the country. The Boston Metropolitan Improvement Commission, created in 1902, was the country's first regional planning organization, while the Suburban Metropolitan Planning Commission, another pioneer, emerged in the Philadelphia area in 1915. Although these organizations struggled to find their footing, new organizations that arose after World War I offered far greater prospects for accomplishment. In 1921, Cleveland created a metropolitan planning commission. In 1922, Los Angeles County organized a regional planning commission that became the largest of its kind in the country. Both had strong civic backing.[3]

Advocates of a regional organization for Chicago felt tremendous energy coming out of New York City. Since passing a citywide zoning ordinance in 1916 and creating the Port Authority of New York and New Jersey in 1921, this city had become a laboratory for new planning techniques. Civic leaders in New York wanted nothing less than a comprehensive plan for the entire region, an area encompassing twenty-two counties in three states, as well as an organization like the Chicago Plan Commission to push for its implementation. Without both a plan and an organization, some warned, the New York area would suffer from piecemeal planning, to the detriment of highways, housing, and the preservation of recreational land.

New York's efforts moved forward under the direction of Charles Dyer Norton, the Chicagoan who first convinced Daniel Burnham, Sr., to prepare a plan for Chicago. Norton, now a Wall Street banker, helped in 1920 to convince the Russell Sage Foundation, where he served as trustee, to provide financing for a regional plan. Two years later, he became chairman of the newly created Committee on a Regional Plan for New York and its Environs.

Experts from around the world soon arrived in Manhattan to provide support. Norton died in 1923, but another former Chicagoan and veteran of the 1909 *Plan*, railroad executive Frederick Delano, took his place as head of the committee.[4] The progress made in New York inspired others. By 1925, thirty professional associations devoted to town and regional planning convened across the country.[5] Social scientists took notice, including the famed "Chicago School of Sociology" at the University of Chicago, which attracted international attention for its scientific approach to study of urban regions.

Even smaller cities began to embrace scientific tools to manage growth. In 1923, Cincinnati, Ohio, became the first city in the country to adopt a comprehensive plan. More than 250 other cities established planning commissions, some of them with paid staff.[6] Creating plans for metropolitan regions seemed to be the next big step in the progression of planning ideas.

Chicago Moves Forward

The champions of creating a regional association in Chicago were swept up in the excitement of the day. In February 1923, the City Club published *Metropolitan Planning for Chicago and its Environs*, laying out a vision for regional cooperation that became the topic of discussion at an event held the following month. More than 200 village presidents and mayors attending the one-day conference deliberated on "whether or not a permanent organization or commission should be created to promote such a planning program."[7]

Mayo Fesler, club secretary, pushed hard for the creation of a voluntary organization that was capable of "directing the growth and improvement of living and working conditions in the Chicago district."[8] Before the end of the day, a committee that included Burnham and Dwight Perkins was put in place to explore the issue. Perkins, who had earned wide respect as the "father" of the Cook County forest preserve, was named chairman.

Generously quoting the late Daniel H. Burnham, Fesler urged the committee not to be constrained by monetary concerns. "It should be comparatively easy to raise in this rich community $50,000 annually for a few years for such an undertaking," he said, adding that "Chicago has always been noted for her willingness to undertake big tasks where small ones have made no appeal to the imagination."[9] At a second conference held

The Chicago Regional Planning Association used this photograph of "two-lane pavement" to illustrate the need to widen roads. Four-lane configurations were considered the "ideal." *(Chaddick Collection)*

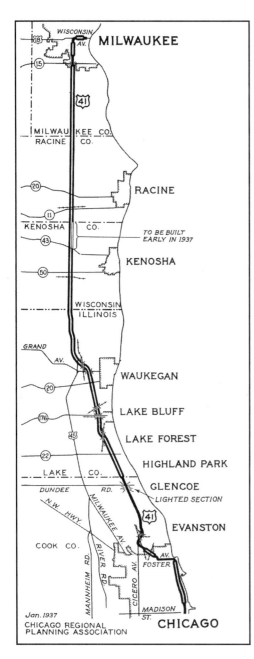

Map of the proposed Chicago-Milwaukee "superhighway" dated January 1937 (today's U.S. Route 41). The push to build this highway began in the mid-1920s. *(Northeastern Illinois Planning Commission)*

on November 2, the planning committee created the Chicago Regional Planning Association (RPA) and installed Perkins as president.

The RPA would serve roughly the same area as that contemplated in the *Plan of Chicago*. Stretching from Waukegan in the north to Gary in the south, a region with a diameter of roughly fifty miles, it would plan for the needs of some 4.7 million people in fifteen counties in Illinois, Indiana, and Wisconsin.[10] A board of directors composed of experts on urban affairs, including Cook County commissioner Charles S. Petersen, University of Chicago professor Charles E. Merriam, city health commissioner Charles Ball, and Daniel Burnham, Jr., would shape the agenda.

Initially, the RPA focused its attention on helping suburban communities deal with the explosive growth of automobile traffic. Roads beyond the city limits were usually unpaved and thus were impassable after storms. Due to the lack of coordination in investment, many paved stretches stopped at county lines, making long-distance driving hopelessly inefficient. In late 1924, the RPA minced no words about the severity of these problems, warning that "[m]ore than a million motor cars registered in Illinois are clamoring for road surface, and nearly half of them are in the region of Chicago," in a newly issued report, *Highways in the Region of Chicago*.[11] To point the way toward the resolution of these problems, the report provided a colorful fold-out map that identified hundreds of miles of roads needing pavement.[12]

Despite its early energy, the new association had some difficulty getting underway. Perkins' health turned for the worse. A gradual loss of hearing left him almost totally deaf. Burnham scrambled to keep his architecture practice solvent, encountering financial woes as Burnham Brothers, the firm he managed with his brother Hubert, struggled to finish a pair of downtown office towers.[13] One of these towers, the Burnham Building, which his firm had designed, had become a financial quagmire. Forced into bankruptcy, he had to sell off assets including the family home in suburban Hubbard Woods.

Hope began to fade that the Chicago RPA's work would match the sophistication of the New York effort. The association's entire budget during 1924 was just $30,000—well short of the $50,000 goal envisioned by Fesler. Staffing amounted to about ten employees and a handful of consultants. Most of the manpower was devoted to regional surveys for planning projects that it hoped to launch in the future. Metropolitan Chicago's planning movement was losing steam.

A streetcar line running through an unpaved roadway in Joliet, circa 1920, illustrates the dismal conditions confronting motorists at the time. This road is today the Lincoln Highway (U.S. Route 30) and equipped with an overpass over the Elgin, Joliet & Eastern Railway tracks in the distance. *(A.G. Kistler photo, Andrew Plummer Collection)*

In early 1925, Perkins announced his retirement, accepting the ceremonial post of honorary president. The executive committee installed Burnham as president and Robert Kingery, a promising young traffic engineer, as secretary. Both turned out to be key appointments, creating a leadership team that remained in place for the next 26 years.

A New Beginning

The RPA's emphasis on civic voluntarism, and on persuasion rather than compulsion, melded well with Burnham's style of problem solving. "We are an association of 'sovereign' municipal bodies, organized to help them carry out their plans in harmony with one another," he wrote. Since these bodies "have full legal authority to plan and build within their own jurisdiction," his association "did not set out to dictate to them, nor to draw 'a plan' for the Region."[14] The RPA would not seek power to tax but would solicit funds from individuals, mostly in amounts of $5 to $100 annually, and from governmental and civic organizations in greater amounts.[15]

Momentum behind the RPA once again began to build, meanwhile, Burnham's own finances improved, allowing him to spend more time promoting the association. Forging relationships at his firm, his golf club in Lake Zurich and on trips to Europe (where he went to study architectural practices), Burnham seemed to derive great satisfaction from his RPA role. After one of the association's luncheons, soon after becoming president, he beamed, "This is about the most intelligent crowd and discussion that I have ever attended."[16] He worked pro bono, as his father had worked on the *Plan of Chicago*, making his civic work into something of a personal crusade.

Also like his father, who came to rely on Edward H. Bennett, Burnham, Jr., put his trust in the skillful engineer Robert Kingery, who attended to details in much the same way as Bennett. Kingery cultivated relationships with the region's mayors and village managers, assembled committees, and lent his expertise to those who asked for it.[17] As the pace of its activity quickened, people began looking to the RPA—and Kingery in particular—for technical analysis and leadership.[18]

Burnham, while clearly energized by the strides his organization was making, believed the RPA needed "some really tangible accomplishments" before winning much publicity for its efforts. The best opportunity for this, he felt, was to further champion highway improvements—a role that would dovetail with his efforts as chairman of Cook County's highway advisory committee. "If there is one basic fault of the present day road and street system, it is probably the scarcity of continuous well-paved traffic arteries," he wrote in an editorial.[19]

Tying Regions Together

In 1926, the association unveiled a proposal for a four-lane divided highway between Chicago's north side and Milwaukee. Building this road—which would later become the Skokie Highway (Route 41)—seemed a natural extension of his father's plans. Getting it built required clearing a wide right-of-way and coordinating actions of numerous agencies and governments over many years—something that had never been done for a major road project in the region. The RPA played a key coordinating role for this and other regional road projects from the 1920s through the 1940s.

Building the Skokie Highway, however, became politically complex. An earlier trucking industry proposal would have widened Sheridan Avenue and Green Bay Road to create a four-lane truck route passing through the middle of several affluent North Shore communities. Strong local opposition led the RPA to instead develop a more rural route farther west, bypassing the town centers. Edward H. Bennett allied himself with the project's opponents, whose effective resistance gave an early demonstration of the coming clash of local environmental concerns with regional transportation goals.

Anticipating that motoring on modern divided highways would become the norm, Burnham, Jr., and fellow highway advisory committee members—Mt. Prospect mayor William Busse, county highway superintendent George A. Quinlan, and Kingery—traveled to Detroit in 1925 to learn about that region's superhighways program.[20] The delegation met with automaker and industry spokesman C.W. Nash, who had high praise for RPA's work, calling it "one of the most constructive efforts that has ever been made in the interests of highway development." The association, he said, was "working together to untangle knots that ordinarily confront a highway program." [21]

The transportation agenda that Burnham and his associates advanced was not without its detractors, even in this early phase of highway planning. Social critic Lewis Mumford did not consider such planning to be authentic regionalism at all, referring to it derisively as "parks and highways planning." It fell far short of Mumford's more comprehensive approach to regional planning, with its emphasis on building autonomous communities in relationship to natural landscapes. Yet Burnham and Kingery saw benefit in their focus on highways, which responded to the obvious public need for high speed automobile and truck travel. They hoped to build a system that would maximize the region's economic potential while protecting local quality of life as much as possible.

Many in the Chicago region shared this opinion. Membership in the RPA more than doubled between 1926 and 1927, reaching 171 people and organizations. Encouraged by this, Burnham felt the time was right to create a new publication, a volume to supplement the *Plan of Chicago*. The book would showcase progress in achieving the plan's goals, while promoting more regional cooperation and investment. In making this proposal, Burnham stopped short of suggesting a new plan for the region, perhaps due to respect for his father's work, his friendship with the still-living Bennett, and his belief in the continuing relevance of the 1909 *Plan*.

In metropolitan New York, meanwhile, the civic community eagerly awaited the completion of a first regional plan, made possible by a half-million-dollar grant from the Russell Sage Foundation. *The Regional Plan of New York and its Environs*, published in 1929 in ten volumes, was perhaps less inspiring than Chicago's 1909 *Plan*, but more heavily grounded in data and technical matter. With this plan in hand, civic leaders formed their own regional plan association to oversee its implementation and conduct further research.

Across the country, the idea of planning for vast metropolitan areas had gained grassroots support. By 1929, regional organizations were in place in fifteen metropolitan areas, and several of these, including Cincinnati, Ohio, and Washington, D.C., were also preparing full-blown regional plans.[22] Of these organizations, however, none came close to matching the Chicago and New York groups in number of staff and population of area served.

Seal of the Chicago Regional Planning Association.
(Larry Lund Collection)

The Travails of a Downturn

The onset of the Great Depression initially did little to dampen the enthusiasm of advocates and scholars of regional planning. By one count, there were sixty-seven commissions or organizations around the country devoted to metropolitan planning in the early 1930s.[23] Much of the energy faded, however, as the national economy continued to spiral downward.

Unlike its counterpart in New York, which had already created a comprehensive plan, the Chicago Regional Planning Association remained burdened during difficult times with trying to raise money to complete its supplement to the *Plan of Chicago*. The money could not be found. The association could not even meet payroll, forcing its entire staff—Kingery included—to accept pay cuts.

Edward Bennett *(center)* with the team that designed the Federal Triangle in Washington, D.C., date unknown. *(Marcia O. and Edward H. Bennett III papers, Special Collections, Lake Forest College library)*

In 1931, with the RPA's budget at its lowest point in five years, Burnham and Kingery were forced to make personal appeals for contributions, mostly without success. In the poor economy, the RPA had no choice but to set aside some of its ambitious goals, such as promoting superhighway construction, and focus on less costly and more basic matters like eradicating blight and promoting zoning.[24] Burnham made the best of this situation by stressing the importance of such work. Regarding the importance of zoning, he noted: "Those who have prophesied as inevitable the steady northward march of the apartment zone from Rogers Park into Evanston and the North Shore suburbs are now reassured that under sound and careful zoning such changes are not inevitable."[25] His journal entries from this period, though, reveal his frustration with having to set aside the association's loftier visions.

New Deal initiatives coming out of Washington did little to lift Burnham's spirits. The "slant on housing" taken by Department of Interior Secretary Harold Ickes (a Winnetka resident whose wife had once served as an RPA board member), Burnham complained, presupposed that it "was necessary to go out in the suburbs to get low-priced land" rather than to build within established areas and where water, sewer, fire, and police services were already available.[26] While acknowledging the fact that "outlying centers are growing at a faster rate than the City of Chicago itself," Burnham worried that suburbs were ill-prepared to handle the population growth.[27]

Meanwhile, Kingery took a leave from the now-somnolent RPA in 1931, summoned to Springfield by Governor Henry Horner to head up the Illinois State Planning Commission, a new agency created to prepare the state for anticipated federally-sponsored public works spending. This commission's members prepared for initiatives that were soon coming from the National Planning Board (later the National Resources Planning Board), a New Deal entity that encouraged state and local governments to control their destiny through ambitious planning.

By early 1933, the commission's final report was largely complete and Burnham pushed Horner to "release Kingery from his duties in Springfield so that he could take up his work actively with the regional *Plan*."[28] Kingery apparently had done all that he was asked, preparing the state for the National Planning Board programs and establishing new channels for communication between various levels of government. Despite his efforts, however, the outcome of this work was ultimately disappointing. Both in Illinois and elsewhere, state planning commissions and the National Planning Board failed to stimulate the kind of comprehensive planning for metropolitan areas that many had wanted. Intergovernmental cooperation would not be as easy as the designers of New Deal programs had anticipated.

Nevertheless, as the economy rebounded and New Deal programs got underway, Chicago began to regain some of its swagger in regional planning circles. Hosting the National Planning Conference in 1934, the RPA basked in the limelight. The newly created American Society of Planning Officials opened its offices in Chicago that same year through the work of board member Charles Merriam. In addition, the city staged a great world's fair, as described in the next chapter. "A Century of Progress," held in Chicago during 1933 and 1934, lifted the spirits of architects and planners.

An Awkward Separation

These accomplishments, while impressive, did not erase the disappointment stemming from the RPA's inability to craft a widely accepted vision for the metropolitan area. By not creating a new comprehensive plan, the group lost an opportunity to build upon the heritage of the 1909 *Plan* and to rally the region behind common objectives in the manner of the recent New York plan. The group's reluctance was probably prudent, given the weakness of the economy and consequent lack of funding. But the lack of progress on the 1909 *Plan* supplement was a sign that something more fundamental had gone wrong.

Another blemish on its record was the fact that the Chicago region now lagged behind other metropolitan areas in planning for highways and airports. The absence of a predictable source of financing for large-scale projects (either from tax levies or private sources) and the increasingly fragmented nature of decision making were largely to blame. By 1935, the metropolitan area had more than 200 communities— more than any other in the country—making regional planning and coordination difficult.[29]

The RPA also had an anemic budget, which, even in the best of times, never exceeded $55,000 per year. In addition, the assumed division of responsibility between itself and the Chicago Plan Commission fostered some contention over which group would marshal the region's civic and business leaders in support of planning. More effective coordination of the two organizations was made difficult by their different agendas, constituencies, and political orientations. Burnham believed that the solution was a merger.

He sensed opportunity for this in 1935 with the appointment of Colonel Albert A. Sprague as chairman of the Chicago Plan Commission. Sprague replaced James Simpson, chairman since 1926, who had succeeded Charles Wacker.

Sprague was a true blueblood, a graduate of an eastern prep school and Harvard College, a former infantry officer, and owner of the Sprague-Warner grocery chain. A familiar face on the Chicago political scene, with two stretches as the city's public works commissioner, Sprague wanted to make the commission less cumbersome and more decisive. Exuding the enthusiasm of Charles Wacker, Sprague set out to make Chicago the "first city in the world." In a *Tribune* interview, he dismissed out of hand objections to a "downtown airport" as "only captious," asserting that objections to airport noise meant "nothing."[30]

Sprague seemed open to giving his advisory body a more regional focus, going so far as to say, "Personally, I think the Chicago Plan Commission will have to include the entire Chicago Metropolitan area in its activities, because the things we are called upon to decide are just as vital to Oak Park and to our neighbors on the north as they are to the City of Chicago." In early 1935, he and Burnham had several discussions about a merger.

The two men talked, but there were tensions. "I do not see how there could be a consolidation," Sprague pronounced, stating a widely held view, "because the Plan

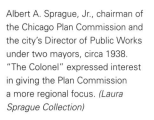

Albert A. Sprague, Jr., chairman of the Chicago Plan Commission and the city's Director of Public Works under two mayors, circa 1938. "The Colonel" expressed interest in giving the Plan Commission a more regional focus. *(Laura Sprague Collection)*

Commission is a creature of the City Council and the Regional Planning Association is a corporation not for profit." Sprague may have been concerned about giving the RPA an upper hand in any merger, as his rivalry with Burnham seemed to intensify. During the merger discussions, Kingery's role became a sticking point. Burnham insisted that his deputy retain a strong executive role in any merged agency, remarking in his journal in July 1935 that "we can't get together unless Colonel Sprague will let Kingery hire and fire who he wishes."[31]

By the end of that summer, all merger hopes had faded. The organizations moved in separate directions, leaving planning for city and suburbs to follow different paths. Yet Burnham continued to feel compelled to carry on the work of his father. In the spring of 1935, he noted in his journal, touchingly, that he was "in tears" after a benefactor agreed to loan the RPA $4,000 for its work.[32] When he placed carnations on his father's grave in Graceland Cemetery in 1936, marking the 24th anniversary of Burnham, Sr.'s death, his great ambition for coordinated planning across the entire region remained largely frustrated.[33]

But regional planning would stay a priority for Daniel Burnham, Jr., Three years later, new federal programs and war mobilization pushed the RPA into its most productive period. Before that, however, Burnham, Jr., enjoyed a personal triumph of another sort, with a world's fair project that paralleled his father's achievement of forty years before.

This rendering offers a striking nighttime view from above, showing the Sky Ride and other illuminated fair attractions. *(Lisa Schrenk Collection)*

3

IN THIS CHAPTER

Forty years after the World's Columbian Exposition, another great fair, the Century of Progress International Exposition, showcases Chicago's capacity to implement visionary plans. Civic leaders work vigilantly to raise funds in the absence of direct governmental support. Daniel Burnham, Jr., takes on responsibilities analogous to those of his father during the 1893 fair, while his brother, Hubert, serves on the exposition's architectural committee. Visitors to A Century of Progress receive an advance look at construction practices that would become commonplace after World War II.

THE "RAINBOW CITY":
A Century of Progress International Exposition

The brilliant illumination of The Century of Progress International Exposition could be seen reflected in the sky for miles during the summers of 1933 and 1934. This celebration of science, technology, and modern architecture reaffirmed the Chicago region's capacity to think big and to create environments that excite and inspire. Held on Northerly Island, in Burnham Park, and along the lakefront south of the Loop—a site prominent in the *Plan of Chicago*— the fair both dazzled and surprised, making it a fitting sequel to the World's Columbian Exposition of 1893.

Two of the senior Burnham's three sons, Daniel, Jr., and Hubert, were called on to help design the fairgrounds. The Chicago Regional Planning Association considered the fair so important for the metropolitan area that it offered financial support from its modest budget. This would be a truly regional undertaking, with much of the responsibility for fundraising falling upon prominent Chicagoans and suburbanites.

A "pictorial map" issued as part of the Century of Progress Exposition, 1933. The L-shaped peninsula created for the event, called Northerly Island *(center)*, was in keeping with the spirit of the *Plan of Chicago*, which envisioned a series of islands and a lagoon along the lakeshore. *(Chicago History Museum)*

Big Plans, Revisited

Originally, the 1933 event was envisioned as a traditional centennial celebration for the city of Chicago. The fair's planning committee, however, feared that it would not attract enough attendees to be viable. A traditional exhibition emphasizing only culture, ethnicity, and history would likely not be successful, as such fairs were considered obsolete. So the fair planners looked instead to showcase innovation in science, technology, and architecture; new manufacturing processes and products; and new materials and building techniques—which they hoped would draw visitors from near and far.

A board responsible for staging the exhibition, headed by Rufus C. Dawes—brother of Charles G. Dawes, vice president of the United States at the time—settled on the theme "Science Finds, Industry Applies, Man Conforms." To create a setting consistent with this theme, the board selected eight prominent local and national designers for the architectural commission. Notably absent was Frank Lloyd Wright, who was passed over because he "could not harness himself for the sake of cooperation." Wright later groused that the fair was "just 1893 with the surfaces changed."[1]

Among the preliminary designs produced by the fair's architectural commission was one by Edward H. Bennett, redolent of City Beautiful and Beaux-Arts themes. Bennett's proposal emphasized the symmetry found in the 1909 *Plan* as well as the 1893 fair's showpiece, the Court of Honor. The fair board ultimately chose the mix of styles that transformed Bennett's classical symmetry into an asymmetrical fairground. The 1933 fair would not recreate 1893's White City, but would be a "Rainbow City" combining Art Deco detailing with other modern styles. In sharp contrast to the neoclassicism of 1893 and its look back to ancient Greece and Rome, this fair would look to the future.

On the financial side, however, problems loomed. The fair would need to cover its costs without direct financial support from government—something no previous world's fair had done. The fundraising effort got off to a rousing start when the fair board issued $10 million in bonds on October 28, 1929, the day before the stock market crash. The organizers also promoted "memberships" entitling buyers to future admissions to the fair. The RPA, urged by Burnham, Jr., made a financial investment that offered it a share of any profits, effectively keeping the organization in the fair's inner circle.

Daniel Burnham, Jr., agreed to serve as secretary of the fair's board and its director of public works. His duties, which included day-to-day planning, were analogous to his father's position in the 1893 exhibition. The board seized on the father-son parallel, publicizing it in announcements to the press.

By all accounts, Burnham performed excellently. Fluent in French, he helped arrange a fact-finding trip to the 1931 Colonial Exposition in Paris. He played a major role in fundraising and wrote several articles for *New York Times Magazine* that drew attention to the techniques used to build the fair's pavilions. These flexible methods, which allowed for quick assembly using low-cost materials such as plywood and gypsum board, later became standard practice in building construction.

Turnaround for Burnham

Burnham, Jr., and his family were rejuvenated by the excitement of the fair. Their financial situation had been grim enough in recent years, with Burnham forced to sell his house in the Hubbard Woods neighborhood north of Winnetka. The family moved to Chicago, eventually settling into an attractive Gold Coast three-flat at 83 East Cedar Street, often renting the third floor to architects working for the family firm. Burnham, Jr.'s oldest son, Daniel III, returned from England to finish school locally. "It is hard to realize how quickly the bottom fell out from under everything . . . and how dumb I was not to realize what was happening," Burnham, Jr., wrote years later in a journal.[2]

Burnham, Jr.'s brother John, an investment manager, had found success in California real estate and managed to sidestep some of the hardships of downturn. Due to his concern over the deteriorating condition of Daniel and Hubert's business, Burnham, Jr., encouraged them to stop work on the Burnham Building, an office tower that risked becoming a financial drain. Daniel expressed a great frustration during this difficult period over the severity of the firm's budgetary problems in his business journals.[3]

The fair helped to smooth things between the brothers. For the family, it was a sequel to the 1893 fair. The Burnhams rallied to its support, bringing along business associates, family, and friends. For Daniel, Jr., it became a consuming passion. His wife Helen promoted the fair on the WGN radio program *The Women's Hour*. His brother John bought ninenteen exposition "memberships" for his employees. And business picked up for the Burnham Brothers firm, which won contracts to design three of the projects for the 1933 exhibition—the Belgian Village, the Firestone Building, and the Sinclair Refining Company Building, the latter with Hubert as principal architect.

Daniel Jr., attended opening-night ceremonies on May 27, 1933, with Mayor Ed Kelly and Governor Henry Horner. The fair's first day saw more than 150,000 visitors fill the 427-acre fairgrounds, packing the lakeside oval just east of Soldier Field. At the precise moment when energy from the star Arcturus was gathered by astronomers, traveling approximately forty light-years away—about the time of the 1893 World's Columbian Exposition—generators powered in part by that energy turned lights on throughout the sprawling grounds.

Visitors came to marvel at the Homes of Tomorrow and the Home Planning Hall, exhibitions demonstrating modern convenience and new building materials and techniques. The Sky Ride, a massive "transporter" bridge, took passengers 219 feet above ground, giving them a thrilling experience while providing a visual identity for

Thousands of fair-goers make their way down the central corridor of the Century of Progress Exposition. This view shows the area between the General Electric pavilion *(right)* and the popular Firestone Pavilion *(top center)*. *(Lisa Schrenk Collection)*

the exposition, much as the Ferris Wheel had done for the first Chicago world's fair.

Margaret Burnham, Daniel H. Burnham Sr.'s widow, travelling from California, received white-glove treatment at the fair and judged the event as "wonderful in every way."[4] Burnham, Jr., tended to the upkeep of pavilions that his firm had designed, including the popular Belgian Village, where he occasionally spent the night so as to remain on the fairgrounds. On one occasion he was awakened by young revelers who had broken in and were trying to upend a statue; he forthwith "put out" the intruders.

A billboard for the Illinois Central Railroad advertises its convenient service to the Century of Progress Exposition. All railroad station agents in the country carried information about the fair. *(Chicago History Museum)*

In the autumn of 1933, Burnham, Jr., sold his share of Burnham Brothers to his brother Hubert and set up shop as D.H. Burnham, Architect, in the Railway Exchange building on Michigan Avenue, where his father once had his offices. When the fair was extended a second year (at President Roosevelt's urging, so impressed was he by its promotion of consumer spending), his new firm received commissions to design three new attractions, including the old Spanish Village, one of a half dozen or more "foreign villages" that were to "dominate" the 1934 fair, according to a contemporary account.[5]

Modern railroading arrived for the fair's 1934 season, when the stainless-steel Burlington Zephyr streamliner ended its nonstop run from Denver to Chicago at the Wings of a Century pageant on May 26. The Zephyr made the trip in a record-breaking 13 hours and 5 minutes—beating the previous fastest time between cities by more than 12 hours. It was a triumph for railroading and for Burlington CEO Ralph Budd, who as a Chicago Plan Commission member had a personal stake in the fair's success.

A Century of Progress closed on Halloween Day in 1934, after drawing nearly forty-million visitors.[6] It was the first world's fair to completely cover its costs, earning a modest profit in the process. More than 300,000 came to the closing ceremonies for a final look at the Rainbow City and the Festival of Illumination, a magnificent light display on the lagoon.

This artistic sketch showcases the Sky Ride, the fair's signature attraction. The Sky Ride, boasting a 1,850-foot span, became an identifying landmark of A Century of Progress, much as the Ferris Wheel had become for the 1893 World's Columbian Exposition. *(Chicago History Museum)*

"Wrecking day" on March 28, 1935, was a sad one for Daniel Burnham, Jr., who noted in his journal that he had felt "low all day."[7]

The pavilions were soon emptied, the landscaping removed, and the ornamentation was stripped, in some cases by vandals and looters. While a few buildings were moved to others sites, none were allowed to remain on the fairgrounds, as stipulated in an agreement with the Chicago Park District. The debt was retired, and in 1942 the Chicago RPA got its promised four-percent share of the profits, a modest $4,000.

The fair proved enormously influential in the development of construction techniques involving asbestos, gypsum board, and plywood, as well as building frames of lightweight steel—techniques that became major elements of the post-war housing boom. It also helped revive interest in major urban expositions. Five years after the fair ended, New York followed suit with its Building The World of Tomorrow fair. In 1949, the Chicago Railroad Fair was held on the former site of A Century of Progress.

Civic Commitment

The energy behind the 1933–34 fair put the strength of Chicago's civic sector on display, showing the determination of private citizens to improve the region's image and its economy. This civic commitment has risen and fallen over the years, often dissipating but always reemerging with vigor to push for new plans in new directions. A Century of Progress was a remarkable demonstration of the activism felt by regional planners in decade after decade.

Fifty years after A Century of Progress, the world's fair bug bit again. Mayor Jane Byrne made plans in 1982 to host an exposition in 1992, the 500th anniversary of

Columbus' voyage to the New World. The Chicago World's Fair Authority was organized under the leadership of noted executive and former Illinois Secretary of Transportation John Kramer, who had served in the James R. Thompson administration. Civic backing for the endeavor began to build.

The city of Chicago won the right to hold the fair and even levied a tax on hotel receipts to pay for it. Plans were drawn for nearly the same location as the 1933 fair. After Byrne lost to Harold Washington in 1983, however, the alliance she formed with the business community fractured and the fair authority was dissolved.

Promotional poster for A Century of Progress as it appeared in the 1933 *Official Guide Book of the Fair* with foreword by fair president Rufus C. Dawes.

More recent preparations for the city's bid for the 2016 Summer Olympic Games involved a more regional approach, with the active participation of suburban officials and events slated for sites across the metropolitan area. However, the core planning area once again concentrated on the south lakefront. This vital area, where the city meets the lake along a picturesque shoreline, remains a testament to the vision of the *Plan of Chicago* and the civic advocacy of two generations of Burnhams, father and sons.

Illinois Central's Green Diamond eases out of Central Station *en route* to St. Louis, circa 1937. Although the streamlined train was new at the time, the metropolitan region was in the midst of long slump in transportation investment. The Chicago Regional Planning Association's pushed to modernize included efforts to eliminate rail-highway grade crossings on newly built divided highways. *(JH Gruber Collection)*

4

IN THIS CHAPTER

Planning for superhighways, subways, and airports shifts into high gear in response to new federal programs and rising anticipation of a post-war development boom. After years of working separately, the Chicago Plan Commission and Regional Planning Association come together to create blueprints for massive public works projects. Robert Kingery proves an effective facilitator of intergovernmental cooperation while he continues to support Daniel Burnham, Jr.'s, dream of creating a "supplement" volume to the famed *Plan of Chicago*.

MASTER ENGINEER:

Robert Kingery and the Push for Public Works: 1936 – 1945

From the late 1930s to the early postwar years, Robert Kingery was at the center of an extraordinary movement to build superhighways, ports, toll roads, and airports throughout the Chicago region. More than any other individual, Kingery laid the groundwork for public investment that changed the contours of the region. The legacy of this quiet but fastidious engineer is commemorated today in two major highways named in his honor.

Kingery's rural upbringing made him an unlikely champion of metropolitan investment. Born in Emporia, Kansas, in 1890, he grew up in Crawfordsville, Indiana, where his father was professor of literature at Wabash College. Kingery's mother, deeply involved in the community's art league, cultivated his interest in landscape painting. After enrolling at Wabash to study the arts, Kingery demonstrated a great perseverance and drive, becoming captain of the college track team. He was a "hard worker" and "consistent trainer" who ran the mile with "a wonderful sprint at the finish, running the last two hundred yards as if perfectly fresh."[1]

Robert Kingery, trained as a landscape architect, conducts survey work, circa 1920. *(Kingery family Collection)*

Throughout his career, Kingery's willingness to exert himself tirelessly for the good of the team became one of his most enduring qualities. After college, he worked as a landscape architect in Chicago for several years and in 1918 joined the Army Quartermaster Department as a civilian engineer.[2] After the war he worked for the Skokie-based Portland Cement Association, a major trade group, where he learned about modern highway and bridge construction.

High Priority Highways

In 1925, Kingery became chief engineer and the first-full time employee of the Chicago Regional Planning Association. Soon, he became general manager, in charge of day-to-day operations. In this capacity, he encouraged collaboration among local governmental entities in the planning efforts encouraged by New Deal programs.

When the governor called Kingery to Springfield in 1931 to head up the newly created State Planning Commission, he divided his time between directorships of this commission and the state's Department of Public Works (a predecessor to the state's Department of Transportation). Despite the workload, he continued to chair the Cook County Forest Preserve District, kept up with much of his RPA work, and remained active in various professional organizations. He had a marked ability to remain focused while juggling activities.

His duties with the state ended in 1936, when he turned to RPA's high-priority projects.[3] One, the Chicago–Milwaukee "superhighway" linking Skokie to Wisconsin (today's Skokie Highway, part of Route 41), was completed in late 1936, save for a few railway-grade separations and about four miles of pavement. It was the region's first divided highway built to serve intercity travel, with two lanes in each direction, a grassy median, and bridges over key intersections.

Kingery and Howard Olson, the RPA's highway engineer, were proud of this new road, having spent more than a decade cultivating the relationships necessary to get it built. Olson "believed it to be the longest superhighway in the nation of four lanes or more."[4] It was "already famous," he said, shortly after its completion in January 1937.[5]

The RPA's next big project was the Tri-State Highway, an expressway "belt route" linking Indiana, Illinois, and Wisconsin. Not to be confused with today's Tri-State

Tollway, it would form an arc through Elmhurst, Mt. Prospect, and Libertyville. It was to be four lanes, stretching from the Skokie Highway in Lake County to Lansing, Illinois, in southern Cook (portions of this road became Route 83 in DuPage County— the aptly named Kingery Highway). Its southern terminus would connect into another highway to South Bend, built by the state of Indiana. Kingery kept quiet about exact routes lest property owners "jump their prices."

With state and federal agencies insisting upon more cooperation between governments, Kingery and Olson hopped from meeting to meeting to keep projects moving forward. The pair helped coordinate a wide variety of Works Progress Administration projects as well as transform Harlem Avenue (today's Route 12/45) through Tinley Park into an arterial road with lengthy stretches of divided highway.

Kingery also led one of the most ambitious railroad relocation projects in suburban Chicago history (see sidebar, next page).

City and Suburbs Go It Alone

Throughout the late 1930s, the RPA continued to plan almost exclusively for the suburban area, while the Chicago Plan Commission attended to the needs of the city. Burnham, Jr., wanted to break down the barriers but made little progress. He had been off the Plan Commission's executive committee since 1935, when it became clear that Albert Sprague Jr., its chairman, felt little urgency in forging closer ties with the region's suburbs and the work of RPA—and the attempt to merge the two organizations failed.

The attractively landscaped Chicago–Milwaukee "superhighway" passes below a pair of railway bridges in Lake Forest, circa 1940. This route, today's U.S. Route 41, was purportedly the longest "continuous pavement" in the country when it opened in 1938. *(Chaddick Collection)*

Congestion Relief for Glencoe and Winnetka

The Chicago Regional Planning Association's efforts to improve transportation infrastructure were a springboard for a massive project to depress the Chicago & North Western Railway and North Shore Line interurban tracks through Glencoe and Winnetka starting in the late 1930s.

This project had been on the drawing board since the 1890s and endorsed by Edward H. Bennett in his plan for the village in 1921. As car and truck traffic grew, the safety and congestion problems caused by trains passing through Winnetka gradually worsened. By the mid-1930s, accidents at street crossings had claimed some thirty-three lives.

The preferred solution, relocating the railroad lines into a lengthy man-made trough, was beyond the financial means of the village. In 1938, Kingery, himself a resident of Winnetka, spearheaded the village's request for $1.5 million from federal sources and leveraged his relationship with Secretary of the Interior Harold L. Ickes, who administered the Public Works Administration that made the Winnetka grant. Ickes also had a home in Winnetka and had once been active in the RPA.

Over the next several years, workers eliminated ten dangerous at-grade crossings, built six bridges, and relocated 3.5 miles of railroad right-of-way while allowing more than 100 trains a day to pass through the construction site. The railroads and the village together contributed about equally to matching funds that brought the total cost to $3.5 million (although Glencoe was included in the project, neighboring Wilmette was unable to raise enough money, so its railroad tracks remained at street level).[6] The project, when finished in 1941, was hailed as a great success of intergovernmental cooperation.

A North Shore Line train stops at the Hubbard Woods station in Winnetka, 1942. This portion of the route was freed of highway grade crossings due to a $3.5 million private-federal-local partnership that put several miles of track into a "depression" below street level. *(Peterson-Krambles Collection)*

To be sure, the *city's* transportation agenda was gathering momentum after a lull of many years. Municipal Airport (later Midway Airport), dedicated in 1931, was gradually improved and became the world's business airport. In 1937, the first portions of the Outer Drive (Lake Shore Drive) were completed, becoming the city's first stretch of divided highway. In 1939, the City Council created the Subways and Superhighways Committee to identify new transportation corridors for future construction.

Work also began on a rapid-transit subway—the city's first—under State Street (today's Red Line), requiring widening of portions of the storied street to 115 feet. Several buildings were demolished to clear 39 feet from the west side of the street to permit digging a "four-track bore" beneath it. The subway, which would require agreements among street car and rapid transit interests, would be partially paid for with a Public Works Administration loan. Ground was broken in 1938, and trains began running in the subway in 1943.

The separate north and south lanes of Cicero Avenue, captured here near the Santa Fe Railway underpass (top center) in Chicago, circa 1935, showcased the future of road building in the region. An automobile is about the cross the bridge over the Illinois & Michigan Canal, a corridor today occupied by the Stevenson Expressway. (A.G. Kistler photo, Andrew Plummer Collection)

The Subways and Superhighways Committee, meanwhile, aimed to jump-start the city's expressway program. The plan that emerged in 1940, unfortunately, was far from comprehensive, lacking details about precisely how and where expressways would be constructed. Although the proposed expressways were attractively depicted on maps, they abruptly halted at city limits with no explanation, as if to suggest that regional considerations had not been part of the analysis. Perhaps inevitably, the committee's work was left to languish.

Nor did the Chicago Plan Commission push for a truly regional agenda. It had made important strides through the late 1920s to implement the *Plan of Chicago*, but struggled to remain relevant during the Depression and ultimately fell victim to the inability of governments in the region to agree on its best role. The fate of this once-illustrious body was of great concern to the Metropolitan Housing Council (MHC), a new player on the region's planning scene. Several years before, MHC led a vigorous debate about the Plan Commission's future while calling for increasing its capacity to work on suburban issues. Chairman Sprague wanted to give it special powers, too, stating that the commission should be able to block ordinances "at variance with the Chicago plan."[7] The *Tribune* heartily endorsed reconstituting the Plan Commission as a way "to prepare for the orderly growth of . . . city as well as suburbs," giving it authority with "supervision over all . . . planning activities in . . . the metropolitan area."[8]

Instead, the opposite was done. The Chicago Plan Commission became an advisory arm of city government, losing its semi-autonomous status. In late 1939, the city passed a law making the Plan Commission—a body of thirty-two members—with an

Ferd Kramer *(Draper and Kramer)*

advisory council of 200. These changes made the commission more nimble, but also inextricably tied it to Chicago's political culture and government, leaving it even less able to vigorously push for policies in the suburbs.

Mayor Kelly, at the urging of MHC president Fred Kramer, dutifully appointed many of the reformed commission's members.[9] Hoping to exert leverage during the restructuring, Burnham, Jr., called on Sprague and "told him flatly" of his desire to rejoin the commission's executive committee.[10] Sprague refused the request. Clearly frustrated, Burnham, Jr., lamented privately in his journal, "… with Sprague as chairman, we are all wasting our time as the commission will never do anything."[11] The men stayed friends and even had dinner together now and then, but Burnham, Jr., was surely pleased when Sprague left the Commission in June 1940, his place taken by civil engineer George Horton, chief executive of Chicago Bridge and Iron Company.[12]

Despite Burnham, Jr's., frustration, the tension between the RPA and the Plan Commission soon melted away. Perhaps due to Horton's leadership, and no doubt also because of the country's deepening involvement in World War II, the two organizations put aside past diferences and pooled resources to solve some of the region's most vexing transportation problems. Plan Commission members felt particular respect for Kingery, making him the commission's principal liaison on regional matters. Soon, the Chicago metropolitan area entered what might be called a "golden era" of intergovernmental cooperation involving trains, planes, and automobiles.

Orchard Place/Douglas Field

The logjam that had blocked airport planning began to break in early 1941, when a special committee of the RPA, Chicago Plan Commission, and Chicago Association of Commerce convened to help the U.S. Army Corp of Engineers identify sites for a large military airport. Accelerating its work after the Pearl Harbor attack, the special airport committee visited at least nine sites in early 1942, including Orchard Place, a small farming community just northwest of the city limits near Bensenville. The committee met with high-ranking Army officials and a young lieutenant named Matthew Rockwell, who greatly admired Burnham, Jr., and Kingery, having worked for them as an RPA intern several years earlier.

At a meeting in Kingery's office in early 1942, the Army Corps met with the special committee and selected the Orchard Place site for the military airport. News broke that the government was condemning 1,347 acres of land, requiring that farmers and other occupants relocate, marking the beginning of a history of displacement that would haunt the airport's neighboring communities to the present day (as discussed in Chapter 13).[13] Soon, crews worked around the clock to build runways, buildings, and hangars.[14] Kingery spent much of his time coordinating construction of a massive Douglas Aircraft Company assembly plant on the site.

A crowd gathers at the Douglas Aircraft plant at Orchard Field, 1943, to commemorate completion of the first Douglas C-54 bomber. Interest in converting the military airfield into a commercial airport grew after the war. *(The Union League Club)*

By the end of the year, Douglas' factory was operating; the first planes took off and landed in spring of 1943. The first C-54 "Skymaster" transport plane rolled down the assembly plant's runway on July 30, 1943. Orchard Field Airport/Douglas Field was home to an Army Air Corps depot, and its hangars were used for holding rare and experimental planes, including captured enemy aircraft. The hangars and airfield—including the administration building, boiler house, garage, cafeteria, health center, paint shop, and parking for 6,300 automobiles—were soon pushed to the limit.

Douglas Field did nothing, of course, to relieve pressure on commercially oriented Municipal Airport (today's Midway Airport), which had seen an explosive six-fold increase in passenger volumes during the ten years ending in 1940. Municipal—the region's only airport with paved runways when America entered World War II—was hemmed in by residential and industrial development and could not easily expand. With large four-engine passenger airplanes under development, the city urgently needed an airport with more and longer runways as well as greater terminal capacity.

In early 1941, George Horton, the Plan Commission's new chairman, and Theodore McCrosky, its newly hired executive director, reached out to the RPA to help create a committee to identify ways to deal with the skyrocketing demand for commercial airport facilities. Burnham and Kingery were key players on this committee, which by the end of the

A United Airlines DC-4 appears ready for boarding at Chicago Municipal (Midway) Airport. When this photograph was taken in 1947, the Chicago Plan Commission had already concluded that Municipal alone was inadequate to meet the region's long-term aviation needs. *(Christopher Lynch Collection)*

year released a report that concluded that Municipal Airport could not possibly meet all the region's needs, even if ambitious efforts were made to expand it. "Instead of a single union air terminal, such as Chicago Municipal, there will [be a need to] develop a series of not fewer than three airports —interconnected by express highways, [and having] fast transportation to the central city, other sections of Chicago, and suburbs," the report concluded.

The airport planners emphasized the importance of a major commercial airport outside the city, perhaps to the south at an improved Ford Airport in Lansing or Rubinkam Airport near Harvey, or to the northwest. Apparently for military reasons, the committee did not comment on the possibility of remaking Orchard Place Airport/Douglas Field into a commercial airport, although that was surely on their minds.

To handle the traffic, the airport committee stressed the importance of a three-pronged approach that involved Municipal Airport, a new downtown airfield, and a massive suburban airport. These three major hubs would be surrounded by dozens of smaller airports specializing in non-commercial traffic. Altogether, there would be seventy-two different airports in the region.[15]

A major airport along the lakefront near the Loop, strongly supported by the business community, had been on the drawing board for years, despite *Plan of Chicago* recommendations for this area to be used as open public space. In the early days of aviation, a dirt landing strip in Grant Park provided perhaps the most-visible evidence of the demand for a close-in airport. Edward H. Bennett suggested in 1916 the construction of a more legitimate airport on a landfill in the lake. In 1929, a group of businessmen pushed for building an "island airport" near downtown, undeterred by the estimated $10 million cost. Alderman John Massen of the 48th Ward suggested dumping refuse into the lake as a way to cut costs.

A lakefront airport seemed almost inevitable during the Great Depression. In 1931, Mayor Anton Cermak appointed a commission led by Merrill C. Meigs to study options for opening an airport, possibly near Montrose Avenue, in time for the 1933 World's Fair. Although that airport was never built, the discussion about the need for a lakefront facility continued.

By the early 1940s, the city's airport problem had reached the point where the Chicago Plan Commission felt compelled to prepare a comprehensive plan for aviation. In 1943, the Plan Commission once again teamed with Kingery's RPA and the Chicago Association of Commerce to study the options. What emerged in 1945 was a document that warned of the risks of over-reliance on airports within the existing city limits. Echoing earlier findings, the study found that, even if Municipal were improved, its facilities would be saturated with traffic in just four years.

A lakefront airport could not possibly solve the problem and would be poorly situated to serve the suburbs. It was now beyond dispute that the region needed a massive commercial airport outside the city. The Orchard Place/Douglas Field military airport seemed ideal for conversion since it was to be decommissioned by the military. The site could be equipped with long runways and was reasonably accessible to the city.

The Plan Commission and RPA championed the site, and Kingery advocated tirelessly on its behalf. The city still had to approve the plan. Ralph Burke, former chief engineer for the city, now retired, led the push to convince City Hall, having been hired to develop an airport master plan that would include terminals and highway links. In 1949, while still on the drawing boards, the city renamed Orchard Place airport after Edward "Butch" O'Hare, a World War II flying ace.

The creation of O'Hare International Airport would still take years. As discussed in Chapter 13, agreements would be negotiated in order for the city to annex the airport land. Commercial operations did not begin until 1955, and the number of scheduled flights did not greatly expand until after a new international terminal was opened in 1958. The big commercial airport proposed for the lakefront, meanwhile, never materialized, although the city did open a small-but-useful facility, Meigs Field, on Northerly Island and adjacent fill in 1948.

Superhighways and Subways

Airports were one thing, but superhighways were another. The Chicago region was falling further and further behind other metropolitan areas in planning for expressways, partially due to the continuing lack of coordinated planning by city and suburbs. By the late 1930s, traffic conditions in many heavily traveled corridors were abhorrent, and forecasts showed that things would grow worse. Although the opening of portions of Lake Shore Drive and the Skokie Highway were commendable achievements, the region still lacked a credible expressway plan in 1939.

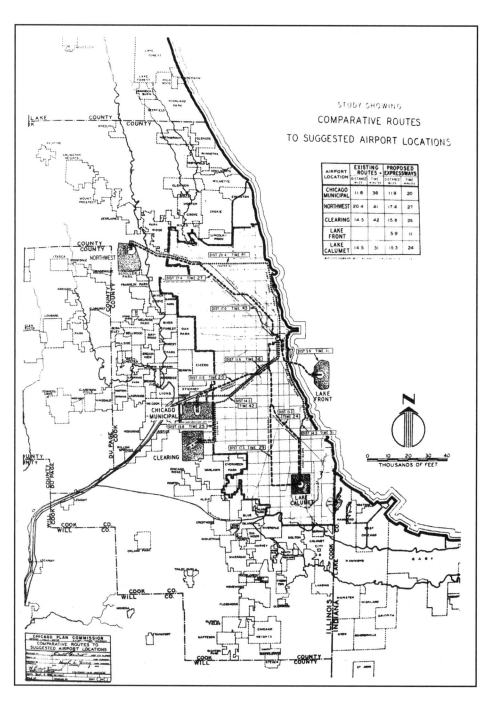

STUDY SHOWING

COMPARATIVE ROUTES

TO SUGGESTED AIRPORT LOCATIONS

AIRPORT LOCATION	EXISTING ROUTES		PROPOSED EXPRESSWAYS	
	DISTANCE MILES	TIME MINUTES	DISTANCE MILES	TIME MINUTES
CHICAGO MUNICIPAL	11.6	36	11.9	20
NORTHWEST	20.4	41	17.4	27
CLEARING	14.5	42	15.8	25
LAKE FRONT			5.9	11
LAKE CALUMET	14.5	31	15.3	24

This map, prepared by the Chicago Plan Commission in the early 1940s, shows a proposed network of expressways serving a system of five commercial airports within or near the city. The prospective airports include a major facility northwest of the city that was to become O'Hare International Airport as well as large airfields at Lake Calumet (an industrial site evaluated once again for airport use in the late 1980s), Clearing (an area dominated by railroad yards), a man-made island in Lake Michigan, and the existing Municipal (Midway) Airport. As this map suggests, the city was busy refining its plans for both airports and urban expressways at the time in anticipation of a post-war traffic boom. As noted in Chapter 13, the debate about expanding the aviation system and improving roadway access to air terminals continues today, although there is no longer formal discussion about building new airports in such close proximity to the city. *(Chicago Public Library)*

By this time, the New York region had already completed three major highway and bridge projects: the Whitestone Bridge, the New Jersey Skyway, and the Henry Hudson Parkway—all three envisioned in its 1929 regional plan. The Henry Hudson Parkway, extending eleven miles, cost a staggering $109 million, twice as much as the Hoover Dam. By the early 1940s, the New York region was also mapping out a system of turnpikes.

The absence of federal funding for expressways clearly had not stopped other cities from building major roadways. In 1940, Southern California celebrated the opening of part of the Arroyo Seco Parkway linking Los Angeles to Pasadena, while Detroit was on its way to completing the Davison Freeway linking Detroit and Highland Park, Michigan. Completed in 1942, the Davison was regarded by many to be the nation's first modern expressway.

Cities across the country sprang into action after President Roosevelt created an International Highway Committee in 1940 to map out a system of interconnected superhighways, which would later become the federally funded Interstate Highway System. Although an expressway map prepared by the city of Chicago's Superhighways and Subways Committee that year was a start, it failed to plan outside the city's boundaries or to spell out details of expressway alignment. The devil was in the details, and the committee provided few.

Several critical years passed before the political machinery began to turn and the Plan Commission and RPA found a way to work together to move planning forward. In March 1943, the two organizations held several conferences, subsequently forming a joint technical committee to lay out an action plan. By the end of the year, the committee made recommendations to the Plan Commission that differed sharply from those prepared by the city in 1940.[16] Several more superhighways, including an "expressway loop" circling the downtown area—bounded by Roosevelt Road, Michigan Avenue, Ohio Street, and the present-day Dan Ryan Expressway—were put on the drawing board. Moreover, unlike the earlier plan, this one envisioned an expressway system extending far into suburbia.

The committee then set out to create a Master Plan of Thoroughfares, complete with charts, maps, and renderings, and organized into separate sections devoted to city and suburbs. This document garnered the support of Cook County and the state before being formally adopted by the Chicago City Council in April 1945. Like the airport plan, this expressways plan was the blueprint for massive public investment after World War II.

By 1946, Cook County had the means, thanks to successful bond referendums, to acquire right-of-way for several expressways beyond the city's boundaries. Robert Kingery, meanwhile, used the master plan to argue for construction of "tollways" through outlying parts of the region. Clearly, city-suburban coordination on public works had improved, erasing much of the earlier frustration felt by Daniel Burnham, Jr.

With a great surge in public-works spending on the horizon, Burnham nonetheless resumed his work on the "supplement" to the 1909 *Plan* that he started years earlier. This undertaking (see sidebar, next page), he believed, would bring renewed relevance to his father's famous work, drawing attention to regional accomplishments while showcasing the RPA's data and analyses.

The war years, however, had forever changed his life. The family's sacrifice was enormous. One of his sons, Daniel III, a naval officer, was wounded during training exercises off the Aleutian Islands. Luckily, he recovered fully.[17] Spencer, his other son, was killed in a Jeep accident on Army maneuvers in North Carolina in late 1943. This death devastated Burnham, Jr.'s wife, Helen. Hospitalized with a goiter and depressed, she died on March 22, 1944. Twenty-one months later, on December 23, 1945, Margaret Burnham, his mother, died at 97.[18]

By the mid-1950s, public-works projects were multiplying. But the civic, collaborative spirit that had made the RPA influential for years was once again dissipating. The organization's effectiveness would never again approach what it enjoyed in the 1930s and 40s, and the era of the Burnhams, father and son, playing central roles on the Chicago regional scene, drew to a close.

The Burnham and Kingery legacy would endure, however, primarily through the persuasive blueprints for airports, tollways, and expressways they helped prepare. What followed was a public-works construction boom on a scale not seen since Charles Wacker's Chicago Plan Commission in the 1920s.

"The Kingery Plan": A Long Awaited Supplement to the Plan of Chicago

The completion of the long-anticipated supplement to the 1909 *Plan of Chicago* must have seemed farther away than ever in 1945. Eleven-plus years had passed since late 1933, when Burnham, Jr., and Kingery met with William E. Clow, the last surviving member of the Merchants Club. The club had set aside money for a publication that would commemorate its civic contributions, especially its role in sponsoring the *Plan of Chicago* before its merger with the Commercial Club. Clow offered to put up money for an "incidental volume" as an addition to the Plan. The gift had been accruing interest and now totaled more than $15,000,

Burnham and Kingery began immediately, outlining chapters and getting a cost estimate from the R.R. Donnelly Company, the same publisher of the 1909 *Plan*. Many people that Burnham asked to contribute material, however, were reluctant to participate, perhaps due to the state of the economy or simply because they felt the day was past when such a document could make a difference. People outside the RPA seemed lukewarm to the idea of publishing the proposed plan supplement.

Hopes for the project rose sharply when the State Planning Commission agreed to underwrite the costs of illustrations in 1936. Burnham now felt that it could be done, writing in his journal, "Clow will put up old Merchant's Club funds ($19,500); we will pay $6,000. This would guarantee that at least 2,000 copies be printed." Later, in 1937, Burnham noted that the text was "practically complete and the maps and artists drawings almost ready for publication," only to see, once again, key deadlines slip.[19] Kingery's hectic schedule was probably a factor. Nevertheless, Burnham's inability to get Charles Merriam or anyone else to jump-start the effort suggests that there was a deeper problem.[20] Then came World War II, when the project had to be put on hold.

Burnham, Jr., resumed work on the project after the war, but progress was slow. The Chicago Plan Commission helped Kingery complete the maps. The engineer, who turned 60 in 1950, was not as resilient as he used to be. Ignoring warnings about his health, he added to his duties by joining the governing board of the newly constituted

Chicago Port Authority in late August 1951.[21] He had been Governor Adlai Stevenson's choice for its presidency, but that post went to a Mayor Kennelly nominee, William W. Huggett. In October of that year, Kingery became gravely ill while in Michigan. Burnham called his contacts in the medical community to ensure that Kingery got the best possible hospital care. But in a few weeks, on November 13, 1951, Kingery died.[22]

The RPA board eulogized its late general manager as a man of "unfailing courtesy and good nature," then promoted Howard Olson, who had been with the organization since its inception, to fill the vacant position. Burnham, Jr., who had worked with Kingery for more than twenty-five years, knew that his friend held the Tri-State Highway "closest to his heart," and asked the Cook County board to rename the Illinois portion of this newly completed superhighway (later part of Interstate 80/94) after his friend.[23] The name change took effect in late 1952.

Four years later, in early 1956, the RPA finally released the 1909 *Plan* supplement, entitled *Planning the Region of Chicago.* Dedicated to the late engineer and to Burnham, Jr., this lavishly illustrated book, called the "Kingery Plan," painted a compelling portrait of change in the region. A lofty and eloquent prose culminated in an inspirational passage exhorting officials to exhibit "leadership, courage, and persistence in a never-ending sequence." The volume described the process to bring plans for the metropolitan area "dream by dream, and step by step, from vision to reality."

The delays in producing the Kingery Plan, however, had taken their toll. Many of the exhibits used data that was more than twenty years old, diminishing the power of its message. Meanwhile, attention was shifting to the creation of an official, state-sponsored planning commission. And the younger, more energetic Metropolitan Housing Council had become a respected and vigorous watchdog over the planning process. The days of the Chicago RPA were quickly drawing to a close.

PLANNING THE REGION OF

CHICAGO

PREPARED UNDER THE DIRECTION OF

THE CHICAGO REGIONAL PLANNING
ASSOCIATION

BY DANIEL H. BURNHAM, JR.
AND ROBERT KINGERY, 1890–1951

EDITED BY
JOHN BARSTOW MORRILL
AND PAUL O. FISCHER

CHICAGO : 1956

Title Page of *Planning the Region of Chicago*, published in 1956, a volume thirty years in the making by the Chicago Regional Planning Association.

A newly minted housing subdivision in Oak Lawn, pictured here circa 1952, shows the enormous scale of residential development in the suburbs after World War II. Oak Lawn's population skyrocketed from 13,000 in 1950 to 49,000 in 1960, making it one of the region's fastest growing suburbs. *(Oak Lawn Public Library)*

5

IN THIS CHAPTER

Spectacular suburban growth and an expanding federal role in metropolitan affairs cause tremendous change in the field of regional planning. The Metropolitan Housing and Planning Council emerges as an authoritative voice and agent of change. The state legislature establishes three agencies—Illinois Toll Highway Authority, Chicago Area Transportation Study (CATS), and the Northeastern Illinois Metropolitan Area Planning Commission (NIPC)—with responsibility for planning the region.

NEW IDEAS AND NEW INSTITUTIONS:
1945 – 1957

As men and women of the armed services returned from World War II, the wheels of regional growth began turning again. Homebuilding surged in metropolitan Chicago, changing the image and dimensions of the suburbs. Housing starts rose precipitously, spurred by a resilient economy and federally backed mortgage insurance. The cost of home ownership fell below that of renting.

Veterans and other first-time homeowners flocked to buy tract houses, with electric heating, spacious backyards, and attached garages or carports for as low as $13,000. New construction was so robust in Arlington Heights, Oak Lawn, and Skokie, that each added more than 30,000 residents in just ten years. Dozens of other communities grew from tiny railroad towns to bustling suburbs. In 1945, Cook County issued long-term bonds for new roads to support development. Soon, construction of the first stretches of long-planned "superhighways" got underway.

Garden "cooperatives" like these in Park Forest, Illinois, catered to middle-income families eager to leave the city after World War II. This newly created community, linked to downtown by commuter trains from nearby Richton Park, was one of the first suburbs in America planned around an autombile-oriented shopping mall. *(Photographer: Hedrich-Blessing; Chicago History Museum)*

In the south suburbs, Park Forest saw more than a thousand residential units sprout up annually after its incorporation in 1948. Some commentators even suggested that such "new suburbs" were changing the essence of American middle-class life. "As far as social values are concerned, suburbia is … classless, or, at least, its people want it to be," noted William Whyte about Park Forest in his seminal book *The Organization Man*.[1] "The expansion of the lower limits of the middle class is … so pronounced in the new suburbs that it almost seems as if they were made for that function."[2]

Suburbs and Expressways

Whether or not one accepted Whyte's contentions, it was difficult to dispute his basic claim that boomtowns like Park Forest—the first community in the country built around an auto-oriented shopping mall—marked a paradigm shift in suburban development. These communities of cul-de-sacs and "ticky-tacky" houses did not merely alleviate housing shortages in older urban neighborhoods, they offered amenities previously unknown to the middle class, while creating an auto-dependent population that quickly grew accustomed to life in spacious, family-oriented subdivisions.

Despite the great surge in automobile traffic, commuter railroads anticipated that business would grow. New trains were added north and west of the city in response to rapid suburbanization and rising congestion. In 1950, the Chicago, Burlington & Quincy introduced bi-level "gallery" cars on its commuter route, the first such cars operated anywhere in the United States.[3] These "ultra modern, air-conditioned, stainless steel" cars were advertised as no less comfortable than the Burlington's well-known Zephyr streamliner cars.[4] Yet, Zephyr-like comfort or not, the fact remained that many first-time homeowners settled into towns without train stations.

The large-scale migration away from rail lines was unprecedented in the region's history. On unincorporated land near the Fox River 35 miles west of the Loop, for instance, a development called Meadowdale grew to more than 2,500 residents in a few years with its own 85-acre shopping center. Prefabricated homes were trucked from Milwaukee by the hundreds and assembled onsite. Meadowdale soon dwarfed neighboring Carpentersville, which annexed it in 1953.

Such rapid development affected travel patterns on a scale unseen since the early days of the automobile, and governments scrambled to keep pace. Using revenues generated through the sale of bonds, the city of Chicago and Cook County worked hurriedly to complete the city's first expressways-without the benefit of federal funds. Civic leaders from throughout the region gathered on December 20, 1951, to mark the completion of the Edens Expressway. A motorcade started from the city's Mayfair neighborhood and continued to Lake-Cook Road, the new expressway's northern terminus, where William Erikson, president of the county board, and Dan Ryan, his highway commissioner, trumpeted the occasion's significance. Also on hand was William Edens, for whom this modern six-lane road was named. Many years earlier, the retired Lake County administrator had arranged for the region's first road-building bonds.

The following year, portions of the Tri-State Highway (today's I-80/94), and Calumet Expressway (now the Bishop Ford Freeway, part of Interstate 94) opened, albeit lacking several bridges still to be built over railroad crossings. Both the Tri-State, which stretched only six miles at the time (from the Indiana state line to Markham, Illinois), and the Edens sliced through lightly populated areas near the edge of the city. Even so, for a region that had seen relatively little change to its transportation system for forty years, these short segments came as welcome indicators that further improvements lay ahead.

These new corridors did not displace many residents. Only when federal help became available could expressways be built deep into the urban core, requiring the relocation of thousands of people in densely populated neighborhoods. Until then, Chicago would further lag behind other major cities in new expressway construction, with traffic tie-ups becoming frightful. On Archer Avenue, Grand Avenue, Milwaukee Avenue, and other routes linking the city to the suburbs, traffic moved as slowly as 4 miles an hour during peak times.[5]

Federal agencies championed such expressway construction, having endorsed—if not yet significantly funded—a national interstate highway system. Washington looked to new roads to become strategic assets in times of war—precisely as the Autobahn had done in Germany during World War II—and to improve civilian mobility. Expressways could also promote a dispersion of population, thereby lessening the probable loss of life after a nuclear attack.[6]

Cook County board president Dan Ryan *(right)*, former board member Clayton F. Smith *(left)*, and board member William N. Erickson, join hands in 1957 at an event honoring Elizabeth A. Conkey for years of service to the board. *(Cook County)*

Few of those pushing for bringing the superhighways into central city districts, however, showed any awareness that inner city population was about to plummet. As late as 1955, the Chicago Plan Commission conducted its work under the assumption that the city's population would grow to six million over the next twenty years. Using these estimates as a guide, Harry Chaddick worked to modernize Chicago zoning laws to prepare for a surge in housing construction. The *Chicago Tribune* put it this way: "There is no doubt that the suburbs are growing faster than the city, but nobody is worrying about it …The rapid suburban growth … is simply the result of the fact that the city is running out of vacant land."[7] The extraordinary scale of expansion fueled the belief that more decisions needed to be made on a truly regional basis.

The Advent of New Institutions for Regional Transportation

By 1953, many regional planning advocates felt that advisory bodies like the Chicago Plan Commission and the RPA would need to make room for agencies with power delegated to them by the state. The combined effect of new federal programs, growing sophistication of state and municipal agencies, and the rising need for intergovernmental agreements made such agencies seem almost inevitable. On July 13, 1953, the state legislature took an important step in this direction by creating the Illinois State Toll Highway Commission (later Authority), a self-funded entity whose main objective was to construct and operate a system of toll roads in outlying areas that would connect the proposed interstate highways. Although the Commission did not have the power to levy taxes, it had deep pockets, quickly selling $415 million in bonds to be repaid from toll revenues.

Building highways into the center of the city would come later, when money became available. Road-builders warned, however, that even if all the expressways and tollways depicted in the Chicago Plan Commission's 1943 map were built, the region's transportation system would be inadequate in just twenty years. In 1954, Momentum for road building accelerated stronger when Dan Ryan was elected chairman of the Cook County board of commissioners. Both Ryan and Bill Mortimer, the new superintendent of the county's highway department, pushed for a much larger grid of transportation routes than what had been previously envisioned. Mortimer's department wanted to add more expressways to the official map and to extend the Logan Square subway (today's Blue Line) to the soon-to-be-opened O'Hare Airport.

But Mortimer felt that the region should not plan on a piecemeal basis. He wanted a comprehensive study of the region's transportation needs and found support for the

Metropolitan Housing Council: An Emerging Voice in Regional Planning

The Metropolitan Housing Council (MHC) established itself as an influential actor on the regional stage in the early postwar era. Unlike the RPA, whose programs emphasized cooperation, but stopped short of proposing changes in the authority of governmental institutions, MHC believed that the greater good required civic leaders to ruffle feathers and take unpopular stances. MHC had been an agent of change since its creation in March 1934, when Elizabeth Wood, the council's first executive director, set out to create a comprehensive housing program for Chicago.

Elizabeth Wood, circa 1940. *(Chicago Housing Authority)*

Wood relentlessly pushed the city to strengthen the Chicago Plan Commission and called for creation of a housing division that would tackle issues related to residential development.[8] Although the Plan Commission resisted this, MHC made progress with the City Council and was instrumental to the passage of the city ordinance in 1939 that reorganized the Plan Commission, making it an arm of municipal government.[9]

Nevertheless, MHC's approach contrasted sharply with that of Burnham, Jr.'s RPA, which continued its conciliatory spirit, with a board consisting largely of men representing units of government. MHC was expressly an agent of change with no formal ties to government. The group was backed by influential civic leaders who felt impatient with current regional planning. Its long-time president Ferd Kramer, a prominent developer, had little interest in a planning process that would drag on for years. Kramer was not shy about voicing his opinions about the need for stronger institutions, even raising the sensitive issue of taxing suburban areas to support improvements in the central city, something the RPA dared not do.[10]

A defining moment for MHC came in 1944, when it sponsored the Chicago of the Future exhibition at the Marshall Field department store, which drew about 10,000 people.[11] Yet the publicity it generated was less threatening to the RPA than MHC's burgeoning regional agenda. In the early 1940s, the organization began pushing for a "regional master plan" to guide housing development and created a list of ten "planning commandments" that the region should observe after the war. One "commandment" was to create policies that would transcend city, county, and state boundaries. According to the organization's official historian, some people believed the Council "had finally gone off into the stratosphere."[12]

MHC's voice grew louder after the war. In early 1948, it officially changed its name to the Metropolitan Housing and Planning Council (MHPC) to better reflect its expanded agenda. Dorothy Rubel, the new executive director, continued to exert pressure on the Chicago Plan Commission, even criticizing it for failing to prepare a master plan for both the city and region as a whole.[13] The RPA took exception to some of MHPC's ideas, especially its belief that the region needed a new agency to put a variety of planning functions under one roof. Burnham, Jr., in fact, was clearly agitated by this prospect, writing in 1949 that he had met with "the Metropolitan Housing boys" and used the occasion to convince a colleague that "we need no more duplicating agencies on regional planning."[14] Despite these objections, support for the idea grew stronger.[15]

As we will see later in this chapter, MPHC, more than any other organization, led the charge to create a new planning commision for the metropolitan Chicago region.

idea from Chicago mayor Martin Kennelly.[16] Soon, a lobbying effort began with this goal in mind, culminating in an agreement to create the Chicago Area Transportation Study (CATS). Signed on January 26, 1955, by Dan Ryan, Kennelly, and Illinois Public Works and Buildings director Walter Rosenstone, the agreement called for a study to forecast the demand for travel and find the best ways to accommodate this demand.[17]

The Chicago Area Transportation Study wasted little time in forming an organization and launching its assessment. Responsibility for major decisions was placed in the hands of a policy committee of appointed officials, which selected a Harvard-trained technician, Douglas Carroll, Jr., as the study's director. Within a few months of its creation, the CATS organization began to collect an enormous amount of data to evaluate the region's long-term transportation needs. By the middle of 1956, it had some 360 people on its payroll, ranging from statisticians to housewives working part time.

Meanwhile, the city, county, and state moved ahead with the expressways already planned and slated for construction. Dan Ryan orchestrated a successful referendum on another bond issue that cleared the way for more road building in Cook County. Soon, attention turned to the Congress Expressway—aligned on the "great avenue" that Daniel H. Burnham envisioned in the 1909 *Plan* as "extending from Michigan Avenue throughout the city and westward indefinitely." Many expected this so-called "West Side Highway" to be completed much earlier—Robert Kingery, when he was director of the state's public works department, had awarded the city $21 million for it back in 1935. After years of wrangling over its proposed path, the city decided to have it follow railroad tracks to minimize the need to relocate people. Finally, in 1955, the first portions were complete. The Congress would become the first superhighway linking downtown Chicago to the suburbs.[18]

In 1956, federal help was on the way. President Eisenhower signed the Federal Aid Highway Act in 1956, authorizing a 41,000-mile coast-to-coast Interstate construction effort, "a vast system of interconnected highways crisscrossing the country and joining at our national borders with friendly neighbors to the north and south."[19] The ambitious system was described at the time as the largest infrastructure project in the world, equivalent to sixty Panama Canals. A system of matching funds, in which the federal government paid 90 percent of the cost, was a boon to state and local governments.

Mayor Richard J. Daley drives a spike to show his support for the new Congress "L" rapid-transit line. When opened in 1958, the Congress became the country's first rapid-transit line operating in the median of a major expressway. *(Chicago History Museum)*

The federal share would be covered by new taxes on fuel—at first just 3 cents a gallon—as well as other auto-related goods such as tires.

As road building kicked into high gear, federal and state officials grew apprehensive over the lack of regional land-use plans to help coordinate development spurred by the new highways. Most of the planning done by highway officials at the time dealt with little more than technical concerns, such as the designs of the roads themselves, the efficiency of the alignments, and the dimensions and locations of interchanges. As work crews cleared large swaths of land to make room for expressways through Douglas, Grand Boulevard, Jefferson Park, West Garfield Park, and other Chicago neighborhoods, important questions about the economic and social implications of these roads remained unanswered.

In spite of the upheaval, there was a presumption at the time that ingenuity and technology would allow highway departments to tackle even the most difficult problems. Yet some planners remained dubious, since the massive infrastructure was not being integrated into an overall plan for the region. Flooding was a persistent problem, and water supply and sewage issues appeared to grow worse each year. Older neighborhoods as well as inner-ring suburbs were beginning to feel the pinch of stagnation and disinvestment. The city of Chicago's population had peaked and begun to fall. Frank Lloyd Wright warned that "the urbanite must either be willing to get out of the city or resigned to blowing up with it."[20]

Chicago Plan Commission member James Downs points to a downtown development project, with *(from left)* Clifford Cambell, Mayor Daley, and Ira Bach (1958). Daley considered his Central Area Plan, released that year, as a sequel to the portions of the 1909 *Plan* that focused on the city center. *(Chicago History Museum)*

The creation of an official regional agency to study and manage land use in the metropolitan area became imperative. Civic leaders and the newspapers joined the chorus of planners who warned of dire consequences if there were not more coordination among local governments. "Many of the city's old mistakes are being repeated in the booming suburban areas," noted the *Chicago Tribune*, adding "well-planned suburbs are being jeopardized by lax standards of adjacent towns."[21]

The Push for a Regional Planning Commission

The campaign to create a "sister agency" to CATS with a focus on land-use and economic development issues was gathering momentum by mid-1955. MHPC, working with the Chicago Plan Commission and Cook County, formed the Metropolitan Area Study Committee to consider the options. The committee was led by Reginald Isaacs, a noted regional planning expert who had served as director of planning at Michael Reese Hospital.

"Suburban Improvement Program" cartoon, December 1958, illustrates popular awareness of the enormous public investments occurring at the time. *(Chaddick Collection)*

This committee's final report, completed in October 1956, called for "legislation to provide planning for the metropolitan area."[22] This helped spur creation of the Randolph Commission, appointed by Governor Stratton, Chicago Mayor Richard J. Daley, and six county boards. The twenty-two person commission, awkwardly named the Northeastern Illinois Metropolitan Area Local Governmental Services Commission, was chaired by U.S. Representative Paul J. Randolph, a prominent Chicago Republican. The best solution to the problem of "disorderly growth," the panel said, was an officially sanctioned organization to develop "superplans" for the metropolitan area.[23]

By early 1957, state and county officials were feeling pressure from Washington to move in this direction. Federal money flowed to local governments for roads, parks, schools, water supply systems, and sewers. Through the Housing Act of 1954, the Department of Housing and Urban Development (HUD) offered grants for councils of government and other regional planning organizations to promote cooperation and shared problem solving. HUD wanted applications submitted by local governments to be screened and reviewed by a regional planning organization, yet no such entity in metropolitan Chicago appeared suitable for this role.

Initially, there was hope of creating an organization with jurisdiction over a massive area, encompassing all or parts of ten counties comprising metropolitan Chicago, including several in Indiana.[24] The roadblocks to such an entity, however, were formidable. Some municipalities feared the preemptive power such an organization might have over local decision making. Others feared the consequences of giving such an organization the power to levy taxes. And Indiana residents had little enthusiasm for an Illinois-based authority.

High-ranking public officials were split on the issue. Governor Stratton supported the effort, but Mayor Daley remained lukewarm, perhaps thinking, as the *Chicago Tribune* put it, that "most of the benefits are likely to accrue to the suburbs."[25] But Daley recognized that he couldn't simply block the effort without proposing an alternative. In any case, he was open to a limited degree of power-sharing, having supported the creation of the Metropolitan Fair and Exposition Authority (later renamed the Metropolitan Pier and Exposition Authority) several years earlier, which ceded power over the convention business to a non-elected board that he could only partially control.

As the effort to draft legislation moved forward in Springfield, MHPC stepped up its lobbying efforts, only to find that other roadblocks remained. To mollify opponents, including Daley, the relevant legislative committee scaled back its proposal to involve just six counties in northeastern Illinois. It also dropped a proposed real-estate tax to support the new organization. Daley loyalists still threatened to block the bill unless it were endorsed by the six county boards and was then approved by referendum. Daniel Burnham, Jr., still in the fray, thought the bill was dead.[26]

Regional planning promoters retreated on their ambition to create a truly sovereign agency, accepting in the end a self-standing "municipal corporation" with little power, no taxing authority, and no guaranteed income from Springfield. This strategy worked, albeit with lasting consequences for the new agency's ability to conduct regional planning. On July 6, 1957, the Illinois General Assembly approved the creation of the Northeastern Illinois Metropolitan Area Planning Commission (NIPC) and provided $50,000 for its operations. Within a year, the RPA was gone (see sibebar below).

Unlike CATS, which became an arm of the state highway department, NIPC would not be formally affiliated with a state agency. It would be governed by a board of nineteen

Both old and new are visible in this photo of a westbound train rounding a curve at Halsted Street on the four-track Garfield "L," circa 1953. The Congress Expressway, which appears under construction *(right center)*, would soon necessitate demolition of the "L" structure. Note the passageway for the expressway through the Central Post Office *(far right)*. *(Peterson-Krambles Collection)*

commissioners appointed for the most part by the governor and the Chicago mayor. Architect Paul Oppermann, former planning director for San Francisco city and county, became the first executive director. A native of Saginaw, Michigan, he had worked for the American Society of Planning Officials and practiced in the Chicago area.

A New Day for Planning

The new agency, NIPC, scored several early victories, attracting federal funds as well as grants from Illinois' transportation department and other state agencies. It solicited local governments for annual contributions and secured some private foundation money for special projects. The agency successfully pushed the state to create subdivision and zoning standards for the region.[33]

Last Days of the Chicago Regional Planning Association

As efforts to create official regional agencies advanced, little life remained in Daniel Burnham, Jr.'s Chicago Regional Planning Association. Revenue plummeted in 1955 and 1956, leaving the RPA, which never had a large budget, with a fraction of the resources it once had. The release of its long-anticipated *Planning the Region of Chicago* report, known as the Kingery Plan (Chapter 4) gave the RPA a publicity boost that strengthened its legacy but did little to solve its money problems.

Only a month before the creation of NIPC, Burnham, Jr., sought a major grant to revive his association's fortunes. A meeting in April 1957 with Chas A. Phelan, an official from the American Civic and Planning Association in Washington, D.C. lifted his spirits. Burnham, Jr., called him "a Public Relations man of the exact type we are seeking for the regional plan." But no grant was offered, and the RPA's relevance continued to diminish.[27]

As the creation of NIPC neared, Burnham, Jr., made a note in his business journal suggesting that he feared the end of the RPA was near. He recounted a report from RPA board member Bill Erickson (formerly Cook County Board president), in Springfield, that there was "such a powerful group in favor of [NIPC] he was afraid it could not be stopped."[28] Another board member, Chester Davis, blamed the setback on the association's failure to publicize its achievements strongly enough and sought redress by suggesting that it submit a letter to A.T. Burch, reporter at the *Chicago Daily News*, to explain its accomplishments.[29] The Regional Planning Association was on the ropes, but Burnham was reluctant to see it dissolved; he proposed instead that it double its dues, believing—improbably—that it could reassert itself while sharing the stage with the new organizations. This strategy was apparently rejected by the board, and plans were made to fold the association into NIPC.

Burnham, Jr., promptly resigned as president, pleading business demands. Besides his objections to the NIPC merger, he likely also had his differences with executive director Howard Olson, who supported the merger. Burnham noted in his journal that he "was surprised that Olie rather favors this and would be glad to get out of the actual

Nevertheless, executive director Oppermann was unwilling to announce a "superplan" without assurance of support for NIPC policies—specifically its effort to link land-use and transportation planning. At issue may have been an emerging rivalry with CATS, which showed little interest in linking its planning agenda to NIPC's. The problem certainly was not helped by the differing philosophies of the two directors. CATS's Douglas Carroll was more inclined to let the marketplace drive development, and consequently more willing to accept the low-density patterns of newly built suburbs, where single family homes on spacious lots were the norm.

"I do not accept the premise that things will be better if we go back to old densities," Carroll once said in a public appearance with Oppermann. "We must evaluate what people want and will want."[34] Oppermann disagreed, and argued instead for the redesign of

management. I have felt for sometime [sic] that his heart is no longer in his job. Therefore, it may be best to wind up the Regional Plan as I certainly do not want the responsibility to put through a reorganization of the same."[30] His decision appeared final.

When the board met for the last time on July 18, the directors voted to formally dissolve the RPA and to have the newly created NIPC assume its lease, accept its assets, and hire Olson and one other employee. At the final meeting on October 24, 1958, Earl Kribben, NIPC's president, compared the association to a "bride" who must lose her name in order to join a marriage. Before an audience of 250, RPA board member Davis presented a plaque to Daniel Burnham, Jr., and lauded him for his "ability and devotion."[31] For the first time since the 1880s, a member of the Burnham family would not be part of the region's planning scene—it was the end of one the country's oldest regional planning associations.

Daniel Burnham, Jr., circa 1957.
(Lyn Burnham Messner Collection)

Burnham, Jr., apparently still felt a yearning to be involved in regional planning. In June 1959, Earl Kribben, first president of NIPC, passed away. Burnham expressed interest in volunteering his services for the NIPC board and visited Chester Davis, who was now on that board, to inquire about this possibility. Burnham offered himself to fill Davis's spot on the agency's board, should the governor wish to appoint him. This overture was successful.[32]

Tragically, four years later, on November 3, 1961, Burnham, Jr., and his second wife, Martha, died in an automobile accident near Lake Zurich. Both are buried in Graceland Cemetery.

State Representatives Abner Mikva, Noble Lee, and Paul Randolph *(left to right)* are cited in 1961 by the Metropolitan Housing and Planning Council for their leadership in securing legislation in support of regional planning. John W. Baird, MHPC president, *(far right)* presented the citations. *(MHPC newsletter, October 1961)*

central cities to moderate the demand for suburban land and to support public transit. Seemingly agitated by Carroll's remarks, he reminded the audience—including Carroll—that his organization "had sole authority and responsibility to coordinate planning for all forms of transportation" in the region.[35]

This latter point clearly had not taken root. Consequently, Oppermann felt he had to wait before launching a new comprehensive plan for the region, which would be the first since the *Plan of Chicago*. His delay, however, did not sit well with the NIPC board.

Despite the apparent CATS-NIPC friction, no one could deny that the years leading up to 1957 had been full of achievement. Several expressways had opened to the public. Enormous investments in public works were underway. Three officially sanctioned regional organizations—CATS, the Illinois State Toll Highway Authority, and NIPC—had their start, and one of them, CATS, had begun a huge planning effort to determine long-term transportation needs.

Mathew Rockwell, executive director of NIPC *(center)*, and Chester Davis, board president *(right)*, recognize Paul Oppermann, the organization's first executive director in 1963. *(NIPC's 1963 annual report)*

Many believed that the first comprehensive vision for regional planning since the *Plan of Chicago* would soon emerge. As the following chapters show, however, the divide between land-use and transportation planning would not be crossed any time soon.

SHAPING A
TRANSPORTATION VISION

Construction of the Calumet *(Chicago)* Skyway, shown here at the Calumet River, was well on its way by November, 1957. Five months later, the six-mile route opened for motor travel. *(Chicago History Museum)*

6

IN THIS CHAPTER

Rapid progress is made building expressways, airport facilities, and new rapid transit lines in expressway medians. In a span of just six years, more than three-quarters of the Chicago region's total current expressway and toll road mileage opens to the public. O'Hare International replaces Midway as the nation's busiest airport, while the commuter railroads make great strides in modernizing their physical plant.

BANNER YEARS FOR TRANSPORTATION:
1958 – 1964

The extraordinary transportation achievements of the Chicago region between 1958 and 1964 dramatically changed the area's political and socioeconomic landscape. Each year, ribbon-cutting ceremonies marked new milestones in the improvement of air, rail, and highway transportation.

The dedications of O'Hare Airport, a multi-county toll road system, the modern Calumet (Chicago) Skyway, and several of the world's busiest expressways showcased the work of transportation planners and ended a more than twenty-five-year drought in large-scale public works investment. In this same period, commuters witnessed the modernization of the commuter railroads, the replacement of the last streetcars with buses, and the completion of the first rapid-transit route ever built in an expressway median in the United States.

Several forces converged to make this period one of such remarkable accomplishment. The Illinois State Toll Highway Authority broke through the political logjams that previously had slowed tollway construction. Mayor Richard J. Daley marshaled financial and political support for bold initiatives in Chicago, even as the city's population fell. County governments, working closely with the city and state, invested bond-sale proceeds into a massive expressway system. Lastly, help arrived from Washington—between 1957 and 1958, the federal government tripled its support to the state for interstate highway construction.

Local opposition to major projects was often poorly organized; when it was not, such opposition was generally ignored—even along inner-city corridors where thousands of residents were destined to be relocated from their homes. Planners working for municipal, county, and state agencies enjoyed the public's trust, allowing these agencies to aggressively use eminent domain, even when it meant destroying established neighborhoods. Until the mid 1960s, enormous progress was made, with massive capital projects moving ahead on schedules that remain remarkably fast by today's standards. The region was on the move, and transportation was its focus.

"A Glorious New Toll Road"

This six-year period of transportation expansion began in earnest on April 16, 1958, wtih the opening of Calumet Skyway (today's Chicago Skyway). This seven-mile "highway bridge," Illinois' first new toll road in more than a century, linked the Indiana Toll Road

Lights from the Calumet (Chicago) Skyway bridge and still-vibrant waterfront industries reflect on the Calumet River, circa 1960. This photograph was taken with 60-second exposure. *(Chicago History Museum)*

and Chicago, allowing the Calumet region's vast steel-producing district to be more effectively integrated with the rest of metropolitan Chicago. The Skyway slashed a full hour off travel time for some automobile trips. Managed by the city of Chicago and financed through bonds, the toll road was heralded as a magnificent engineering achievement.

On the day it opened, the weather was unseasonably warm. "The luck of the Irish is with me," Mayor Daley quipped after arriving in the official motorcade, before addressing a crowd of 300. In his speech, Daley hailed the Skyway as "another step forward for Chicago's progress."[1] The first vehicle to cross the big bridge towards the city was a school bus carrying disabled children, who displayed a "Congratulations Mayor Daley" sign. The children had watched the Skyway being built from the Jane A. Neil School for the Handicapped on the South Side.[2]

Massive concrete supports along I-90 south of 79th Street, circa 1958, await the next phase of construction. *(Chicago History Museum)*

The Skyway's massive steel bridge over the Calumet River rose so high that some motorists feared for their safety. "Since God helps those who help themselves, let's all cooperate to prevent this glorious new toll road from ever becoming a 'death' road," the *Chicago Daily News* remarked.[3] The day unfolded without incident, but traffic was so heavy that a jam occurred near the west end of the route.

Less than two months later, on June 20, 1958, the city celebrated another milestone with the dedication of the world's first rapid-rail transit line in a multi-lane expressway median. Running through the center of the Congress Expressway, the new line let the CTA abandon the old Garfield Park elevated. Once again, Daley basked in transportation glory, taking part in a ceremony at the new Halsted Street station attended by hundreds, then lunching with hundreds more at the Palmer House. For its sheer innovation, the *Chicago Tribune's* Hal Foust compared the new line to the city's first elevated trains of 1892.[4]

Meanwhile, the Illinois State Toll Highway Authority (ISTHA) made progress in the suburbs. Work on the East-West Expressway, which linked Hillside (at the endpoint of the Congress Expressway) to a rural location west of Aurora near Sugar Grove, proceeded at a furious pace, passing as it did through lightly populated areas. Its completion on November 21, 1958, offered more ribbon-cutting ceremonies for Mayor Daley, who was joined this time by Governor William G. Stratton at a variety of celebrations. Motorists could travel nonstop for the first time through the western suburbs, needing only to slow down to pay 30-cent tolls along the new tollway's twenty-twp miles.[5] This superhighway (today known as Reagan Memorial Tollway, part of Interstate 88) did more than expedite travel, it paved the way for extraordinary population growth in DuPage County. By flowing into the Congress Expressway, it let motorists make a thirty-six-mile uninterrupted trip from Aurora to downtown Chicago.

The symmetrical design of the newly completed Tollway Oasis in Lake Forest appears in this June, 1960 photo. Four of these rest-stops, built in the International Style, lined the new Tri-State Tollway. *(Illinois Tollway Photo)*

These projects were impressive enough, but involved far less mileage than that of the Northwest and Tri-State toll roads that were nearing completion. The Northwest Tollway stretched seventy-six miles from O'Hare to Rockford and on to Beloit, Wisconsin. The Tri-State was a ring road reminiscent of those envisioned in the *Plan of Chicago*, stretching from near the Wisconsin state line to the Kingery Expressway three miles to the west (the latter route, part of the old Tri State Highway, was completed in 1952). By late autumn of 1958, lengthy portions of these roads had opened to traffic.

The last stretches opened on December 28, 1958, bringing ISTHA's network quickly up to 187 miles. The entire system was completed in just twenty-seven months, a pace that some builders of urban area highways had previously considered impractical if not impossible. Where traffic once crawled, it now moved "fast and free," generally at speeds exceeding a mile a minute. "The Tollroad's impact already is felt," the *Chicago Daily News* noted the day after the Tri-State opened, "in new traffic patterns, requests for motel building permits, and soaring property values adjacent to tollway entrances and exits."[6]

By this time, federal funding became a major part of the equation. A system of matching funds became available in 1957 (with the federal government paying 90 percent of the costs, and state and local agencies the remainder), allowing work to commence on many Interstate Highway projects around the country. Robert Moses, who famously planned and promoted superhighways in New York, believed that "this new highway program will affect our entire economic and social structure…. The appearance of the new arteries and their adjacent areas will leave a permanent imprint on our communities and people."[7]

An attendant hands a motorist an "Illinois Tollway Pioneer" souvenir to commemorate the opening of the East-West Tollway on November 21, 1958. The new route allowed for a 35.5-mile uninterrupted trip between Aurora and Maywood. *(Chicago History Museum)*

Moses wasn't alone in ascribing such importance to the new highways. Soon large swaths of land, sometimes several blocks wide, were being cleared for construction. In 1958, federal support to Illinois for road building surpassed $100

million for the first time.
The following year, it
soared to more than
$180 million—a tenfold
increase over ten years.
By the beginning of
1960, great progress was
made on the Northwest
Expressway (today's
Kennedy), an extension
of the Eisenhower (I-290)
to Rolling Meadows,
and the North-South
Expressway (today's Dan
Ryan Expressway).

A construction crane used to
support Chicago's massive
expressway program has a
special occupant, mayor Richard
J. Daley, who is apparently
pretending to be testing its lifting
mechanisms, circa 1959. As this
photograph suggests, the mayor
used the region's roadbuilding
achievements to maximum
political advantage, basking in the
spotlight at carefully staged events
held to draw attention to various
construction milestones. *(Chicago
History Museum)*

The enormous economic impact of the region's superhighways was painfully obvious
to the commuter railroads. Already facing large deficits over its system in 1954, the
Chicago & North Western took drastic measures to protect its passenger business.[8]
In 1955 it began to replace its half-century-old rolling stock with new streamlined
bi-level gallery cars, double-decked and air-conditioned.[9] In 1956, a few weeks after Ben
Heineman took over as chairman, the North Western retired the last of its aging steam
locomotives, replacing them with sleek diesel units.[10] The line also closed many inner-city
stations for the sake of faster service. By 1958, observers of the local rail industry were
calling the C&NW "the Chicago Miracle."[11] Other railroads in the region followed suit in
the next few years, and by the early 1960s the region's commuter rail system was hailed
as the country's best.

Heineman recognized that the construction of the Northwest Expressway—and
its proposed transit line to O'Hare—posed a particularly serious threat to his passenger
business. Adding insult to injury, the superhighway required tearing up and relocating
a lengthy stretch of C&NW tracks. Mayor Daley was also aware of the highway's
impacts, publicly voicing concern for the thousands of people that would be relocated
for construction. Unlike most other inner-city expressways, which ran mostly parallel
to existing streets, the Northwest cut a diagonal through the street grid, requiring the
relocation of residents on a scale previously unseen in the city.

Cancelling the Northwest Expressway, however, was hardly an option. Part of
the city's plans since 1927, when the "Avondale Highway" between downtown and
the northwest suburbs was proposed, the Northwest now had federal funding as part
of the Interstate Highway System. Business and political leaders knew the expressway
was critical to the expansion of O'Hare. Seeking to minimize the disruption caused
by its construction, the mayor demanded that the right-of-way be kept to an unusually

The Congress rapid-transit line nears completion in the Congress expressway median, circa 1958. *(Illinois Department of Highways Photo, Andrew Plummer Collection)*

narrow width. Cook County highways chief Marshall Suloway found this demand extremely difficult, as he wanted the road to be wide enough to accommodate a median-strip transit line to the airport. Suloway's solution was to eliminate the customary grass-covered embankments, instead building vertical retaining walls along the road that allowed its footprint to be relatively narrow.

Walls and all, the Northwest Expressway opened on November 4, 1960. The *Chicago Daily News* described it as the "envy of the world's planners" and a "Model for the World."[12] At a ceremony at the expressway's Lake Street overpass, five-hundred people fought the blustery weather to hear Mayor Daley praise this great milestone. Dan Ryan, who had pushed for this road for years, noted that "those of us who are representatives of the public should congratulate not ourselves but all of the taxpayers." The day also featured a sixty-five car motorcade including Governor Stratton.

This "dream road" was a boon to commercial airlines, which were relocating many of their flights from Midway Airport to O'Hare at the time. Anticipating that the road would stimulate travel to the newer airport, American Airlines placed half-page newspaper advertisements congratulating "forward-thinking Chicago."[13] A bus trip from the Chicago Loop to the air terminal, once more than an hour, now took just twenty-five minutes.

Motorists, however, still could not travel all the way through Chicago by expressway. That would have to wait for the North-South Expressway, another project long championed by Dan Ryan. The affable county board president, however, died on April 8, 1961, at the age of 66, after attending mass with his wife.[14] Ryan's death prompted an outpouring of sympathy from public officials and ordinary citizens. "He was a big man in the biggest county in the country," noted *Chicago Daily News* political writer Charles Cleveland, who "had as few enemies as anyone could in politics."[15]

Ryan's absence was felt at the December 15, 1962 ceremonies to mark the completion of the North–South Expressway. With fourteen lanes, including separate express and local lanes, this expressway—deemed the "Gateway to Chicago Southland" by the newspapers—was considered to be the widest in the world. Constructing this road required clearing two full city blocks for most of its length, then lifting it onto an extraordinary series of pylons immediately south of downtown.

Dan Ryan's widow, Mildred, presided over the ribbon-cutting ceremony for the road, now named after her late husband. The ceremonies went without a hitch, but traffic backed up severely on the Congress Expressway as curious motorists slowed down for

Mildred Ryan stands with two of her grandchildren, Dan and Marcy Ryan, and an impressive group of dignitaries at opening ceremonies for the expressway named for her late husband, December 15, 1962. In the front row (l to r) are Cook County commissioner Edward Sneed, Chicago alderman Robert Miller, Mayor Richard J. Daley, a young Dan Ryan, Mrs. Ryan, Governor Otto Kerner, county board president John Duffy, county highway superintendent William Mortimer, and county commissioners Seymour Simon and John Touhy are also present. *(Cook County Highway News)*

The spacious dimensions of the Dan Ryan expressway, with separate local and express lanes, appear in this photo looking northward from 35th Street, circa 1968. The superhighway required clearing a two-block-wide corridor through much of Chicago's South Side, effectively dividing white and black neighborhoods. *(Chicago History Museum)*

a look at the magnificent new route. A *Chicago Sun-Times* headline proclaimed that "Dan Ryan Would Love It." A journalist surmised: "If the proposition of naming the expressway after him had been put to him while he still lived, he would have cracked a typically self-deprecating joke and laughed it off."[16]

Mathew Sielski, of the Chicago Motor Club, optimistically reported that the new expressway would neither worsen Loop congestion nor hurt the commuter railroads. "Commuters now using trains will return almost to a man once they have looked over the new road," noted a *Daily News* writer in an article about Sielski's views.[17]

By early 1963, work was underway on the Southwest Expressway (later renamed the Stevenson), which some would consider an even more remarkable piece of engineering than the Dan Ryan, requiring the construction of several miles of pylons to elevate the road high above industrial areas. Unlike other expressways of this era, the Southwest required relocating very few households—most land in its path was occupied by industry or railroads along the Sanitary and Ship Canal. This pleased the mayor, who recognized that the public's mood was turning negative toward more urban expressway building. When it opened in 1964, the Southwest would be hailed as a marvel and deemed the city's safest and most modern expressway, albeit lacking the express bus lanes envisioned in an earlier plan.[18]

These public-works investments were widely understood to have enormous social and economic implications. Nevertheless, policymakers failed to grasp the extent to which they would accelerate the decentralization of population—particularly the outward flow of the middle class—and have far-reaching implications for urban neighborhoods and the suburban environment. The vulnerability of once-vital inner city neighborhoods came to light in New York through the writings of activist Jane Jacobs, whose 1961 book *The Death and Life of Great American Cities*, became a major work in the field of urban planning. Yet in Chicago a serious debate about these issues was still several years away.

An Air Terminal "Second to None"

As residents took their first drives on new expressways, another major initiative, the development of O'Hare International Airport, moved briskly ahead. A city in itself, O'Hare covered 6,700 acres of land, with its own zip code, power plant, and expressway; it was connected to the city of Chicago by a 200-foot-wide sliver of land along the Northwest Expressway. This annexation, which kept the airport under city control, arose from a deal between Mayor Daley and long-time Rosemont mayor Donald Stevens. In exchange for Stevens' approval of the annexation, Daley agreed to provide the village with much sought-after Lake Michigan water.

O'Hare was in development for more than a decade. In 1958, a new international terminal and a customs and immigration building allowed for dramatic expansion of flight activity. Boeing 707 aircraft, unable to take off on Midway's short runways, began using the terminal, and soon the city enjoyed nonstop service to Europe. In 1959, Chicago issued the largest bond in its history to finance further expansion, which would give Chicago, in Daley's view, "a jet air terminal second to none in the world." By 1961, many airlines were moving flights from Midway to O'Hare, and work was underway on massive new passenger facilities.

The big day was March 23, 1963, when the mayor, Governor Otto Kerner, Senator Paul Douglas, the nephews of "Butch" O'Hare, and President John F. Kennedy helped make O'Hare what a *Tribune*

An American Airlines newspaper advertisement of 1960 illustrates the important role of the new Northwest Expressway in the development of O'Hare International Airport. *(Chaddick Collection)*

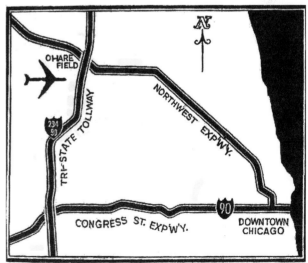

NOW AMERICAN'S JETS AT O'HARE ARE MORE CONVENIENT THAN EVER!

President John F. Kennedy lays a wreath at a monument to Lt. Commander Edward (Butch) O'Hare during the dedication of O'Hare International Airport, March 23, 1963. Mayor Daley *(left)* looks on. *(Chicago History Musuem)*

writer called "the most dedicated airport in the nation."[19] The ceremonies inaugurated a new rotunda in the International Style, with five restaurants, and terminals with tinted glass walls and modern passenger amenities. A three-terminal complex, arranged in a horseshoe-shaped configuration, was served by a new bi-level road with one level for flight arrivals and another for departures, a first for U.S. aviation. Kennedy called the new O'Hare "a fine story in Chicago-industry-Washington cooperation," said Kennedy, and it made O'Hare "one of the wonders of the world" and "a tribute to Mayor Daley."[20]

The complex, funded largely by proceeds from airline-backed bonds, was the city's newest public-works showpiece. Architects lauded it for its unity of design. Construction boss Walter Metschke was cautiously laudatory: "As far as I know," he said, "there's never been anything like it." By the following year, virtually all major airlines had relocated most flights from Midway, and work began on a giant parking garage—one of the largest in the world—and a hotel adjacent to the terminals.

Motorists dine at an Oasis on the Illinois Tollway System, circa 1965. This photo was used for publicity purposes. By today's standards, traffic appears remarkably light in both directions. *(Illinois Tollway photo)*

Farewell to Earlier Transportation Choices

The Chicago area's new highways and rapid transit service came on line as older services disappeared. Buses replaced the last Chicago streetcars on June 21, 1958. The CTA gave up on its wooden rapid-transit cars the same year. The Chicago, Aurora & Elgin Railway, once a familiar part of the Loop elevated system, abruptly ceased passenger service on July 3, 1957, stranding commuters downtown. The line lay dormant for several years as efforts to revive it continued, until the "Roarin' Elgin" was finally abandoned in 1963.

This series of graphs shows the region's expanding expressway system since the mid-1950s. The pace of construction was particularly impressive for the ten-year period 1955–65.

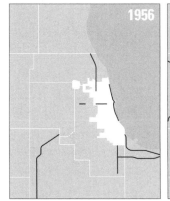
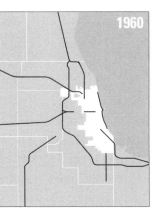

Construction workers pour concrete for the parking garage—one of the largest in the world—at O'Hare International Airport, circa 1973. *(Chicago History Museum)*

The Chicago, North Shore & Milwaukee Railroad—the North Shore Line—closed down in January 1963, leaving the Loop elevated system entirely to the CTA. Commuter trains of the Rock Island and the Chicago & Western Indiana (C&WI) lines, both linking downtown to the south suburbs, became hopelessly unprofitable after the Dan Ryan Expressway siphoned riders. The Rock Island soon petitioned for large-scale service discontinuations, and C&WI's run between old Dearborn Station and Dolton ended in 1964. It was the last route to disappear before public funding of commuter railroads began in the 1970s.

Clearly, over the six years from 1958 to 1964, there was a tectonic shift in Chicago transportation. By 1964, Chicago felt less like a big city surrounded by smaller suburbs linked to downtown by commuter and electric railways, and more like a giant metropolis interwoven with state-of-the-art expressways and tollways. Growth along the new superhighways encouraged travel between communities, in many cases making their boundaries invisible. And O'Hare, although within city limits, became a suburban growth machine, bringing prosperity to dozens of outlying communities and increased revenue to the city.

Transportation planners wanted more—much more—and thought that another round of highway construction was just around the corner. As we will see in the next chapter, things did not turn out as they had planned. "Expressway revolt" reared its head and the costs of building highways escalated sharply. The federal government failed to provide funding for major urban expressways beyond those already approved in the initial Interstate Highway System.

For the next several decades, the region's transportation system, with a few notable exceptions, seemed almost frozen in time. The debate over the environmental impacts of road building, meanwhile, gradually grew in intensity.

An artists's rendering of "busway" terminal proposed for the Southwest (Stevenson) Expressway, circa 1964. Today the CTA Orange Line follows this route. *(Graham Garfield Collection)*

7

IN THIS CHAPTER

The Chicago Area Transportation Study (CATS) completes a sophisticated analysis that calls for a near doubling of the region's previously planned expressway mileage, together with a modest expansion of the transit system. The plan, a product of hundreds of thousands of interviews and state-of-the-art computer analysis, lifts the CATS agency to national prominence. But few of the proposed highway improvements, including the Crosstown Expressway, are built, signaling a dramatic change in attitudes about big urban public works projects.

MAXIMUM MOBILITY:

The Chicago Area Transportation Study

I t was a red-letter day in Chicago-area transportation history—September 6, 1962—when a plan like none before it, the Chicago Area Transportation Study (CATS), was released in its final form. Rooted in data from more than two hundred thousand interviews, and sophisticated analyses from a mainframe computer, the study likened a transportation system to the "assembly line of urban society."[1] It envisioned a greatly expanded grid of superhighways across the metropolitan region, placing them roughly three miles apart in the city and four to six miles apart in the region's outer areas.

The rigorous process that CATS followed to prepare the plan brought it national prominence, establishing the agency as a model for effective transportation planning in a metropolitan area. Douglas Carroll, Jr., the organization's executive director since 1955, the year of its founding, insisted CATS adhere to a high degree of scientific rigor, even if it meant spending huge sums to collect and analyze traffic movements throughout the region. With Roger Creighton, the study's assistant director for research and planning, he assembled a research team that used complex statistical tools and the most modern information technologies available.

A worker displays signs alerting motorists to the Chicago Area Transportation Study's ongoing field survey of travel patterns, circa 1956. This picture, discovered in the Municipal Reference Library in Chicago, is one of the few known photographs from the initial CATS traffic survey. *(Chicago Area Transportation Study)*

Carroll, at 38, was already a widely respected figure in the urban transportation field by 1955. Born in Minneapolis in 1917, he moved with his family as a boy to the northwest side of Chicago. After attending Dartmouth and serving in the U.S. Navy during World War II, it was off to Harvard University's Graduate School of Design, where Carroll became, in 1947, only its third graduate with a doctorate in city and regional planning. His views were influenced by Walter Gropius, an architect of international acclaim as founder of the Bauhaus movement in Germany. Gropius designed the Harvard Graduate Center in 1948 and taught at Harvard during 1949-50.

After several years in the thriving automobile production center of Flint, Michigan, Carroll spent time as a research project director and lecturer in political science at the University of Michigan. He became director of the Detroit Metropolitan Area Traffic Study in the early 1950s, where he conducted what is considered the first major urban transportation study of its kind—an undertaking that involved data collection and analysis on a scale never before seen in a U.S. metropolitan area. Several years after the Detroit study's completion in 1953, he set out to produce an even larger study for Chicago.

Upon his appointment as director of the new CATS organization in 1955, Carroll wasted no time getting down to business. His staff accepted without complaint the inconveniences of modest office facilities, at first quartered in the State of Illinois Building on North LaSalle Street. In January, 1956 the study relocated to a vacant bank building, more recently a night club, at 4812 West Madison in the Austin neighborhood on Chicago's West Side.[2]

Although Austin was a quiet, middle-class neighborhood on the west side, some considered the location of questionable merit given its distance from the Loop—six miles from State Street—and it was already showing signs of decay, neglect, and "white flight." For many on Carroll's staff, however, the excitement of working for such a progressive agency apparently outweighed the limitations of the location. According to Roger Creighton, "The human atmosphere at the bank was exciting," but the building was "a dump."[3]

CATS was both an organization and a study. It was, in effect, an agency of the state that operated in a fishbowl, with Democrats and Republicans watching it carefully while seeking ways to exploit its potential for political advantage. The Cook County Republican Organization, led by Governor William G. Stratton, oversaw all hiring. The situation changed somewhat after Richard J. Daley, a Democrat, succeeded Martin Kennelly as Chicago mayor just a few months after CATS was founded. This weakened the Republican organization's influence—but the hiring remained distinctly partisan.[4]

Carroll's team produced forecasts suggesting the city and suburbs should prepare for dramatic increases in population. The forecasts projected—too optimistically, as it turned out—that by 1980 the region's population would top 9.5 million people with 4.6 million jobs. (The actual counts for 1980 were 7.5 million people and 3.4 million jobs).[5] In anticipation of rapid growth, the CATS planners assumed people throughout the region would welcome new highways, even if it meant clearing paths through their neighborhoods. To make his point, Carroll, speaking to the *Chicago Tribune*, noted that rush-hour speed was as low as four miles an hour on Irving Park Road and other thoroughfares.[6]

Carroll felt strongly that regional transportation planning should not be done in piecemeal fashion, as it historically had been; it should account for the wide range of factors affecting people's demand for travel. His team pioneered new techniques to evaluate how changing land-use patterns would affect the need for transportation facilities in the future. This work required an enormous amount of data, but rather than following the typical method of counting vehicles passing observation points to determine travel behavior, the staff collected travel data directly from drivers and transit riders. During 1956, CATS expanded its staff to 350 people—many were temporary hires for the travel surveys—with half the cost paid by the federal government.

Interviews were conducted on trains and buses, in homes and taxicabs, and at designated points along roads. Dozens of homemakers, who worked part time, canvassed the city and suburbs with clipboards in hand, conducting interviews to ascertain travel habits. Others worked in teams, staffing "traffic stops" along arterial roads. One particularly busy group conducted several-thousand interviews in a single day on North Lake Shore Drive. Still others examined aerial photos and property maps as well as home and business addresses to compile critical land-use information.

By late 1956, nearly two-thirds of an expected 57,000 interviews in private homes were complete, as were most of the expected 200,000 interviews with drivers at roadside stops and more than 5,500 interviews with truck and taxi drivers.[7] Commuters boarding trains were given cards to complete and submit. It was a personal and detailed approach to gathering data rarely undertaken by public agencies.

The human side of interviewing showed up in sometimes humorous mistakes. A woman of "grandmotherly years" was recorded as spending a morning on the golf course followed by an afternoon at a bowling alley and an evening at a night club. The interviewer had transposed symbols—the day of fun had been experienced by the lady's grandson.

Surveyors conduct interviews along Lake Shore Drive in what is apparently a publicity shot, circa 1956. Drivers were asked their origin, destination, trip purpose, and other questions to collect data for accurate travel demand forecasts. This picture, discovered in the Municipal Reference Library in Chicago, is one of the few known photographs from the initial CATS traffic survey. *(Chicago Area Transportation Study)*

This CATS illustration displays "desire lines" of travel by rail and rapid transit (trips desired for personal and business travel) in the late 1950s. Note the heavy concentration of trips along the major commuter railroad lines to the south, west, and north. Similar data was compiled for auto and truck trips. *(Chicago Area Transportation Study)*

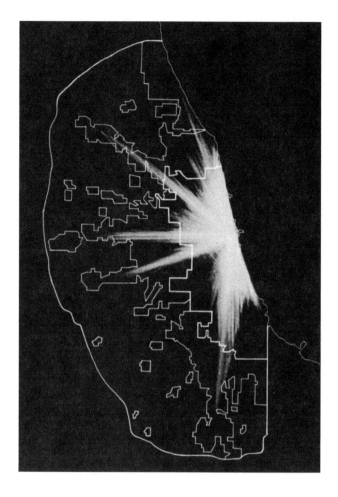

A cat disappeared during another interview. That night, driving on a dark road, a CATS interviewer felt his neck clawed and heard eerie sounds, then saw the missing cat jump out the car window. "I still don't know its color, size, or its destination," he told the *Tribune*, supplying his interviewer's perspective. "I'm sure glad it changed to a walking trip."[8]

Problems aside, the interviews produced a mountain of information— "trip origin and destination data"—to be key-punched onto computer cards over many months.[9] At a time when most data collected by planners was little more than information displayed on color-coded maps, the CATS approach was considered state-of-the-art. "It is impossible to convey adequately the arduous nature of the work of collecting data for a transportation study," Creighton said years later.[10]

Carroll's insistence on analyzing data for the entire region simultaneously in order to find the optimal transportation grid presented a logistics problem: no computer in the Chicago area could be found to perform the desired computations. This meant delivering computer tapes to a General Electric computer facility in Cincinnati, Ohio. When a Datatron computer finally arrived at the CATS offices, the front stairway had to be disassembled to move the computer into the basement and to install an additional air conditioner.[11] Bob Vanderford, the data processing supervisor, likened the giant machine to a mechanical desk calculator, recalling that "the number of calculations to be made were so great that the computer would be busy for over a year."[12]

As the study progressed—CATS would produce the first transportation plan in the country that used a mainframe computer—other agencies were busy preparing plans of their own. In 1958, the Chicago Transit Authority unveiled its own grand scheme—the "New Horizon for Chicago's Metropolitan Area" report. It called for new transit corridors, including subways under Wells Street and Jackson Boulevard, a "busway" in the Southwest (Stevenson) Expressway, and rapid-transit lines down the medians of several other superhighways. CATS took these proposals and integrated them into its analysis as it searched for the optimal configuration of transit lines.

After extensive computer modeling, the CATS staff released the first volume of its study, which described its survey findings, in late 1959 and the second, describing the models developed as well as predictions, in mid-1960. Due to the necessity of public hearings, revisions, and policy committee approvals, the third and final volume, which offered its transportation plan, was not released until September 6, 1962.[13]

The final volume's recommendations were extraordinary, calling for an entire network of new divided highways, spaced roughly three miles apart throughout the city and every four-to-six miles in the outer areas of the region. When completed, the imagined expressway network would form a massive grid of high-speed highways across the metropolitan region, nearly doubling the mileage of the system then being constructed. New rail transit lines would also be built, although their primary purpose would be to maintain the number of people commuting to downtown Chicago. The plan's main focus was on automobile travel, which it considered "the best general purpose tool for meeting individual travel needs."[14]

Corridors of Tomorrow

The newly released plan, known by CATS planners as the "L-3 scenario," envisioned an expressway system with many more route miles than those presently in service. A new expressway would extend west from the north end of Lake Shore Drive to the Edens and Northwest (Kennedy) expressways. Another, shaped like an L, would run south from the Northwest Expressway near O'Hare Airport to 65th Street in Bedford Park and then turn east to the Dan Ryan Expressway, a distance of twenty-six miles.

It also proposed, the Crosstown Expressway, extending north-south in the vicinity of Cicero Avenue through Chicago's West Side. This route was envisioned in the 1943 expressway plan as a link between the city's Mayfair neighborhood (where the Northwest/Kennedy and Edens expressways meet) and Oak Park, where it would connect with the Congress (Eisenhower) Expressway. But CATS had it continue south to Oak Lawn at 95th Street, where it would turn east to meet the Dan Ryan Expressway, offering north-south traffic a speedy alternative to the Ryan and the Kennedy.

Additionally, it identified new expressways through suburbia, including a twenty-six plus-mile north-south route through central DuPage County and contiguous areas.

Chicago Area Transportation Study, Volume III, with recommendations for expressway and transit–system expansion.

Proposed Expressways in the Chicago Area Transportation Study

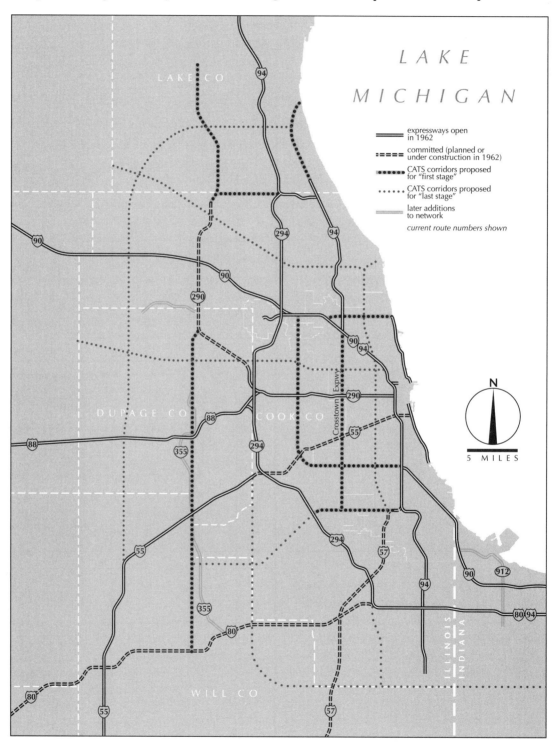

Expressway engineers pose for a photograph with Illinois Governor Otto Kerner *(right)* next to an oversize "button" at the dedication of the Reversible Lanes Automatic Control (REVLAC) system on the Kennedy Expressway in November 1961. The new system was considered a milestone in traffic management innovation. Pictured here *(from left)* are Roger Nusbaum, deputy chief engineer, Illinois Division of Highways, William Payes, director of the Illinois Department of Public Works, an unidentified man, and Kerner. *(Andrew Plummer Collection)*

(This, as I-355, became one of the few plan proposals actually built.) Another proposed highway would extend west from the Tri-State Tollway along Lake-Cook Road to near State Route 53, where it would turn north. Yet another would become an extension off the Edens Spur from near Glencoe to the Great Lakes Naval Training Center. Remarkably, these projects were additions to the Interstate Highway projects already completed or soon to be complete—and all of the CATS additions would be built within twenty years. The L-3 proposals were to be full-scale freeways with off and on ramps designed to keep travel moving at posted speeds.

The 1962 plan's recommendations for public transit mostly echoed CTA's New Horizon plan of a few years earlier, calling for rapid-transit routes in the medians of the Northwest (Kennedy) Expressway and the South (Dan Ryan) Expressway. The Southwest (Stevenson) Expressway, under construction at the time, was slated for a high-speed bus corridor. Some of the transit proposals were original, however, such as the acquisition of the right-of-way of the beleaguered North Shore interurban railway to create a CTA rapid-transit connection to Skokie. Midway Airport would be served by extending the Englewood rapid-transit line west along 63rd Street.[15]

Momentum Shifts

Media coverage of the plan was lighter than anticipated due to competition from other stories, including a railway strike, tension over Cuba, and even the first day of school.[16] The lack of media interest, however, was also prescient: the delay in releasing the CATS recommendations clearly affected the plan's prospects for implementation.

Proposed Expressways in the Chicago Area Transportation Study *(opposite page)*
This map depicts the present-day expressway system and the additional routes proposed in the 1962 CATS transportation plan. CATS envisioned a grid of expressways roughly three miles apart in the city and roughly six miles apart in the suburbs, all built in various phases. The lack of political support for building this expanded system was evident by 1963, although the proposed Crosstown Expressway *(center)* remained the subject of debate for many more years.

This model of the Crosstown Expressway shows the controversial route's proposed design. The narrow dimension of this design may be in response to rising neighborhood opposition. *(Chicago History Museum)*

By late 1963, the dynamics of the federal and state partnership for highway construction shifted away from massive projects that tore through dense urban neighborhoods, as these "urban dislocations" threatened to provoke "expressway revolt" in Chicago and other major cities. CATS officials experienced difficulty getting elected officials to embrace and promote its plan. In the end, the time lost before the plan's release, between 1960 and 1962, proved enormously detrimental.

Weeks before the plan's official release, when its recommendations were well known, Joseph J. Cavanagh, president of the Chicago Motor Club, accused Mayor Daley of backing off because the plan was "unpopular politically." He was particularly critical of the mayor's hesitancy to push for the Crosstown Expressway.[17] Cavanagh argued that the Crosstown was critically needed to alleviate "intolerable" congestion resulting from "traffic now detouring by way of the central business district, overloading the Congress and Northwest expressways."[18] The bypass was also needed by motorists traveling between the Edens and Chicago Skyway, Cavanagh stated.

Editorialists at the *Chicago Daily Tribune* argued that the entire CATS effort was misguided, stating that the plan's proposed transit improvements were a mere "afterthought" and accusing Carroll's policy committee of being "capable of thinking only in terms of automobiles."[19] The paper warned that the new expressways would put the city "in danger of developing into a gigantic slum with a fringe of expensive housing along the lake shore and at the outer edges," and "encourage the sprawl of the suburbs, giving the metropolitan area some of the less attractive aspects of Los Angeles."[20]

By the mid-1960s, many local leaders, including Mayor Daley, were skeptical of the need for further expressway construction. Speaking to the American Transit Association, Daley noted: "We must exercise the greatest diligence … We must be extremely careful that we do not destroy or adversely affect any of our fine neighborhoods by a program of mass demolition."[21] The mayor, in fact, distanced himself from the new CATS plan, stating only that such transportation improvements would be "considered in light of other considerations of importance to the city."[22] Many officials in Springfield, including Governor Otto Kerner, followed Daley's lead.

Public reaction was not entirely negative. CATS succeeded in having all 153 suburban communities within the study area publicly endorse the plan. Joe Cavanagh, head of the

Chicago Motor Club, enthusiastically supported new roads. Nevertheless, it seemed at times as if the job of promoting the plan was left solely to Douglas Carroll.

Nor was the Northeastern Illinois Planning Commission a spirited supporter, having been, in its view, kept in the dark until a relatively late stage. The federal government, meanwhile, showed increasing concern about urban area transportation plans that were undertaken without careful attention to other metropolitan goals. Legislation passed in 1962 (discussed in Chapter 10) made aid for highways in urban areas conditional on the establishment of a regional planning process, one carried out cooperatively by states and local communities. This stance helped shift the momentum toward rival NIPC.

Recognizing the political consequences of massive land clearance, the city asked CATS to study more modest options, such as making improvements to existing roads instead of clearing land for new ones. Streets could be widened and stoplights eliminated by closing off crossing streets and building overpasses at regular intervals.

Even so, none of the CATS plan's proposed highway projects moved forward during the next two decades, although none died more spectacularly than the Crosstown. The Chicago Motor Club did its best to promote it, holding meetings with community leaders and organizations throughout the city's west and south sides. An "action group" led by Cavanagh recommended an engineering study to carve out the best route, with the project's $48-million cost to be covered by federal highway funds.

Mayor Richard J. Daley came to embrace the Crosstown project, even calling it the "Roadway of the Future"—until he felt the fury of community groups, especially those in the Logan Square neighborhood, through which the proposed highway would run.[23] Governor Daniel Walker, coming to office in 1973, stood behind the community groups, bolstering their case. What little momentum was left behind the road disappeared with Daley's death in 1976. The project was officially canceled in 1979 when Mayor Jane Byrne and Governor Jim Thompson transferred the funds earmarked for the expressway to the CTA for a rapid-transit extension to O'Hare (today part of the Blue Line) and a new route (today's Orange Line) to Midway.

Limited Success

The 1962 plan's mass transit proposals fared better than its expressways. With federal support, the CTA built rapid-transit routes in the medians of the Dan Ryan Expressway to 95th Street (opened in 1969), the Northwest (Kennedy) to Jefferson Park (1970) and to O'Hare (1982). "Skokie Swift" service was launched

A CTA train ends its trip at O'Hare International Airport, 1984. This long-anticipated rapid-transit extension was partially paid for by funds freed up by the cancellation of the Crosstown Expressway. *(Chicago History Museum)*

The Skokie Swift station at Dempster Street bustles on this overcast day, circa 1965. The rapid-transit branch (today's Yellow Line) opened on an abandoned segment of the "North Shore Line" interurban railway on April 20, 1964. *(CTA)*

by the CTA in early 1964. However, none of the new transit lines envisioned for the downtown area, including the much-touted Wells Street subway, materialized.

After languishing for decades, the proposed expressway through DuPage County saw partial completion with the first portions of the North-South Tollway (Interstate 355, which was later renamed the Veterans Memorial Tollway) in 1989. The busway in the middle of the Stevenson Expressway was never built, although the CTA Orange Line commenced rapid transit service to Midway Airport over part of this route in 1993.

Many lessons can be taken away from the first CATS planning effort. The research behind the plan was path-breaking. University of Illinois at Chicago economist John F. McDonald notes that the effort put the agency, figuratively, "at the head of the transportation policy analysis class."[2] Some go so far as to consider 1956—the year CATS conducted its initial surveys—the "founding year" of the field of transportation policy analysis.[2] New York completed a plan in 1969 that included a transportation component, but the sophistication of its analysis paled in comparison.

There has also been criticism. CATS failed to anticipate how the population and population density of the inner city would decline, while that of the metropolitan region would grow, quite slowly, over subsequent decades. By 1980, there simply were not enough people or jobs in the city to justify all the investment in new corridors—particularly expressways—that the plan proposed. David Boyce, who has studied the legacy of the first CATS plan, notes that its innovative use of surveys and forecasts changed the transportation field, but also that the effort "lost its way" when making recommendations on the design of the network. "No one picked up on its network design principles," he concludes.[26]

The study also suffered, McDonald notes, from a "curious imbalance" between the research findings and the recommendations. The focus was on new expressways, but the plan provided few details about how they would be built. Transit improvements were recommended on a largely ad hoc basis. Apparently, the CATS Policy Committee had many road builders, but few members able or willing to articulate the importance of their plan to the public.

Nevertheless, the failure to build any additional expressway mileage within the city—most notably the Crosstown Expressway—beyond the initial Interstate System has left Chicago with some of the worst traffic congestion in the country. In 2006, discussion about building the Crosstown once again arose, possibly as a truck-only route. Debate has also been ongoing and vigorous, even heated, about the need for a north-south expressway through Lake County, an extension of Route 53, to relieve congestion.

In spite of the controversies, CATS' subsequent work brought it many accolades. For decades, its twenty-two-member Council of Mayors advised the Policy Committee, playing a critical role in the creation of regional transportation plans and transportation improvement programs—both required by the federal government as a condition for funds. CATS adeptly used civic groups and concerned citizens as sounding boards on transportation issues, allowing them to serve on task forces to help guide planning for arterial roads, bikeways, handicap access, and an array of other needs.[27]

Most of the 1962 *Plan*'s creators did not stay long in Chicago to witness firsthand its ultimate fate. Douglas Carroll left for New York a few years later to lead the Tri-State Transportation Commission, where he spent the rest of his career.[28] Cook County highway superintendent Bill Mortimer retired. Chicago public works commissioner George DeMent left the Policy Committee. Carroll's assistant director, Roger Creighton, left for Buffalo to head a planning study.[29]

Their successors, who replaced Carroll, says highway historian and retired CATS deputy director Andrew Plummer, found implementation of the 1962 plan "an almost impossible task."[30]

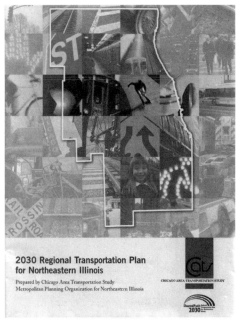

2030 Regional Transportation Plan for Northeastern Illinois

Prepared by Chicago Area Transportation Study
Metropolitan Planning Organization for Northeastern Illinois

CHICAGO AREA TRANSPORTATION STUDY

The Chicago Area Transportation Study's 2030 Regional Transportation Plan (2003), its last major planning document.

An "L" train on the Douglas route passes over the canopies at the south end of Union Station in 1952. This line was later replaced by the subway that is today part of the Blue Line. The canopies, however, remain almost unchanged. *(WC Janssen Collection, Krambles-Peterson Archive)*

8

IN THIS CHAPTER

In the early 1970s, public transportation faces financial distress and political turmoil. The Regional Transportation Authority (RTA), created in 1974 after a campaign that split city and suburbs, strengthens planning for public transportation but does not alleviate the sector's financial woes. A major reform of the RTA in 1983 sets the authority on more solid footing by creating new "service boards" to operate commuter rail and suburban bus service. The new Metra and Pace agencies vie for funding with the long-established Chicago Transit Authority.

REGIONALISM ON THE RAILS:
The Regional Transportation Authority

B uses, streetcars, rapid transit lines, and commuter trains serving the Chicago region were for many years operated by a panoply of private companies that had no agreements among themselves to allow passengers to transfer among the various lines. Riders who traveled on several modes to reach their destinations often had to buy separate fares for each portion of their journey.[1] Making matters worse, the physical integration of the different companies was often poor, resulting in awkward and time-consuming transfers between various parts of the system.

When Burnham and Bennett began work on their *Plan of Chicago* in 1906, they quickly recognized that the system needed much better integration. They outlined the benefits of consolidating the six downtown railroad terminals into two and constructing a new streetcar line circling the downtown district. At the time, many held out hope that the transit system would be unified and brought under municipal or public ownership. However, a 1907 referendum to create such a system, supported by the city's Democratic mayor, Edward Dunne, failed.

Samuel Insull *(center)* walks on a station platform with Leslie Grant *(left)*, date unknown. Insull's major investments in rapid transit systems dramatically improved service. *(Chicago History Museum)*

Electric-utility magnate Samuel Insull became a major player on Chicago's transit scene in 1911 by taking over the first of several rapid transit lines he would acquire, all of which he eventually assembled into the Chicago Elevated Railways Company (later Chicago Rapid Transit).[2] The spirited industrialist, owner of the Commonwealth Edison Company, was prominent in civic affairs, and was a member (and later president) of the Commercial Club and "subscriber" to the *Plan of Chicago*. In the transit business, however, Insull acted not as a reformer, but as a businessman, accepting company stock in lieu of payment for electric bills.

Insull gradually gained control of a vast elevated railroad network, restored it to good repair, and expanded its service—partially to expand the market for his electric power companies. Over the next ten years, thousands of daily riders benefited from the improvements. Insull pushed for the unification of his and other privately operated transit companies and is credited with having saved the Oak Park "L" and the South Shore interurban railway from economic ruin.

For their part, Chicago politicians also felt pressure to unify the transit system. After some controversy, the state General Assembly passed a bill in 1929 to merge Chicago Surface Lines (the streetcar company) and Insull's Chicago Rapid Transit, on the condition that the merger be approved through a citywide referendum. Citizens feeling the effects of the Great Depression—but hopeful a merger would create new jobs through the expansion of the rapid transit system—strongly supported consolidation, allowing the referendum to pass easily in 1930.

But Insull's investments collapsed in 1932 under the weight of the national economic downturn, and the necessary financing for the merger evaporated. Amid fevered accusations of impropriety, Insull fled to Greece and, in the midst of a great deal of publicity, was extradited to the United States before he was found not guilty on all counts. (Historians who have studied Insull, including biographer Forrest McDonald, generally offer a sympathetic view of Insull, arguing that his only real "crime" was believing so passionately in the future of his companies).[3] Meanwhile, the bankrupt companies, the city, the Illinois Commerce Commission, and a federal judge tried to untangle the transit system's problems, although the parties could not reach agreement on what should be done. Matters dragged on for the next thirteen years.

As the bankrupt transit companies' future looked uncertain, the Illinois Commerce Commission acted on a City of Chicago petition in 1935 ordering the three transit companies to provide transfers between one another's routes at specified points. To inaugurate this new policy, ceremonies were held at the Ravenswood "L" stop at Kimball and Lawrence.[4] Transfers from the "L" to streetcars would cost riders nothing more than the normal "L" fare of ten cents, but those transferring from street car to "L" would pay the car fare of seven cents and an additional three cents.[5] The transfer policy proved hugely popular, with more than seventy thousand riders a day using them in the first month, more than twice the projected number.[6] The companies gradually expanded their programs, with transfers to motor coach buses added at twenty-seven elevated stations in early 1936.[7]

Efforts to reorganize Insull's Chicago Rapid Transit and Chicago Surface Lines, meanwhile, remained deadlocked in legal and financial confusion. By early 1945, a frustrated federal judge, Michael Igoe, announced that he saw no alternative but public ownership over the system.[8] Amid concerns that the system could otherwise be auctioned off in piecemeal fashion, the state legislature passed the Metropolitan Transit Authority Act in April 1945, creating the Chicago Transit Authority, subject to approval in a referendum in Chicago and in the suburb of Elmwood Park.[9] Although turnout was low, the referendum easily passed, setting up a new public agency to buy the bankrupt companies.[10]

An "L" car on the Stock Yards branch appears through the famous Union Stock Yards gate in 1954—just three years before this lightly-used branch was closed. *(HM Stange Collection, Krambles-Peterson Archive)*

The CTA: Struggling from the Start

Selling CTA bonds to finance the acquisitions proved more difficult than anticipated. It was not until 1947 that that CTA raised enough money to buy Chicago Surface Lines and the Chicago Rapid Transit. Five more years passed before Chicago Motor Coach, which ran buses on the boulevards, came into the authority's fold. Although the bonds issued were guaranteed by "farebox" revenues, the legislation did not provide the agency with other funds or any tools to raise additional revenues, leaving it in a precarious financial state. Nevertheless, the agency managed to sustain itself for many years largely by exercising its freedom to raise fares.

An aggressive modernization program after World War II bolstered the CTA's reliability and image. Modern buses replaced aging streetcars, hundreds of new rapid transit cars entered service, and dozens of "L" stations were closed.[11] Several lightly patronized branches of the "L" were dismantled. By the late 1950s, however, most of the readily achieved financial advantages from these efficiencies were realized, while further cost reductions proved difficult. Attention shifted to construction of new lines, including the "Skokie Swift" (1964), and median routes in the Dan Ryan Expressway (1969) and the Kennedy Expressway (1970).

Saddled with the cost of operating an expanded system, the agency's financial condition took a sharp downturn. The CTA's 1969 budget was the agency's last to meet operating costs through farebox revenue, and even a forty-five-cent fare increase in 1970 proved too little, too late to balance its budget. Chicago's mayor Richard J. Daley, who, as a state senator, had co-sponsored the original act creating the CTA, grew concerned over the authority's deteriorating budget situation.

Mayor Richard J. Daley helps turn a "key" to commemorate the opening of a modernized "L" station on the CTA's Englewood Branch (part of today's Green Line), at 63rd and Ashland, circa 1972. Milton Pikarsky is standing at right. *(Chicago History Museum)*

When the CTA's chairman, George DeMent, died in 1971, Daley went outside the city bureaucracy to replace him, appointing Michael Cafferty, a nationally known transit expert, as chairman. Cafferty took to his responsibilities with great energy and assembled a coalition of elected officials who successfully arranged for a state bond issue that allowed for the CTA's first major modernization in fifteen years. Despite its improving physical plant, deficits continued to mount. After Cafferty died unexpectedly in 1973, the agency's future again became cloudy and transit advocates looked to Springfield for a solution.[12]

While the region's roads felt the strain of rising automobile traffic, many began to see transit investments as essential to maintaining a balanced transportation system. The state's newly adopted constitution called public transportation "an essential public purpose for which public funds may be expended."[13] Governor Richard B. Ogilvie, eager to modernize and professionalize public administration, understood that only new public strategies and policies could save the Chicago area's transit system.

Through the early 1970s, the Illinois General Assembly regularly bailed out the CTA with short-term subsidies, a practice that suited Mayor Daley and elected officials of both parties, but left others, particularly Republicans, uncomfortable. As the subsidies grew, George A. Ranney, Jr., Ogilvie's deputy budget director and point man on transit matters, felt that the GOP was right not to "trust the city with that amount of money."[14] Considering ad hoc subsidies to be bad policy, Ranney and Ogilvie envisioned a transportation agency with stable revenues, one that would direct public transportation in the context of broader metropolitan goals.

As support for a new authority grew, funding problems began to cripple suburban bus companies, and cost escalations pushed some commuter railroads to the brink of collapse. The railroads wanted subsidies for their commuter services, even while retaining the option to sell their assets to make stockholders and owners whole. But as the companies continued to post losses, elected officials and transit riders became convinced that dramatic action was required.

Painfully, the RTA Is Born

With fears of the system's collapse growing, Ranney assembled a task force to push for the creation of a regional transportation agency. The group was skeptical of two proposals under consideration at the time, one to create a suburban counterpart to the CTA (which the commuter rail companies wanted) and another to create a "superagency," a kind of CTA-turned-regional that would run the entire metropolitan system, including the commuter trains.

Ranney's task force rejected these options in favor of a Regional Transportation Agency (later Authority), or RTA, to purchase service from transit providers rather than buy them out.[15] This approach followed a middle course that the task force hoped might attract bipartisan support. It would maintain private ownership of most suburban bus companies and commuter railroads, while letting them cover their costs through subsidized contracts.

The political scene in Springfield, meanwhile, remained volatile.[16] In late 1972, independent Democrat Dan Walker, running for governor on a reform platform, took advantage of voter outrage over a new state income tax and narrowly defeated Ogilvie. Sensing opportunity in the transition, the task force cleverly made its RTA report available to the public just four days before Walker took office, presenting the new governor and General Assembly with a proposal they could hardly ignore. The proposed RTA would receive $126 million in subsidies in 1973 and tens of millions annually thereafter.[17]

Commuters walk along the platform at the Chicago, Burlington and Quincy Railroad station in Western Springs in the spring of 1972. The "Q," like other railroads, sought financial relief from state and local governments to offset the rising deficits of its suburban operations. *(Ed DeRouin Collection)*

George A. Ranney, Jr., a key figure in the creation of the RTA, circa 1974. *(Chicago Metropolis 2020)*

Initially, Mayor Daley stood opposed to the RTA proposal, apparently fearing he would lose control of the CTA. As it became increasingly clear that the beleaguered CTA could not survive without more state support, the mayor's opinion changed. By June 1973, he was expressing willingness to "accept any way of financing" the new regional authority.[18] Republican W. Robert Blair of Park Forest stepped forward as the chief sponsor of the RTA in the General Assembly. As Speaker of the House, Blair apparently envisioned using the issue as a springboard for his gubernatorial ambitions.

Intrigue was the order of the day when Rep. Harold Washington, then a rising star in the Democratic Party, unexpectedly added a utility tax plan to the RTA bill. Washington's move left Blair "visibly upset," throwing the issue into chaos, the *Chicago Tribune* reported. After the utility tax was dropped from the bill, more turmoil arose when Blair, learning belatedly that his home district constituents opposed the effort, wavered in his support. Under fire at home, he gave only "lip service" to the RTA, "insuring its defeat," noted the *Tribune*. Blair reversed his earlier position that the agency could be created without a referendum.[19] The newspaper accused Blair of reneging on his promises to "6.5 million citizens…who want and desperately need a Regional Transportation Authority."[20]

With hopes of softening the suburban opposition, Ranney, Jr., and CTA chairman Milton Pikarsky drafted revised RTA legislation requiring that the agency be approved through a referendum in six counties comprising the metropolitan area. In the months leading up to the vote, groups on opposing sides battled to sway public opinion. The RTA Citizens Committee for Better Transportation, led by Ranney, publicized the agency's benefits, while the "kNOw RTA" Committee, led by Rep. Cal Skinner (R-Crystal Lake), tapped into historically deep suburban suspicions about Chicago and its motives for supporting this regional authority. Many suburbanites opposed the RTA out of concern they would be forever obligated to subsidize the CTA's seemingly endless financial needs.

Citizens groups were concerned not only about having to fund public transit. Some feared the RTA would hasten the assimilation of their communities into a metropolitan government. Save Our Suburbs (SOS), a feisty group of homemakers, feared unwarranted governmental intrusion in local affairs, making allegations of political conspiracy that linked the RTA to creeping socialism. On the opposite end of the political spectrum, the *Chicago Metro News,* an African-American publication with a largely urban readership, analyzed the issue from a black nationalist perspective. Anticipating eventual black political control of the city, the *Metro News* foresaw the RTA succumbing to the control of white suburbanites. Rev. Jesse Jackson, head of Operation PUSH, took issue with this position, telling black leaders not to automatically oppose Daley (who supported the RTA) on such matters, because "sometimes [he] is right."[21]

Then there was Eugene Schlickman, a state representative from Arlington Heights, who considered the RTA to be out of synch with ongoing efforts to better integrate regional transportation and land-use planning being led by the Northeastern Illinois Planning Commission (NIPC). Earlier, in 1972, he proposed making the CTA the transit provider for the entire region as a way of "testing the water" for the regional concept.[22] As he had expected, City Hall wanted no part of this proposal. When the RTA proposal emerged, however, the Republican did not like what he saw, judging it too hasty an approach to a complex issue.

A 1974 cartoon in the *Chicago Daily News* shows the newspaper's support for the creation of the Regional Transportation Authority.

NIPC's executive director, Matthew Rockwell, shared Schlickman's skepticism. He argued that the new regional authority would undercut his organization. The RTA would become another regional organization within an already unsettled political and economic environment. Furthermore, Rockwell doubted the RTA could monitor its own operations, likening this to "having your bookkeeper do your audit."[23]

Former governor Ogilvie, however, came out of political retirement to campaign vigorously for the RTA's creation. On the day before the vote, March 19, 1974, the *Chicago Daily News* editorialized, "Not since the new state constitution was approved 3½ years ago has an issue so important...gone before the voters."[24]

The margin of passage was a mere 12,989 votes out of 1.3 million ballots cast. In the city of Chicago, the referendum won a clear victory, with some 71 percent in favor, in 48 of 50 wards. The collar counties were as clearly opposed, with the "yes" vote ranging from a high of 25 percent in DuPage and Lake counties to just 9 percent in McHenry County. Voters in suburban Cook County, where 41 percent supported the RTA, proved to be a critical swing constituency. Support for the RTA came primarily from voters working in Chicago, earning high incomes, and living in the close-in suburbs.[25]

The Losers Seek Recourse

The losers did not concede to the narrow majority's wishes. Twelve suburban senators demanded a recount and drafted legislation to allow counties to secede from the RTA. "The thirteen [British] colonies had the guts to stand up and opt out and the people of these five counties may be forced to take drastic measures," declared Senator Thomas Hanahan, a Republican from McHenry.[26] The succession movement was led by none other than Speaker of the House Blair, apparently trying to regain support in his district. Blair tried to amend the RTA law to weaken it, a move denounced by the *Chicago Tribune* as "Brutus" stabbing the RTA, gutting the legislation in a "perfidious manner."[27] The next day Blair was lambasted at a Republican platform hearing for trying to kill the RTA, acting to "further divide the suburbs and the city."[28]

Chicago Tribune headline, December, 1974.

Judge rules against RTA

A few weeks later, Blair's amendments were quashed in the House.[29] However, disagreement over who would become chairman of the new authority lingered on for months. The newly created RTA board, half city and half suburban appointees, was required to select a chairman from outside its ranks. City members pressed to give the post to Milton Pikarsky, chairman of the CTA. Although suburban appointees opposed this, they had no candidate of their own.

After almost nine months of disagreement, suburban board members relented, allowing Pikarsky to become chairman in early 1975. Finally, the RTA's leadership was up and running.

Evolution of the Suburban Rail System *(opposite page)*
This map shows the changes in the suburban rail passenger routes since 1950, including routes discontinued and added since 1985. Counties that are not part of the Regional Transportation Authority system are shaded. Note how the abandonment of two electric interurban railways, the Chicago, Aurora & Elgin (CA&E) and the Chicago, North Shore & Milwaukee (CNS&M), affected mobility north and west of the city. Subsequent commuter rail expansion, most notably Metra's routes to Antioch and Manhattan, has closed sizeable gaps in service.

Pikarsky, a native New Yorker and civil engineer, had done little to warrant suburban suspicion, although his ties to the city were extensive. He had been on the city's staff since 1960 and was appointed commissioner of public works in 1964. Pikarksy had great aptitude for creating and running area-wide infrastructure systems—he had overseen an expansion of O'Hare Airport, construction of the Stevenson Expressway, and building of new rapid transit lines.[30] Some wondered, however, whether he was the right man for an agency that needed heavy salesmanship—he was not known for being politically savvy.

Tough Early Years and Eventual Reform

The new agency nonetheless made notable progress under Pikarsky, negotiating purchase-of-service contracts with bus lines and commuter railroads while stabilizing service throughout the system. A newly instituted "universal transfer" between CTA and the suburban bus system proved popular, and federal money allowed for rehabilitation of the severely deteriorated Rock Island commuter rail line.[31] The RTA inaugurated new suburban bus routes, albeit without much market research beforehand nor strong ridership once in operation.

Evolution of the Suburban Rail System

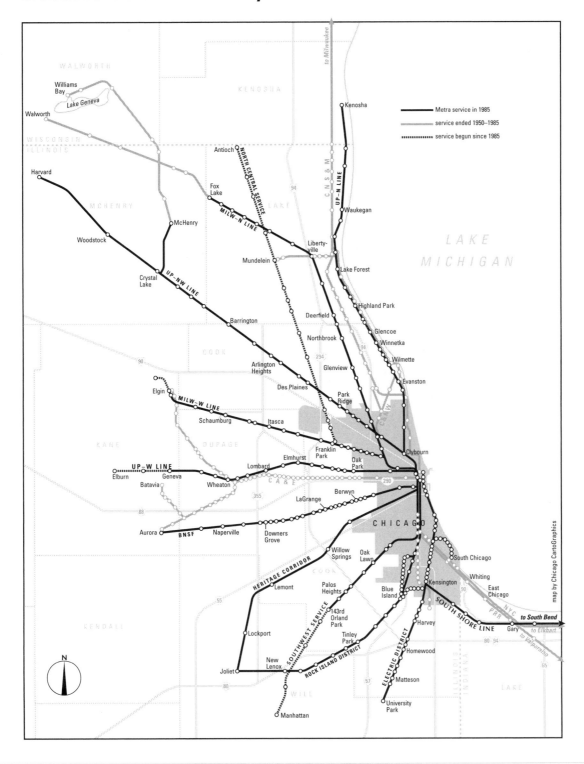

Legend:
- Metra service in 1985
- service ended 1950–1985
- service begun since 1985

map by Chicago CartoGraphics

All of this was soon overshadowed by unresolved funding issues. A presumption that the RTA would impose tight fiscal controls over the CTA, making it "more efficient without necessarily trying to run it," as George A. Ranney, Jr., had hoped, proved unfounded.[32] The original RTA Act contained few fiscal controls. Even if this were not the case, it remains debatable whether the authority would have enforced controls with much vigor. Board appointees were evenly divided among city and suburban residents while its chairman was a city appointee, giving the city an effective majority and—importantly—making it unlikely the board would say "no" to the CTA.

Milton Pikarsky, who served successively as chairman of the Chicago Transit Authority and the Regional Transportation Authority, walks along a trolley bus, circa 1975. *(Chicago History Museum)*

The RTA performed two basic functions. In the suburbs, it managed contracts with the private commuter rail and local bus operators; in the city, it wrote checks for the CTA with little supervision of that agency's finances or operations. The result was an inability to address the disturbing rate of cost escalation at the CTA.[33] By 1977, the RTA's dedicated funding (largely a 3/32 share of state sales taxes collected in the six counties) was no longer sufficient. Seeing no other option, the board used its statutory power to enact a 5 percent regional gasoline tax, which, in a political compromise to gain support of suburban board members, was agreed to be in effect for just two years.

Frustrated by the agency's problems, suburban board members united to remove Milton Pikarsky as chairman in 1978.[34] Pikarsky's loyal patron, Richard J. Daley, had died, but his successor Michael Bilandic was no pushover on such matters. Bilandic agreed to the ouster on condition the board accept either of two choices for chairman: Lewis Hill, the city planning commissioner, or Marshall Suloway, the city's public works director. The board opted for Hill, who upon taking office announced that he was not "disowning" Chicago or its mayor, but neither would he be "following someone else's dictation." In any case, the politically astute Hill did not make tight financial management a priority. Within a few years, the region would feel the effects of the agency's light management.[35]

With the two-year gas tax set to expire in 1979, the board opted for a 1 percent regional sales tax as its replacement, but needed legislative approval. RTA board members got what they asked for, but only in Cook County. In the five collar counties, they settled for ¼ percent, but in doing so lost the subsidies based on sales taxes the legislature had previously granted. Predictably, the new tax revenues proved insufficient and financial crisis continued to dog the RTA.

The severity of the crisis was greatly magnified when CTA unions went on strike during the holiday season of 1979. The agency cut rapid-transit service back to rush hour and sent managers and staff to run the trains. Service was limited to peak periods, and then only on a handful of rapid transit lines, while bus service was suspended entirely. In the end, labor achieved its wage demands, making the CTA's unionized personnel among the best paid of any transit system in the country.[36] The service disruption and expensive labor settlement cost the agency dearly, not just financially but politically, as it continued to lose the support of local governments throughout the region.

To deal with these latest budgetary problems, CTA and the suburban bus operators increased fares by 50 percent, while commuter rail fares doubled in 1981. Most suburban bus routes shut down briefly when the RTA failed to make needed subsidy payments. The commuter-rail fare increases provoked suburban outrage, and ridership overall fell by about 40 percent. Some riders, particularly in Evanston and Hyde Park, shifted to CTA rapid transit and express bus routes.[37] Several thousand suburban commuters chartered school buses to avoid paying the higher fares.[38]

The perennial political and financial crises grew worse when allegations revealed that the RTA was now diverting money from the suburbs to help the CTA, in violation of its legal requirements. More problems loomed when several commuter railroads plunged into bankruptcy, raising questions about the continuation of commuter service on several routes. The future of commuter service on the Rock Island was left in limbo when the judge sorting out the railroad's bankruptcy decided

Chicago & North Western commuter train on the Lake Geneva line departs McHenry, Illinois, in 1975. Soon after this photo was taken, service to the Wisconsin city was eliminated on account of its being outside the boundaries of the RTA district. *(Mark Llanuza Collection)*

This illustration by cartoonist Joe Fournier in 2008 describes the burden felt by mayor Richard M. Daley on account of the transit system's woes. *(Joseph Fournier Collection)*

in 1980 that the railroad should be liquidated. To preserve service, the RTA bought the portion of the railroad between Chicago and Joliet. Soon, the agency was buying more railroad property, this time to assure the continuation of service on the bankrupt Milwaukee Road routes. Several failing suburban bus companies were also brought into the agency's fold.

Throughout all of this, sentiment grew that the RTA could not succeed if it continued serving as both a funding agency and a transit provider. Some felt its record in fulfilling these dual goals was wholly unsatisfactory. In 1980, the Metropolitan Housing and Planning Council (MHPC) initiated a move to transform the RTA into a financial oversight agency, while creating new entities to manage commuter rail and suburban bus service.[39] Over the next several years, other influential players, including Governor Jim Thompson and the CATS Council of Mayors, began to think along similar lines. In 1982, the mayors' council chair, Florence Boone, village president of Glencoe, proposed creating separate operating units for commuter rail and suburban bus. Although this proposal was not enacted, it added fuel to the debate about a major restructuring.[40]

In the summer of 1983, the composition of the RTA board was changed due to reapportionment, for the first time giving the suburbs a majority. Yet many continued to believe that more fundamental change was needed. By the fall, the General Assembly passed the RTA Amendatory Act, which removed the RTA from day-to-day responsibility over transit operations by creating two new "service boards"—Metra for commuter rail and Pace for suburban bus. These entities were given authority comparable to that of the CTA.

The newly reconstituted RTA would provide planning and financial oversight of the service boards, while the CTA, Metra, and Pace would directly receive most of the sales tax revenues, according to a formula based on where the taxes were raised, whether in the City of Chicago, suburban Cook County, or one of the five collar counties. The service boards as a whole had to recover at least half their costs from fares and other revenues, meeting budgetary targets set by the RTA board. The service boards were not permitted to offer automatic cost-of-living allowances in collective bargaining agreements, which had exacerbated the CTA's financial problems. In exchange for this improved oversight, lawmakers restored a state subsidy they revoked in 1979.

For some years, these financial arrangements worked fairly well, helping to restore some fiscal responsibility to the region's public transportation system. Metra gradually increased fares to cover half its operating costs through the farebox and added new services. In 1996, the railroad introduced service on the "North Central" route to Antioch in the far northwest suburbs, creating the region's first new commuter rail line in more than fifty years. Meanwhile, federal funds became available for rapid transit improvements, including the rehabilitation of the Green Line to Oak Park and the city's South Side.

Even as these improvements were enacted, the system's riders and transit advocates continued to ask for more effective unification of service across the entire region-wide system. Calls for a "universal farecard" allowing travelers to use one payment system for CTA, Metra, and Pace trips, grew in intensity. Transit advocates also pushed for more convenient connections between commuter trains and CTA rapid transit in downtown Chicago. Neither issue, however, could be easily resolved. The universal farecard was hampered by a variety of operational complexities, as well as the need for revenues lost through discounts to be offset with other revenue sources. In addition, better connections between commuter rail and city trains could be achieved only with major new capital funding, which was not available.

Postscript

By the early 2000s, weak growth in sales tax revenue and staggering pension costs conspired to once again undermine the system's fiscal health. In addition to the usual calls for more funding, mass transit critics and

Metra's bi-level "gallery cars," shown here in the yards south of Union Station, soldier on after more than a quarter century of service. Many of these high-capacity cars entered service through the auspices of private railroad companies prior to the Regional Transportation Authority's formation in 1974. *(Ronald Walker Collection)*

supporters alike looked to change the formulas that apportion the sales tax revenues among the CTA, Metra, and Pace. As the funding crisis worsened in 2006, the CTA threatened drastic service cuts.

Democratic state representative Julie Hamos of Evanston investigated the imbalances between funding and service in various parts of the region.[41] She criticized the RTA for failing to better coordinate the city and suburban systems.[42] As a condition for giving the system more money, Hamos insisted that the service boards become more accountable for spending and reduce their pension costs.[43] After CTA unions agreed to reduce costs, Hamos drafted a bill to increase sales tax rates and give the RTA more "oversight authority." The evening before this bill was to be ratified, Governor Rod Blagojevich held the process hostage. He promised to veto the bill unless senior citizens were granted free ride privileges throughout the entire system. Recognizing that refusal would trigger another crisis, the legislature acquiesced, passing the revenue reforms in 2008 but sapping them of their full potential.

Despite its stormy life, the RTA is generally viewed as a notable example of city-suburban cooperation. Its work to stabilize and rationalize regional transit service appears to have helped to maintain a system that is older and far larger than most others in the country. The RTA's thirty-five years of work appears also to have helped to fuel the revitalization of downtown Chicago. Today, the service boards handle substantially more passengers than any other system in the country, except New York's.

At the same time, the RTA's presence on the regional scene has complicated efforts by the regional planning agencies to integrate transportation and land-use planning. As discussed in Chapter 12, the proposals in 2004 to create a "super agency" handling all the region's planning functions hit a roadblock. By then, the RTA had become too big a bone to swallow in the reform of regional planning and thus would remain an entity all to itself.

SHAPING A
COMPREHENSIVE VISION

Planners review a stormwater detention facility in suburban Woodstock, circa 1951. The group includes planning consultant (later NIPC director) Matthew Rockwell *(left)*, Howard Olson of the RPA *(center)*, and Ira Bach *(second from right)*. *(Chicago Tribune)*

9

IN THIS CHAPTER

Matthew Rockwell, newly appointed executive director of the Northeastern Illinois Planning Commission, leads an ambitious effort to create a comprehensive regional plan, the first since the 1909 *Plan*. The planners evaluate five regional designs including the preferred Finger Design, a scenario that emphasizes public transit in suburban growth corridors. By selecting the most popular design, NIPC hopes that state and local authorities will embrace and implement its vision for the region.

MATTHEW ROCKWELL AND THE FINGER PLAN:
1964 – 1966

Matthew Lafflin Rockwell's appointment as the second executive director of the Northeastern Illinois Metropolitan Area Planning Commission (NIPC), in February 1964, energized the agency's staff and rekindled optimism about its mission. With regional planning energies shifting from transportation toward more-comprehensive efforts, Rockwell set out to create an "armature" to guide the metropolitan area's growth. Assembling the new regional plan would require one of the most ambitious efforts since Burnham and Bennett prepared their important work more than a half-century before.

Rockwell, who had joined the NIPC staff ten months earlier, seemed the right man for the job. He had deep roots in the metropolitan area and, at 49, an impressive record of service in planning and architecture. He served as president of the American Institute of Planners local chapter, and as an executive at the American Institute of Architects. Rockwell moved effortlessly between the two professions, much as Burnham had done generations before. A native Chicagoan and descendant of Matthew Lafflin, one of the city's early settlers, Rockwell possessed a deep perspective on the region's history and problems.

Mathew L. Rockwell with his trademark bow-tie. *(Northeastern Illinois Planning Commission)*

Rockwell was profoundly influenced by Burnham, calling him a "shining light" who "led me . . . into the study of architecture and planning."[1] In the late 1930s, Rockwell complemented his architectural studies at the Massachusetts Institute of Technology with an internship at the Chicago Regional Planning Association, where he came to know and admire Daniel Burnham, Jr. The RPA was a "marvelous" organization, Rockwell once said, fondly recalling his work for Robert Kingery, whom he considered a "great residuum" of information.

When the U.S. entered World War II Rockwell joined the Army, taking up the duty of planning military encampments—a process which he compared to laying out large cities. Perhaps as a result of the experience, he was appointed in 1943 to a civilian team planning for a military airfield outside Chicago, which would eventually become O'Hare International Airport. After the war he entered private practice and his career took off. By the late 1950s, his firm, Stanton & Rockwell, enjoyed great success creating plans for communities across the country, establishing him as a national planning authority.

A Fresh Start for Planning

Rockwell's appointment at NIPC offered a fresh start as the organization navigated its way back to the center of Chicago's regional planning stage. His predecessor, Paul Oppermann, had been a controversial figure, openly criticizing CATS, which was at the time earning accolades for its sophisticated data analysis. Oppermann was outspoken about the region's planning problems and a perceived lack of cooperation from CATS. Yet he delayed having his agency put its full energy behind a comprehensive plan. NIPC board member John Baird, a prominent real estate executive, said of Oppermann that he tended to "study things to death." Other NIPC commissioners also felt that the time had come for NIPC to promote a new set of policy priorities for the region.[2]

NIPC officials including board president Chester Davis *(second from left)*, gather before a NIPC exhibit, circa 1958. After Earl Kribben's death in 1959, Davis succeeded him as board president. *(American Planning Association)*

The Metropolitan Housing and Planning Council, vigilant as always on the regional scene, created the Committee on Urban Progress in late 1963.[3] This blue-ribbon committee, chaired by Baird and Allen Stults, president of the American National Bank & Trust, probed the question of why so little headway had been made in advancing a metropolitan agenda. NIPC president Chester Davis apparently learned of this committee from a newspaper article, which irritated him greatly and prompted a call to Oppermann requesting that he call Baird to learn more.[4] His concerns were justified—in a matter of weeks, the committee expressed its view that, under Oppermann, NIPC "ignored its legislative mandate" to create a comprehensive plan.[5]

As the new director took charge, the Urban Progress committee felt its qualms about the organization's leadership melt away, although it would soon have much more to say about governance in the region. Rockwell quickly earned the respect of the NIPC board, taking advantage of opportunities to promote the commission's involvement in regional governance issues. With the arrival of the Kennedy administration, and the creation of several new federal programs to address urban problems, optimism about the prospects for regional planning rose in Chicago and throughout the nation. Whereas money flowing from federal programs was previously earmarked for highway projects, now funds were becoming available for more comprehensive undertakings—precisely the kind of work Rockwell wanted to do. In 1964, federal aid for mass transit systems was added to other programs that provided incentives for metropolitan areas to engage in comprehensive planning.

In addition, the federal government's new "three-C" rule issued in 1962—in language that only a lawyer could appreciate—mandated "a continuing and comprehensive transportation planning process … carried out cooperatively by state and local communities." This rule pushed planning organizations to bridge the gap between land-use and transportation planning. In other major cities, new regional organizations sprouted up, such as the Tri-State Regional Planning Commission in metropolitan New York in 1962. Similar commissions emerged in Boston and Philadelphia.

More good news came in the form of an expanded federal "Section 701" program, which gave funds for a wider array of planning and public works projects undertaken by local and regional entities. Suddenly, NIPC had the authority, and the funding, to weigh in on matters that were previously beyond its control. The agency's staff mushroomed from just nineteen during Oppermann's tenure to more than one hundred. New field offices put NIPC technical advisors closer to the suburban clients that needed them. Still more growth lay ahead as federal funds became available for water quality management planning through the "208" program.

The agency's fortunes continued to rise as its rival, CATS, struggled to promote its 1962 transportation plan. As that plan did not appear to be compliant with the "three-C" requirements, NIPC received federal funds, passed through the state highways department, to create a comprehensive plan. Rockwell now had the opportunity to create a basic blueprint—an "armature" as he liked to call it—that would put the region on a path to realizing carefully articulated development goals.

An armature—a wire frame used by sculptors working with clay—was a favorite Rockwell metaphor. He kept a wire figure on his desk, a small armature in the shape of Auguste Rodin's figure *The Thinker*, using this in presentations to help audiences appreciate his agency's work. Within a few years, that image was synonymous with NIPC's planning process.

Recognizing that NIPC could not achieve its goals without additional help from Springfield, Rockwell strongly supported a controversial bill to give NIPC the authority to levy taxes—legislation that was resoundingly defeated in July 1965. Nevertheless, he made his point: NIPC had shed its docile image and now flexed its muscles. Less than two weeks after the defeat of the NIPC tax bill, the Committee on Urban

A Pattern for Greater Chicago (1963), called for sweeping changes in regional governance strategies. (Northeastern Illinois Planning Commission)

Progress issued its highly anticipated final report— *A Pattern for Greater Chicago*. In addition to calling for sweeping initiatives to combat blight in "Metro Chicago," it sought to strengthen NIPC by giving it certain responsibilities assigned to CATS, including the power to develop both a transit plan and an integrated transportation strategy for the region. *Pattern* made the case that better governance required just one regional agency rather than various agencies involved in planning.[6]

Another proposal, to create "special service districts" with the authority to levy taxes raised the ire of local officials. However, by far the most ambitious—and controversial—proposal was for an agglomeration of governments, including Chicago and Cook County, into a super entity to reduce duplication and inefficiency.[7] It was an idea that University of Chicago scholar and city alderman Charles E. Merriam put forth more than forty years earlier. It was also mentioned in the 1909 *Plan*. However, to recommend it at a time when city-suburban relations remained strained—and Mayor Richard J. Daley was accumulating greater power to direct federal urban-renewal funds— would invariably cause acrimonious debate.

A city-county consolidation, of course, had enormous political implications. With a primarily Democratic city and heavily Republican suburbs, it would put the two parties on a collision course.[8] John Woods, mayor of Arlington Heights, led a chorus of opposition to an "amalgamation of municipal functions into one superagency."[9] A Hinsdale newspaper offered more nuanced criticism stating "If we must abandon local identification and local authority in the process of making garbage cheaper, we are not sure we have a bargain."[10] At a conference held to discuss these proposals, opponents dug in their heels and the idea of a city-county consolidation quickly fell out of favor. In one way, however, the *Pattern* report achieved its purpose by drawing attention to the need to rethink the roles of planning institutions so that the Chicago region might become something more than an uncoordinated amalgam of local governments.

The momentum behind comprehensive regional planning grew during 1966 as new urban-renewal legislation emanated from Washington. A new law required that all

A 1965 cartoon depicts the politics of NIPC public hearings on the agency's forecasts for employment and population growth. (Northeastern Illinois Planning Commission)

applications submitted by local governments for certain types of federal aid be reviewed and approved by a regional planning agency. This so-called "A-95 review" strengthened NIPC's influence over the flow of federal money to local governments for infrastructure, housing, and openspace preservation, giving the agency authority to perform "advisory reviews" of grant applications. Local governments also received the right to comment on such applications, which often put NIPC in the business of resolving disputes between neighboring communities.

NIPC was quick to take on this responsibility. With the largest budget in its history, and a board comprised of such policy heavyweights as Ted Aschman, nationally known planner and close friend of Mayor Daley; Dick Babcock, zoning expert; Harold Mayer, a noted researcher at the University of Chicago; and John Baird, NIPC could get things done. The agency moved forward confidently, despite lacking the legal (or fiscal) authority to require local governments to adhere to its plans. With its power to make recommendations on federal funds, the agency would encourage local governments to work with it for the benefit of the region.

Making the *Plan*

To launch the long-anticipated comprehensive plan, Rockwell divided the work into several phases, starting with creation and analysis of scenarios (or "schemes" or "designs") for the region. NIPC conducted analyses to assure that proposed regional designs were able to accommodate population and employment growth anticipated through 1990. The study area encompassed the six counties, 3,600 square miles that included an area about three times larger than the planning area of the 1962 CATS transportation plan.

The task of "scenario building" proved to be quite labor intensive. In effect, NIPC looked at the metropolitan area as though it were a giant game board, with the critical pieces being people, jobs, and infrastructure. With computer-based mapping still years away, this painstaking work required that designs be laid out by hand on table-sized maps, with calculations done on adding machines. NIPC made sure its designs were capable of meeting the needs created by the projected growth in population and employment. By early 1966, its planners had settled on five regional scenarios for further analysis (see sidebar, next page).

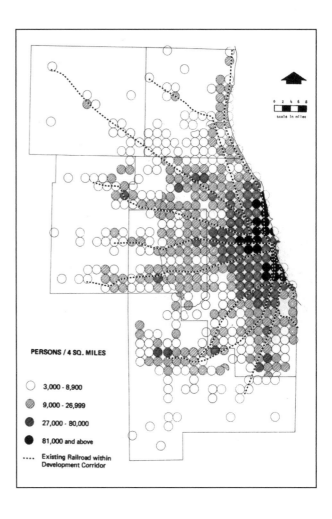

PERSONS / 4 SQ. MILES

○   3,000 - 8,900

▨   9,000 - 26,999

●   27,000 - 80,000

●   81,000 and above

····   Existing Railroad within Development Corridor

This map, appearing in a 1981 publication prepared for NIPC's 25th anniversary, shows the region's population still heavily concentrated along rail corridors, a development pattern the agency sought to reinforce when adopting the 1968 Finger Plan. More dispersed development patterns, however, were by this time prevalent.

Five Designs for the Future

Planners at the Northeastern Illinois Planning Commission evaluated a variety of scenarios for the metropolitan area's long-range development. The *Trend Design* depicted an unconstrained development pattern, showing suburban outflow from the central city that would occur if the region's development patterns were left largely unchecked, with no guiding regional plan. Neither this nor its close counterpart, the *Dispersed City Design*, produced development patterns that the planners found acceptable.[11]

A third scenario, the *Finger Design*, placed most new commerce and housing in "fingers". These were corridors along commuter rail lines, with extensive open space areas left between them. This pattern allowed a large portion of the suburban population to live near transit, with good rail links to numerous urban centers. The "wedges" between the fingers, which contained fields, woods, cemeteries, private estates and other open areas, put residents of the fingers into close proximity to recreational and natural areas. The Finger Design drew upon the same principles that inspired the 1947 Plan of Copenhagen.[12] (See illustration on page 137).

Another method of configuring high-density development around open space was offered by the *Multi-Town Cluster Design*, a scenario that proposed numerous and diverse "multi-towns" or "community clusters" outside of Chicago, with populations ranging from 10,000 to 100,000. Intensive urban development would occur at intersections of expressways. Each cluster would nonetheless develop a distinct identity and offering residents access to nearby open space connected into a series of "linear parks."

A final design, the *Satellite Cities-Greenbelt Design*, saw the region's "satellite cities"—Aurora, Elgin, Joliet, and Waukegan—become magnets for suburban growth. These industrial cities, each thirty to forty miles from downtown Chicago, were in many ways independent of Chicago. Each would grow to the size of Cincinnati or Milwaukee. All four satellites and Chicago would be joined by a web of newly built high-speed commuter railroads and expressways.[13] This satellite design, inspired by the famous *Greater London Plan* of 1944, would preserve a great opening, or greenbelt, between the four cities and Chicago, a wide swath of fields, woods and large estates—areas large enough to support abundant wildlife.[14]

As noted, the first two scenarios, both largley extrapolations of existing trends, were found to be unsatisfactory. They were eventually dropped, leaving three more visionary designs for further study and public comment. The Finger Design was most highly favored, however, by those who wanted to maintain a strong central city, promote the use of public transportation, and combat suburban sprawl.

As racial issues in the region became more explosive, NIPC felt a need to consult several noted planners to assess how the three most preferred designs would affect patterns of segregation and housing (see Appendix D). Although the Finger Design fared well in these reviews, racial issues increasingly haunted regional planners. Concerns about the inner city, particularly about the declining physical deterioration, rising crime, and high unemployment in public housing projects—which were by this time largely African-American—grew more intense. Suburban resistance to racial integration was a backdrop of the famous

Gautreaux vs. Chicago Housing Authority case, a 1966 court ruling mandating that all public-housing residents be given vouchers to move to more integrated neighborhoods. Inevitably, many suburban leaders began to link regional planning with racial integration.

Another issue facing NIPC planners was the dearth of assistance they received in evaluating the transportation impacts of the various designs. CATS declared that its 1962 transportation plan would accommodate any of the five scenarios, making any adaptation of this earlier plan unnecessary.

The lack of participation by CATS was irritating, although not surprising, to the NIPC staff. The CATS study area for its 1962 plan covered just the inner third of the six counties, an area already densely developed. This inner area would not see much population change under any of the three NIPC scenarios, which focused more heavily on shaping growth in the outer portions of the region. Larry Christmas, NIPC research director at the time, believed that the CATS findings "may have been entirely different" had it looked at the larger region.[15]

The Choice Train

With its three preferred regional designs ready for public review, NIPC put together an innovative mobile exhibit—the Choice Train. It began with Matthew Rockwell approaching the Chicago & North Western Railway in 1966, asking if his agency might borrow a couple of passenger cars for the summer. The C&NW generously agreed, loaning a pair of parlor cars that had until recently been used on its famed "400 series" intercity trains. These were specially outfitted with renderings and models displaying the three regional designs.

The Choice Train's exhibits would allow NIPC to describe its planning goals and encouraged people to select the scheme they liked best.[16] Creating it, however, was no simple matter. Overhead luggage racks were removed to make way for meeting room, while a portable generator was brought on board to illuminate the exhibits. Propane gas cylinders were used to run the air conditioners.[17] And several employees were hired to run the Choice Train that summer. NIPC public relations specialist Lorenz "Larry"

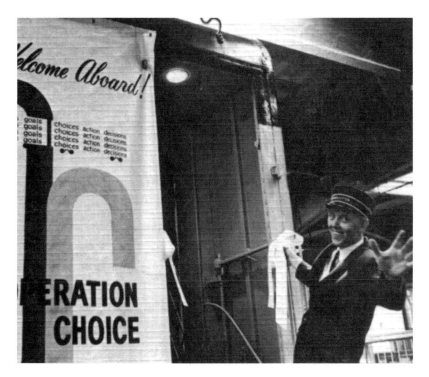

NIPC planner Larry Aggens performs his duties as "conductor" of the Choice Train, at Northwestern Terminal in downtown Chicago during the summer of 1966. *(Northeastern Illinois Planning Commission)*

Aggens became conductor. Aggens served as official host and supervisor of all logistics and public relations. Volunteers from the League of Women Voters and the American Association of University Women helped to administer questionnaires.

NIPC shrewdly arranged for the train's stops to become publicity opportunities for local officials. The host mayor could mingle with constituents aboard the train, then join NIPC staff in one of the cars to discuss the regional plan. Folding chairs could be set up in the train for these talks. At each stop, hundreds would view the exhibits and vote on the plan they preferred. A public hearing would be held near the end of the stay to let people share their thoughts on the various regional designs. Each scheduled station stop— there were twelve in total—would last six days. On the seventh day, the train would travel to the next town.

Mayor Daley and city planning director Ira Bach joined Matthew Rockwell for the Choice Train's grand opening at Northwestern Terminal in June 1966. NIPC considered the mayor's participation to be something of a victory, as it suggested that the city of Chicago stood squarely behind the planning effort. But, as discussed in the next chapter, regional planning was in more peril than the festive occasion suggested. Indeed, just months before the Choice Train send off, Rockwell complained about "well-meaning but distracting ladies" who were "somewhat diverting" work on the comprehensive regional plan.[18] Regional planning's opponents were emerging from the most unlikely places, and the upheaval would soon test NIPC's resolve.

This aerial view of the waterfront and the densely built Loop commercial district illustrates the vibrant urban qualities that have enhanced Chicago's reputation on the world stage. Efforts to promote the recreational role of the south lakefront, a goal emphasized in the *Plan of Chicago*, are evident in this dramatic September 15, 2007 scene, which offers a clear view of the Burnham Harbor, Grant Park, and Museum Campus. Extensive residential development throughout the Greater Loop, a phenomenon unanticipated by planners a century ago, has brought new vitality to areas situated near these prominent public amenities. *(Larry Okrent Collection)*

The frontispiece of the *Plan of Chicago*, a watercolor by Jules Guerin, shows an imaginary-but-geographically accurate bird's-eye-view of the Chicago region. Burnham and Bennett envision a unity of city and country—a region with a dense urban core, rich cropland, and bands of woodland and wetlands all coming together along the magnificent Lake Michigan shoreline. The city is linked to smaller towns and villages by the sinuous lines of roads that reach like arteries into the hinterland. (Plate 1 from the *Plan of Chicago*)

Michigan Avenue is shown from above in this sketch by Jules Guerin appearing the *Plan of Chicago*. This northward view from the vicinity of Randolph Street shows the avenue's anticipated role as a major north-south axis through the city center. The widened avenue is envisioned as an elegant promenade crossing the Chicago River on a bi-level bridge. Interestingly, the planners, including architect Daniel H. Burnham, who was involved in the early development of the skyscraper, prefer to depict a series of low-slung Parisian-style buildings running to the horizon. In fact, much of the area depicted here would later be filled with enormously tall buildings. (Plate 112 from the *Plan of Chicago*)

This diagram of highways in the *Plan of Chicago* shows a web-like structure of roads around the central city, with numerous radials crossing over concentric rings and "circumferential" highways. The dotted lines indicate critical links still needed to create a fully interconnected and unified region. The *Plan* anticipates the eventual alignment of high-speed arterial roads and highways but it does not consider the profound way that motor travel would change the character of urban life. (Plate 40 from the *Plan of Chicago*)

A poster created for the Century of Progress International Exposition in 1933 depicts the U.S. Government Building, one of the architectural showpieces of the World's Fair situated on Northerly Island. The fluted towers, each 150 feet high, represent the three branches of federal government: executive, legislative, and judicial. *(Courtesy of Posters Plus, www.postersplus.com)*

approved as of September 1, 1932
A Century of Progress
Rufus C. Dawes
President
© *H.M. Pettit.*

This guide to the grounds of the Century of Progress Exposition in 1933 serves as an illustrated map of the World's Fair, showing the many special buildings and attractions on Northerly Island (the future site of Meigs Field airport) and adjacent grounds, as well as the Field Museum, Shedd Aquarium, and Soldier Field. The curved south lakeshore leading to Jackson Park along with the smokestacks of East Chicago appear in the distance. This drawing illustrates the dramatic meeting of land and water that provoked Daniel H. Burnham to produce a scheme for a naturalized south lakeshore as far back as 1896, which he and Edward H. Bennett later incorporated into the *Plan of Chicago. (Lisa Schrenk Collection)*

A Century of Progress

INTERNATIONAL EXPOSITION
CHICAGO
1933

Adler Planetarium . . . G-1
Administration Bldg . . G-9
Agricultural Group . . . G-4
American Radiator . . . E-16
Amusements Group . . . D-16
Anthropology Group C-16
Bathing Beach G-2
Bendix Lama Temple . . F-15
Bus Terminal H-9
Byrd's Polar Ship . . . G-10
Century Dairy Exhibit . G-5
Chrysler Building C-17
Court of Nations G-3
Dancing Pavilion F-4
Edison Memorial F-10
Electrical Group F-9
Field Museum . . . . I-9 to 13
Firestone Area D-16

Fort Dearborn D-16
General Exhibits E-14
General Motors Bldg . C-17
Hall of Science F-12
Hollywood E-12
Illinois Building G-12
Industrial Arts C-17
Lincoln Group D-17
Main Entrance H-8
Mayan Temple C-17
Music Group D-13
Sears-Roebuck Bldg . G-11
Shedd Aquarium I-6
Sky Ride . . . . . F-8 to F-13
Soldier Field G-12
Standard Sanitary . . . E-16
States Group F-7
Travel & Transport . . . C-17

U. S. Government Bldg. F-7

Copyright 1932, H. M. Pettit—Evanston, Ill.
Rand McNally & Co., Publishers and Distributors, Chicago

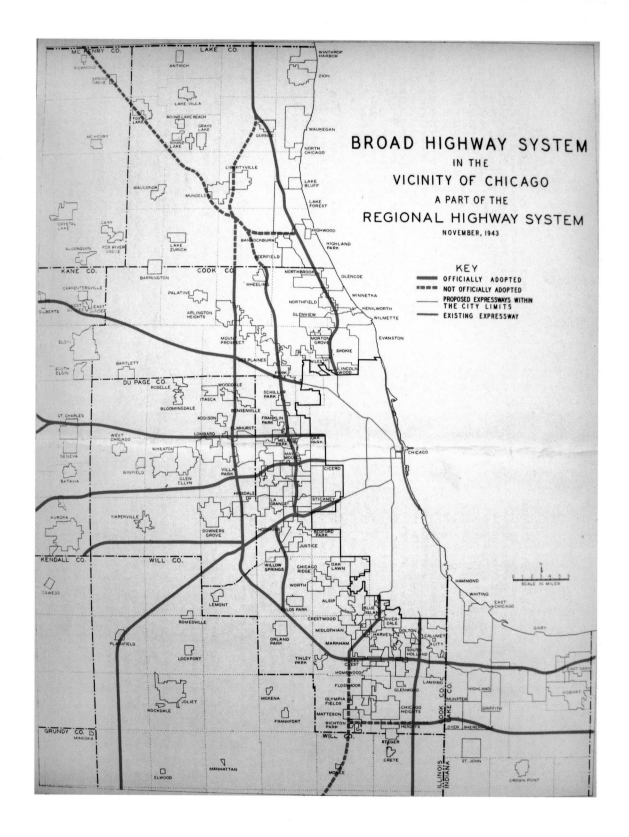

This regional expressway plan map, issued by the Chicago Plan Commission in 1943, expanded upon an earlier plan that showed the proposed routes stopping at the city's boundaries. The plan framed the imminent growth of suburbia, showing the paths that future motorists would take from the city's center to the furthest reaches of the metropolitan region. Much of the system was quickly built once funding for expressway construction became available in the mid-to-late 1950s, albeit on routes somewhat different than those depicted here in various parts of region. *(Chaddick Collection)*

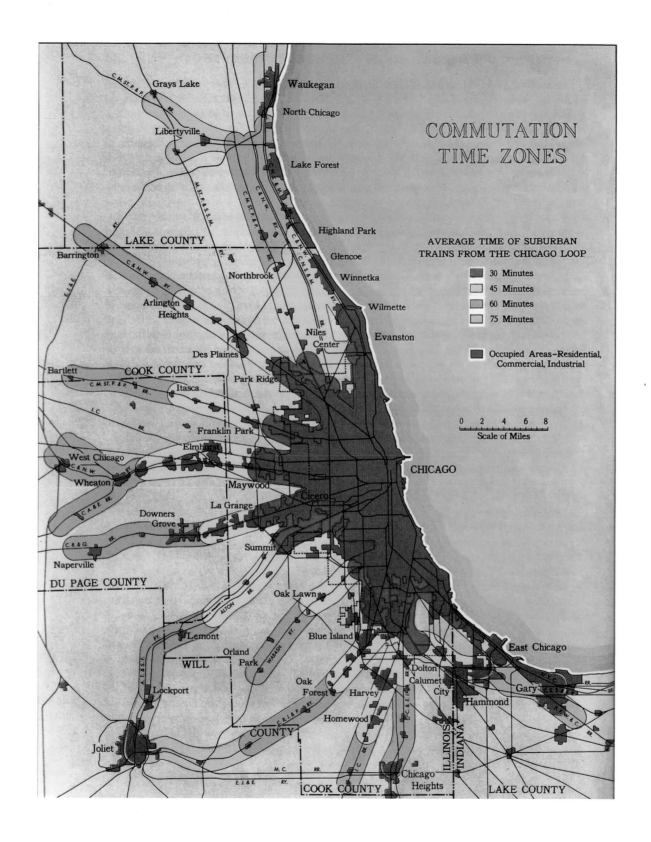

COMMUTATION TIME ZONES

AVERAGE TIME OF SUBURBAN TRAINS FROM THE CHICAGO LOOP

- 30 Minutes
- 45 Minutes
- 60 Minutes
- 75 Minutes

Occupied Areas—Residential, Commercial, Industrial

0 2 4 6 8
Scale of Miles

Grays Lake
Waukegan
North Chicago
Libertyville
Lake Forest
Highland Park
LAKE COUNTY
Glencoe
Barrington
Winnetka
Northbrook
Wilmette
Arlington Heights
Niles Center
Evanston
Des Plaines
Bartlett
COOK COUNTY
Park Ridge
Itasca
Franklin Park
Elmhurst
West Chicago
Wheaton
Maywood
Cicero
La Grange
Downers Grove
CHICAGO
Naperville
DU PAGE COUNTY
Summit
Oak Lawn
East Chicago
Lemont
Blue Island
Orland Park
WILL
Dolton
Calumet City
Gary
Lockport
Oak Forest
Harvey
Hammond
Homewood
COUNTY
ILLINOIS
INDIANA
COOK COUNTY
Chicago Heights
LAKE COUNTY
Joliet

This "data map," appearing in the Chicago Regional Planning Association's *Plan for the Region of Chicago* (1956), shows travel times to the Loop's railroad stations on the region's commuter rail system. The historic rail lines, indicated by their initials (e.g., CB & Q), show the strong radial pattern that would later become the backbone of the 1968 comprehensive plan (Finger Plan). Even as the RPA produced this map, however, it was busy promoting plans for regional highways to accommodate the rising demand for auto travel in an expanding suburbia. *(Larry Lund Collection)*

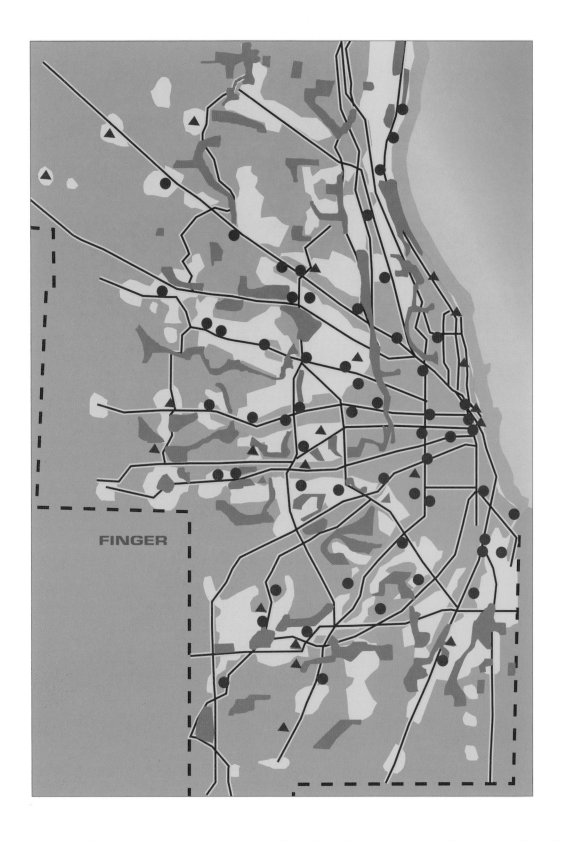

FINGER

This artistic rendering shows the spatial scheme adopted by the Northeastern Illinois Planning Commission in its General Comprehensive Plan of 1968, often referred to as the Finger Plan. The plan would concentrate development in corridors ("fingers") along regional commuter-rail lines *(the map's olive green colors indicate high density)*, making public transportation a primary mode of travel in suburban areas. Yet, even as the plan was issued, major residential and commercial development was occurring at considerable distances from the railroad lines in the wedges between the "fingers"—an area that the plan wished to reserve as open space. *(Northeastern Illinois Planning Commission, adapted by Omar Garcia)*

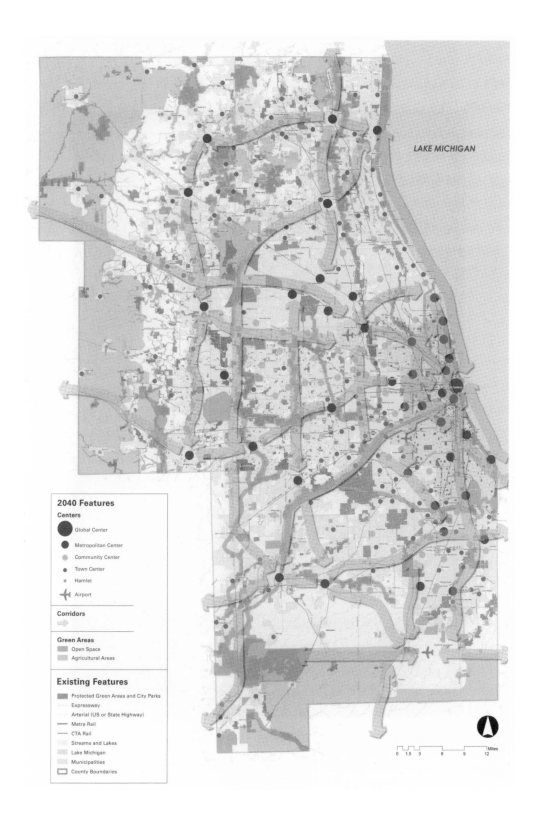

2040 Features

Centers

● Global Center

● Metropolitan Center

● Community Center

● Town Center

• Hamlet

✈ Airport

Corridors

Green Areas

Open Space

Agricultural Areas

Existing Features

Protected Green Areas and City Parks

Expressway

Arterial (US or State Highway)

Metra Rail

CTA Rail

Streams and Lakes

Lake Michigan

Municipalities

County Boundaries

LAKE MICHIGAN

0 1.5 3   6   9   12   Miles

This 2040 Regional Framework Plan map, adopted by the Northeastern Illinois Planning Commission in 2005, shows a hierarchy of centers and corridors in the region. The result of a five-year-long public outreach initiative called Common Ground, the centers-based framework provided NIPC with a strong spatial concept upon which to build its subsequent forecasts and land-use plans. This effort considered the potential impact of a new south suburban airport near Peotone *(see symbol at bottom right)*. But the effort became something of a parting act, as NIPC would soon be dissolved into the new Chicago Metropolitan Agency for Planning (CMAP), which quickly launched a fresh effort to create its own regional plan. *(Northeastern Illinois Planning Commission)*

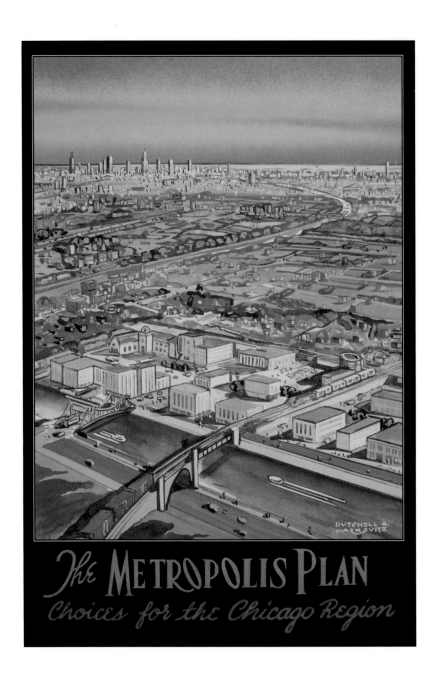

The Metropolis Plan

Choices for the Chicago Region

This illustration promoting the Metropolis Plan completed by artist Mitch Markovitz in 2003 conveys a balanced harmony of cities and countryside in soft pastels. The non-profit Chicago Metropolis 2020, created by the Commercial Club, advanced the heritage of the club's 1909 *Plan of Chicago* while using detailed maps and compelling images to demonstrate the region's future potential. Metropolis 2020 publicized the possibilities of more-aggressive planning and sought to overcome what it saw as the too-constrained approach of the region's official planning agencies. *(Chicago Metropolis 2020)*

2030 Metropolis Plan Concept
Six County Metropolitan Chicago Area

Legend

CTA Rail Line
New CTA Rail Line
Metra Rail Line
New Metra Rail Line
New Bus Rapid Transit (BRT)
Expressways
New Expressways
Arterials
Regional Centers
Protected Open Space
Urbanized Land
Counties

Chicago Metropolis
2020
One Region. One Future.

0   5   10 Miles

Source: Chicago Metropolis 2020 Technical Report

The Metropolis Plan map, shown here, was the product of sophisticated modeling that looked to the year 2030. The Plan, finished in 2003, emphasized transforming arterial roads into multi-modal corridors with "bus rapid transit" (BRT) service (*as denoted in brown lines*) while concentrating population in revitalized "regional centers" along commuter rail lines (*which appear in blue*). While reminiscent of NIPC's Finger Plan, this initiative was backed by proposals for aggressive implementation, including new legislation and the creation of a consolidated regional agency to restrain sprawl. (*Chicago Metropolis 2020*)

Several signs erected by the grass-roots organization Shut This Airport Nightmare Down (STAND) remind passing motorists of the strength of local opposition to the proposed South Suburban airport in Peotone, Illinois. The airport is envisioned as being built on the farmland appearing in the distance of this March 2009 photo, and much of this land is now owned by the state government. Despite the strength of the opposition in some areas, many neighboring communities support the airport's construction due to its job-creating potential. *(Cyrus Khazai Collection)*

An aging West Towns bus at the Keeler Garage in Chicago serves as a rolling billboard for supporters of a March 19, 1974 referendum for the creation of the Regional Transportation Authority. After a flurry of press coverage "for" and "against" the agency's creation, the referendum narrowly passed; strong support in the city more than offset an overwhelmingly negative vote in the suburbs, setting the stage for protracted political conflict. *(G. Krambles Photo, Krambles-Peterson Archive)*

Two Federal Express freighters at O'Hare International Airport provide an unlikely backdrop for tombstones at the St. Johannes Cemetery in suburban Bensenville in May 10, 2009. For months, lawsuits surrounding the proposed relocation of the cemetery served as roadblocks to runway additions and improvements at the south end of the airfield. A court ruling finally cleared the way for the city to proceed with the disinterment and reinterment process. *(J. Schwieterman Collection)*

A crossed-out photograph of Mayor Richard M. Daley leaves little doubt about the Village of Bensenville's stance on the O'Hare Modernization Program. Several hundred homes in the vicinity of this sign had been condemned and vacated to make room for airport-related improvements. The sign, removed only a few weeks after this photo was taken in May 2, 2009, attempted to draw parallels to the fate of Bensensville and that of tiny Meigs Field on Northerly Island in Chicago. *(J. Schwieterman Collection)*

Chicago's image as a "Global City" is captured in this contemporary view from Balbo Street looking north toward the wall of skyscrapers along Randolph Street. The lights of a Metra Electric train departing Van Buren Street Station appear in the foreground, with the Prudential Building *(center)*, Prudential II *(center right)*, and Aon Building *(right)* in the distance. The Trump Tower, still under construction, looms at left-center. Although Burnham and Bennett envisioned consolidating rail operations into two major terminals, there are still four such terminals in the heart of the city. (*Piush Dahal and Ronald Walker Collection*)

Columnist at Bat: No Hits, No Runs, One Big Error

CHICAGO DAILY NEWS

Saturday, December 10, 1966

THIRD PAGE
News Scope

An End to Urban Sprawl

3 Plans for Chicago's Future

By Robert L. Dishon

Finger Plan

A Complex of Corridors with Wedges of Farmland

Employment

Open Spaces

Residential

Commercial Centers

Transportation

Satellite Plan

A Ring of Populous Cities in 4 Outlying Counties

Employment

Open Spaces

Residential

Commercial Centers

Transportation

Multiple-City Plan

Clusters of Communities Varied in Culture and Size

Multiple

Commercial Centers

Employment

Residential

Open Spaces

Transportation

6-County Effort

Urban Sprawl Attack Mapped

This full-page *Chicago Daily News* spread of 1966 showed three regional designs studied by NIPC: the Multi-Town Cluster, Satellite Cities-Greenbelt, and the Finger.

137

This "help wanted" sign in the South Chicago neighborhood, circa 1980, reveals the long decline of heavy industry in the region. *(American Planning Association)*

10

IN THIS CHAPTER

The Northeastern Illinois Planning Commission adopts its landmark Finger Plan, in 1968, which concentrates future suburban development in carefully planned commuter-rail corridors. But new threats to NIPC emerge as local elected officials begin to question its power and influence. Citizen groups, most notably Save Our Suburbs, rise in opposition. A scuffle involving Oak Brook leaves NIPC more politically cautious. Federal and state funding for regional planning diminishes as new policies displace the programs of the 1960s.

HARD TIMES FOR REGIONAL PLANNING:
1966 – 1979

As the Choice Train traveled through the Chicago area during the summer of 1966, NIPC collected an enormous amount of information about the people's preferences for its regional plans. Exhibits on the train showcased the agency's technical sophistication while demonstrating its commitment to public participation. Visitors commented on the three regional "designs" under study, sharing their hopes for the region while helping the agency settle on a long-range plan.

But the train also provided opponents a ready-made opportunity to bring media attention to their cause. The problem arose soon after the train arrived in Highland Park—its first stop. Protesters packed public hearings to vent their anger over the regional planning effort, trying to persuade people that the entire effort was an affront to their local government's right to self-determination. Although few in number, opponents seemed at times to receive as much attention as the exhibits themselves.

Save Our Suburbs

The most vocal of these groups was Save Our Suburbs (SOS), a Winnetka-based volunteer organization whose members were distrustful of anything that smacked of centralized power. Led by two suburban housewives, this spirited group made up for its small numbers with its enthusiasm and with effective strategies that tapped into the Chicago region's historic distrust of institutions that threaten local control. The fact that NIPC's plans were endorsed by Chicago's political establishment only deepened the organization's suspicions. The most active SOS members found time and energy to follow the Choice Train from stop to stop to make sure their opinions would be heard. Taking a page from the playbook of Vietnam war protestors, SOS members understood the value of well-staged political theater.

The group had particularly strong beliefs about the effects of regional planning on their right to self-governance. It developed some surprisingly effective populist rhetoric to counter NIPC's planning discourse. The SOS argued that adopting any comprehensive plan would require that local elected officials forsake their constituents' interests in favor of non-elected bodies like NIPC. By its very nature, the group argued, regional planning threatened personal liberty and private property and trampled other constitutional rights.

Indeed, the phrase "Save Our Suburbs"—or SOS—had been around for years and tapped into a deep social and cultural wellspring of civic distrust. It was a rallying cry for suburban GOP leaders who raised opposition against Mayor Richard J. Daley's so-called "Morrison Hotel Gang," which set the Democratic slate for the 1958 elections.[1] But SOS did not gain prominence until the 1960s, when Eileen McIntosh, a Winnetka resident, founded an organization with the name.[2] McIntosh used her position as vice president of the Women's Republican Club of New Trier Township to assemble a wide network of suburban residents who perceived regional institutions threatening their local governments.

Operating from McIntosh's home, Save our Suburbs was sustained by a small group of women who attracted donations of money, materials, and printing.[3] McIntosh relied heavily on Adeline Dropka, a Brookfield village trustee who became the group's chief spokesperson, appearing at public meetings and in the media.[4] Dropka

A 1978 drawing from the Save Our Suburbs organization illustrated its concern over the expanding reach of government programs. *(Chaddick Collection)*

once estimated that several-thousand people were involved in SOS, but offered no credible evidence to substantiate this.[5]

Save Our Suburbs painted with a broad brush, denouncing not only regional planning but a host of other policies it felt interfered with the rights of everyday citizens to shape the future of their communities. It opposed municipal "home rule," which allowed local governments to impose tax increases without first gaining approval through referendum, and virtually all forms of federal funding to communities, especially those giving regional agencies like NIPC influence over distribution. All this populist agitation posed significant problems for NIPC's attempts to gain public support for its plans. Rockwell tried to reach out to the group, but to no avail.

The Choice Train's scheduled public hearings became the preferred SOS target. At the meetings, SOS supporters looked for cues for when to applaud or to express disapproval, which sometimes amounted to chanting "urban renewal" over and over again—a phrase intended to elicit images of urban planning gone wrong but considered more polite than booing. SOS gave "scripts" to its speakers and allies while its members often took seats in a diamond configuration to create the impression that they were unaffiliated.[6] At one meeting, the calculated disruptions became so loud that the local mayor abruptly cancelled the gathering and escorted the embattled hearing officer past an angry mob. A group of high school students in attendance looked on in bewilderment. Reporters scurried to interview the agitators, only to find that they preferred to read from their scripts rather than carefully explain their views.[7]

The SOS's opposition baffled many planning professionals, who felt that the group was unjustified in its conspiratorial tone and cynicism toward metropolitan planning. Aggens, the Choice Train conductor, who later directed NIPC's public participation program, believed the group's "extreme rhetoric as well as violent confrontation" had replaced "civic discourse."[8] Yet the SOS message hit a resonant chord with many suburbanites, putting NIPC on the defensive.

Concerned about the intensity and negative tone of opposition at these hearings, some elected officials criticized NIPC for riling up the "metro government crazies" for no good reason, putting their credibility among their own constituents in danger. Even Mayor Daley, who attended the Choice Train's grand opening, had serious misgivings. In private, the mayor criticized Aggens for helping design a program that bypassed elected officials and went directly to the people. Daley reportedly fumed that such tactics were nothing less than "a threat to the Republic."[9]

'Anti-Plan' Hecklers Force Meetings to End

Chicago Tribune headline, November 5, 1966.

By mid-October 1966, SOS had generated such negative rhetoric around the NIPC process that Aggens and other NIPC staff approached public meetings with some trepidation and, at times, a sense of dread. At one hearing, twenty-one out of twenty-eight statements submitted as testimony did not even comment on the regional designs, focusing instead on the legality of NIPC and demanding its "abolition."[10] The hecklers "attributed powers to the commission which simply don't exist,"[11] NIPC assistant director Robert Ducharme complained to the *Chicago Tribune*, adding, "If they would read the legislative act which created the commission, they would realize their fear is misplaced."[12]

Moving Forward with the Finger Plan

Despite the vocal opposition, NIPC gathered feedback from an estimated 8,000 people before summer's end. The agency weathered the SOS onslaught and gave every part of the region a chance to have its voice heard. In December 1966, the *Chicago Daily News* ignored the skirmishing and published a full-page description of the three designs,

Bob Ducharme, *(left)* assistant director of NIPC, Gerald R. Weeks, chairman of the DuPage County Board, and Thomas Dorn, former president of the DuPage Mayors and Managers Conference, study a map of the Aurora and Naperville boundary, circa 1976. *(Northeastern Illinois Planning Commission)*

replete with the reporter's endorsement: "Regional planners have found the answer to ending troublesome urban sprawl."[13]

The extensive public feedback lent credence to Rockwell's view that the region should promote more compact forms of urban development relying on suburban public transit. Government agencies and civic groups showed particular enthusiasm for the Finger Design, due to the orderly patterns of growth it would presumably foster, its reliance on existing transportation corridors, and its ability to strengthen the central city.

Not everyone was convinced that the Finger Design was best. Some observers felt the scenario deviated too far from prevailing land-use trends to be effectively implemented. Larry Christmas, NIPC's director of research, preferred the Multi-Town Cluster Design and believed that Rockwell felt the same way, Christmas had already prepared a plan for the DuPage Country forest preserve district, that called for land conservation along the DuPage River and Salt Creek. These waterways, and the Fox River, flowed southward, perpendicular to the rail corridors and the open space "wedges" of the Finger Design.[14]

After evaluating the public comment, however, NIPC planners came to the consensus that the Finger Design was best. It promised efficient transportation by putting workers close to job centers and putting consumers close to retail centers that were accessible by public transit and private car.[15] In addition, the design performed best overall in a number of technical evaluations prepared by staff.[16] The Finger Design would require less public expenditure on land and infrastructure than the other designs.[17]

Yet as the agency integrated this feedback into its final report, more trouble loomed. NIPC's role in federal funding, specifically NIPC's "mandatory reviews" of federal grant applications, further energized the agency's opponents. Suburban leaders began to resist this perceived interference with local autonomy and sought ways to get federal funds without NIPC intervention or review.

As a result of local agitation, legislators in Springfield attempted to end NIPC in June 1967, through a House bill to repeal the 1957 law that created the organization. Although easily defeated by a House vote of 85-39, the reprieve was hardly encouraging. More than a dozen bills that year sought to limit NIPC's influence or independence in some way, with several passing. One reaffirmed NIPC's role as strictly advisory.[18] Another required that thirteen of the nineteen NIPC commissioners be elected officials. Still another shortened the agency's name to the Northeastern Illinois Planning Commission, eliminating from its name the words "Metropolitan Area," which played on fears that it was a "metro government."[19] Rockwell made the best of it, expressing hope that the legislation would "end speculations that metropolitan planning will lead to metropolitan government and the loss of autonomy."[20] But the reconstituted board would feel considerably more pressure from local officials promising more fiery politics.

A few weeks after the bill to kill NIPC failed, Republican Cook County Board President and future governor Richard B. Ogilvie openly criticized the agency, claiming that it was not truly representative of the six-county area it was created to serve. To make his point, Ogilvie appointed fellow Republican Floyd T. Fulle, a twenty-three-year county board veteran, to the NIPC board. Fulle, who had earlier called some of the agency's proposals "utopian," promised he would work to prevent NIPC from becoming "too powerful."[21] The appointment did not bode well for the agency or its plans.

Ogilvie then set out to create a council of governments in Cook County, one that would provide an alternate forum for discussion and problem solving in the region's largest county. But Ogilvie stressed that this council would "in no

Richard B. Ogilvie, future governor of Illinois, at a Union League Club Luncheon, circa 1963. Ogilvie was Cook County Sheriff at the time. *(Union League Club)*

way be a form of metropolitan government,"[22] and announced that it was specifically designed to "protect our present individual governmental bodies from the creation of metropolitan government." No one doubted that he was targeting NIPC.

Not surprisingly, Rockwell voiced misgiving about Ogilvie's effort. NIPC was on its way to solving its representation problem, he protested, making the proposed Cook County council unnecessary, even disruptive to his agency's work. Rockwell also stressed that NIPC "was an antidote to metro government" rather than a regional government itself. Ogilvie created the council anyway, in October 1967 convening a kind of congress of 600 Cook County governmental units to choose an advisory board.[23]

In fact, Ogilvie was building on a strong movement toward councils of government. In 1958 the Northwest Municipal Conference—metropolitan Chicago's first large council of government (COG)—began operation in Arlington Heights. The DuPage Mayors and Managers organization came into existence four years later. These organizations, which brought suburban mayors together in a common forum, had mostly amicable relations with NIPC. Much of their work was devoted to "sub-regional planning" meant to compliment NIPC's work, as well as joint purchasing of public services. The Cook County COG, conversely, was far more ambitious—and it represented almost three-fourths of the region's population.

Despite all the turbulence, NIPC labored over its comprehensive plan through early 1968. Staff integrated the most desirable aspects of the Multi-Town Cluster and Satellite designs into the Finger Design, making it, in the *Chicago Tribune*'s words, "a diluted version" of the original design.[24] In April 1968, the commissioners formally adopted the Comprehensive General Plan which, for obvious reasons, was popularly called the Finger Plan.[25] It became the region's first officially adopted comprehensive plan.

Heralding a Great Milestone

The Finger Plan was at first well received and NIPC commissioners were pleased with their agency's work. The scholarly Regional Science Research Institute reviewed the plan and declared that its "value per study dollar was colossal," and that the "the story of NIPC must be one of success."[26]

The plan was presented in a very modest format, belying its years of research and sophisticated methodologies. It included a simple map and a few pages of policies bound in a light cardboard cover carrying the title *A Concept of Order*. A much more substantial methodology document accompanied the plan, but the plan itself was the "armature" that would guide local governments. NIPC intended to build upon it, filling it out with functional plans to address all major aspects of regional development. Indeed, NIPC would remain busy over the next decade assembling supporting documents.

Rockwell heralded the plan's completion as a significant milestone and, by 1969, felt the time was right to ask the state to name NIPC as the region's official metropolitan planning organization, replacing CATS. The federal designation of metropolitan planning organization—MPO—identified the agency that would prepare the region's official transportation plan for federal funding. Wrestling the designation from CATS would allow NIPC to achieve a full integration of transportation and land-use planning, giving the agency a central role and enhancing its prestige.

Rockwell's bid to make his agency the MPO failed. Nevertheless, his agency continued to derive considerable influence from its role as a federal gatekeeper, or at least coordinator, for grant applications.

GRANT APPLICATIONS REVIEWED BY NIPC

Billions of Dollars Applied For

Number of Applications

1.5

1.0

0.5

1000

500

1971 1972 1973 1974 1975 1976 1977
Federal Fiscal Years (July 1-June 30)

This graph from a NIPC annual report shows trends in grants requested and reviewed by the agency, 1971-77. *(Northeastern Illinois Planning Commission)*

By late 1969, it had reviewed 345 applications for some $459 million in federal funds.[27] It had enough influence to raise its hopes for the Finger Plan, even through the plan was "an advisory tool"—an "armature"— municipalities weren't required to follow.[28] Floyd Fulle promised that the organization would place greater reliance on "persuasive salesmanship" than it had in the past.[29] "I think it is safe to say," crowed commissioner and state Rep. Eugenia Chapman, impressed with the strides it was making, that "the Northeastern Illinois Planning Commission is here to stay."[30]

Searching for a Consensus

Over the next several years, increasing political and financial difficulties frustrated NIPC, while the state and local political scene dramatically changed. In the spring of 1968, one of NIPC's main supporters in Springfield, Governor Otto Kerner, resigned to become a federal judge. Republican Richard B. Ogilvie won the special election to finish Kerner's term. Ogilvie sought to modernize government but remained skeptical of proposals to shift planning authority from local governments to regional agencies. And with the election of Richard Nixon to the White House, federal urban programs gradually lost their regional orientation.

Ultimately, the Finger Plan failed to elicit the response that its creators had hoped for. Although different in nature from the 1962 CATS plan, it suffered much the same fate. Local political leaders did not embrace it as their own. Across the country, regional plans were confronting similar difficulty with implementation. Many of the recommendations of the New York RPA's second plan, approved in 1968, as well as a San Francisco Bay Area plan of 1970, were largely ignored.

A variety of factors were to blame, including a lack of real federal backing for regional comprehensive plans. Federal laws that tied transportation funds to conformity with local and regional plans lacked strong enforcement mechanisms.[31] In many parts of the country, highway departments fulfilled the "three C" requirements

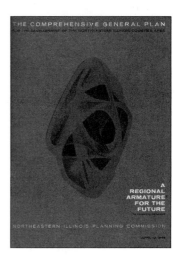

NIPC General Comprehensive Plan (Finger Plan) of 1968.

through separate agreements made directly with local governments, bypassing regional planning organizations. In the Chicago area, there was a particularly wide separation between land-use and transportation planning agencies. CATS took no significant action to discourage transportation development in the areas designated as open space in the Finger Plan. In fact, its 1971 interim plan added outlying expressways to the 1962 plan—a glaring contrast to the Finger Plan. These highways were designed to accommodate a sprawling metropolitan growth pattern without consideration of NIPC's spatial scheme. The entire CATS document made just one minor mention of the Finger Plan.

Other regional institutions similarly chose to ignore the plan. The Metropolitan Water Reclamation District continued to build its facilities on the assumption that open areas would receive typically sprawling development patterns, regardless of what NIPC wanted. For the most part, municipal governments pursued development objectives with little heed to the Finger Plan. County governments produced land-use plans that by and large supported development in areas prescribed by NIPC as open space.

NIPC could do little to discourage local governments' approval of light industry, office, and research parks along expressways, where the Finger Plan called for open

The NIPC Planning Committee convenes to hear a presentation on an application for federal funds. The agency's budget reached its peak in the mid-1970s. This photograph appeared in NIPC's 1976 annual report. *(Northeastern Illinois Planning Commission)*

space.[32] Construction boomed along the "East-West Corporate Corridor" (I-88) and the "Golden Corridor" (I-90) ignoring the plan's call for "wedges" of open space in these areas. Similarly, the agency had little leverage to push for dense development along commuter rail lines. In one instance, the Barrington Area Council of Governments persuaded Rockwell to allow its area to become an official exception in the Finger Plan, remaining a low density area despite its proximity to commuter rail service.[33]

NIPC did indeed attempt, often courageously, to get the local governments to go along with the regional plan, using what little enforcement power it had as a clearinghouse for federal funds applications. The agency routinely challenged applications for projects that violated the spirit of its plan, even when the irritated towns threatened to withhold their annual contributions to NIPC. Such confrontation, however, could only be pushed so far. When Schaumburg sought a federal grant to expand Higgins Road to support the construction of Woodfield Mall—a giant shopping center in the midst of a planned low-density area—NIPC staff voted to *support* the application.[34] An attempt to stop a major shopping center by opposing a grant application for widening a road seemed a backhanded way of implementing the regional plan. The political costs were far too high, and the commissioners voted according to staff recommendation on the Schaumburg project.[35]

By the mid-1970s, it was clear that the region lacked the necessary tools or political will to implement NIPC's vision. The "corridors of development" that were to contain the main population centers began to fill in at lower-than-anticipated densities. With new housing and commercial projects oriented primarily to automobiles, rather than rail lines and transit hubs, the frontier of suburban development shifted outward in scattershot and unplanned fashion. The growth of Schaumburg—a community at the intersection of several superhighways,which added more than 29,000 residents during the 1960s—exemplified the development patterns that were fast becoming the norm.

The rapid decentralization was especially dispiriting in the face of growing signs of regional stagnation. The metropolitan area's population grew much more slowly than NIPC had forecast. Although the number of jobs grew at a faster pace than the population, many were in outlying suburban areas and primarily in the service sector, which accelerated migration to the region's periphery. Meanwhile, aging industrial districts near the city center began to spiral downward, including the vast steel-producing district extending through the city's southeast side to northwest Indiana.

The rapid outward migration of people and jobs was guided neither by the NIPC plan nor any other regional "concept of order." It was driven by the market under the auspices of local governments, which approved it acre-by-acre and subdivision-by-subdivision. But the Finger Plan's fate disappointed NIPC leadership. In his resignation letter as NIPC chair in 1970, John Baird said bluntly: "We have to come face-to-face with the hard reality that … the legal structure within which our society operates has clearly NOT accepted planning as an important, much less an essential activity." He added, "Further planning without great chance of plan implementation would only represent a wasted effort."[36]

John Baird stands at the podium with Mayor Richard J. Daley at the grand opening of the Choice Train, on its "inaugural stop" at Northwestern Terminal. This photograph appears in NIPC's 1967 annual report. *(Northeastern Illinois Planning Commission)*

The Con-Con

The problems facing regional planning advocates came into sharp focus as the state constitutional convention called into session in late 1969. The convention sought to enhance the ability of local governments to chart their fiscal and political destiny through more autonomous long-range capital and financial planning. A secondary purpose was to explore whether the state should amend the constitution to strengthen regional institutions and/or create new ones to better coordinate development in metropolitan areas. Now, the shortcomings in the state's legal structure, so regretted by John Baird, were about to get some needed attention.

Making constitutional changes, however, was no simple matter. In Illinois, a constitutional convention, or "Con-Con," requires separate approvals by both the General Assembly and by voters, the latter through a state-wide referendum. Elections are then held to select one delegate from each legislative district. These delegates hear testimony, deliberate, and draft a new constitution, which often takes the form of amendments to the existing one. The process can last for months.

There have been few Illinois Con-Cons since 1870, and these enacted only piecemeal changes to the state's foundational document. High among the priorities for the 1969 effort was a concern to give local governments authority to raise revenue from various untapped sources and to enhance the collaboration opportunities among governments to solve common problems. Con-Con proponents sought to authorize municipalities to enter intergovernmental agreements, including boundary agreements and other agreements to share costs and revenues.

The Commission on Urban Area Government (CUAG), created to find ways to strengthen government in metropolitan regions, became an influential voice in the state constitutional convention convened in 1969. Pictured here *(from left)* are Norman Elkin, executive director of the commission; state representative Robert G. Day; Governor Richard Ogilvie; Robert J. Lehnhausen, director of the state's Department of Local Government Affairs; and Edmond W. Wilson, co-chairman of the commission. *(Norman Elkin) Collection*)

The proposals to give larger local governments "home rule" powers, including the power to raises taxes without direct voter approval, captured the spotlight at the outset of the convention. Richard M. Daley, 28, son of Chicago's mayor, used the convention as an opportunity for political grandstanding. He led the home-rule supporters, while Governor Ogilvie, who was not a delegate, expressed concern that home rule could lead to excessive taxation on local citizens. Daley, acting on behalf of Chicago interests, called foul, tearing into the governor for "misusing the power of his office" to influence the convention's discussions.[37]

When the debate turned to regional cooperation, attention focused on the recommendations from the state's Commission on Urban Area Government (CUAG), which had worked with both governors Kerner and Ogilvie through the late 1960s and received active support from the Metropolitan Housing and Planning Council.[38] CUAG recommended the creation of a "regional policy framework" to deal with large-scale development problems. At the time, the state legislature was trying to identify sub-regional areas for program administration, so the regional framework

Representative Eugene Schlichman (R-Arlington Heights), chairmen of the NIPC Advisory Committee, at a hearing. *(Eugene Schlichman Collection)*

seemed a logical next step.[39] Another closely related idea was to establish an elected "regional commission" with authority to plan for the delivery of services in each of the state's metropolitan areas. Modeled on a special taxing authority for Minnesota's Twin Cities metropolitan area, this commission (or "development council") would review and approve all major projects in the six-county area, distributing a percentage of sales tax revenue from larger retail and industrial developments to less-affluent areas.

In typical fashion, suburban mayors and other local officials vehemently opposed this proposal, leaving it with little hope of passing. Save Our Suburbs, its rhetoric sharpened by its struggles against NIPC, issued a seventy-page booklet warning that such ideas would transform the country into the "United Socialist States of America." Apparently to provide legislators political cover, CUAG recommended that any proposed commission be approved by referendum in the pertinent counties—the usual political bargain struck when proposals for regional action threaten the powers of local governments.[40]

All in all, the proposed amendments intended to strengthen the powers of local government succeeded, while those that would strengthen regional governance failed. "Home rule" and allowances giving municipalities the power to enter local boundary agreements all made it into the new constitution. But by increasing the powers of *local* governments, the Con-Con may well have added difficulty to the efforts of *regional* agencies to implement plans.

More Controversy

Rather than lobby personally in Springfield for legislation pertinent to NIPC, Matthew Rockwell worked closely with a legislative advisory committee. Whether or not his "hands-off" approach to the political arena was wise, Rockwell could always count on allies in Springfield. Among them was Eugene Schlickman, Republican representative from Arlington Heights, who led Rockwell's advisory committee and made NIPC's cause a political crusade. In 1973, he successfully pushed for a bill that again changed the composition of NIPC's board, making local elected officials even more dominant.[41] In another effort that same year he attempted to give the agency the authority to levy taxes, although this bill fell short.[42] Later, Schlickman's legislative committee held off an effort to allow Kane and McHenry counties to "secede" from NIPC.[43]

The help of a few allies notwithstanding, NIPC was soon to have more salt rubbed on its wounds. Federal funding coming through the HUD "701" program gradually diminished, inflicting more financial pain. Across the country, comprehensive land-use planning continued to fall out of favor as it came to be considered an expensive endeavor that should be pursued only after more pressing needs were satisfied. During the 1970s, planners' attention gradually shifted from regional problems to the deteriorating economic and social condition of central cities.

In the midst of these trying times, another controversy stoked the long-simmering resentment over NIPC's federal grant application reviews. In 1976, the commission announced that it would, as part of its federal grants review process, "raise a flag" on any of fifty-three suburban communities with less than 2 percent minority population that failed to study the need for affordable housing.[44] This policy was put to the test when Oak Brook applied for a $750,000 grant to improve 16th Street adjacent to the Oak Brook Mall. Affordable housing advocates complained that Oak Brook's housing stock was affordable only to the wealthy and urged NIPC to reject the application. NIPC opposed the application not simply because the community lacked affordable housing, but because Oak Brook was obviously seeking to become a major employment center while not permitting affordable housing for most people working there. Half of NIPC's commissioners held this position, while half presumably thought it would set a bad precedent to use housing as a criterion for a road project. With the commission split, the agency did not endorse the application.

NIPC staff continued to press the matter. Planning director Larry Christmas joined other housing advocates to urge the Illinois Department of Transportation to not approve the project. The backlash was fierce. Lawsuits were threatened, and an investigation was demanded. John McCarron of the *Chicago Tribune* observed that "aggressive village managers had little use for NIPC's opinion on how a new shopping center would affect storm water runoff." State Senator Jack Schaffer scoffed that NIPC planners "don't build bridges. They don't teach children ... They are anonymous bureaucrats whose principal function appears to be shoveling smoke."[45]

The state, in the end, approved the application, but the hostility engendered between NIPC and the handful of local governments opposing it did not relent. Undaunted, NIPC once again asked the state to name it as the region's federally designated Metropolitan Planning Organization, replacing CATS. The DuPage Mayors and Managers Conference strenuously objected: "The Chicago Area Transportation Study has developed a structure for direct participation ... so we can have an impact on the final decision. Too often, we have not had this opportunity in other regional planning matters," it noted, in an obvious jab at NIPC.[46]

Angered by the Oak Brook incident, Save Our Suburbs again brought its sharp rhetoric into the fray, hurling allegations that the federal government was now prying its way into their living rooms. The "ladies from Winnetka," as Rockwell once called them, always well prepared, presented several thousand signatures to Republican members of the General Assembly, spurring the creation of the Joint Committee on Regional Government in 1978. At this committee's three public hearings, speakers warned about the "dangers of federal regionalism" and "federal usurpation of local government's constitutional powers and prerogatives." NIPC and the Regional Transportation Authority were singled out for "having power over duly elected local governments."[47]

In early 1979, the Joint Committee recommended the creation of a new commission to "guard the sovereign rights, powers, and duties of the State of Illinois and its people." It asked the state to issue a resolution denouncing the proliferation of regional governments and demanded the abolition of federally supported regional councils. Its target was the "A-95 review" program, which since 1966 gave NIPC the authority to review local applications for federal funds.

Talk of "sovereign rights" and powers seemed to signal declining public support for regional planning. In 1976, the Illinois governorship went to Republican James R. Thompson and remained in Republican hands for the next twenty-seven years. Meanwhile, Ronald Reagan, presidential candidate, was promoting smaller government and "new federalism," foreshadowing an even greater withdrawal of federal support for regionalism.

Matthew Rockwell, circa 1975. *(Northeastern Illinois Planning Commission)*

Goodbye to Matthew Rockwell

Matthew Rockwell maintained a calm demeanor throughout the decade's storms and refused to abandon his expansive vision for NIPC. The agency's technical documents and functional plans met with considerable success, while NIPC staff continued to provide valuable population and job forecasts, delivering these to CATS for travel modeling in its Regional Transportation Plan. NIPC model ordinances, particularly for natural resource management, were used heavily by local governments. Across the country, regional agencies looked to NIPC as an innovator.

John Calloway, news director at WTTW and future host of the *Chicago Tonight* program, moderates a public meeting of NIPC using state-of-the-art electronic voting technologies and local public television to gather opinion on regional development in 1977. *(Northeastern Illinois Planning Commission)*

The agency issued a revised comprehensive plan in 1978, essentially an update to the 1968 plan. The revised plan, however, showed just how far the pendulum had swung. The agency no longer tried to use its political leverage to encourage large-scale change in development patterns. It no longer pushed to promote job and population growth along "corridors of development" as in the Finger Plan. NIPC now acknowledged that development would spread out in all directions, restrained only by the extent of communities' "facility planning areas." These state-regulated areas determined the permitted extent of waste water facilities. They appeared as shapeless blotches on the NIPC plan map but were considered a kind of *de facto* framework for planning.

The skirmishes took an emotional toll on Rockwell, who resigned in 1979 after sixteen years at the helm. He later expressed his frustration, telling the *Chicago Tribune*, "Unless quantum steps can be taken [in shoring up funding and recruiting more effective commissioners], it would be better to turn NIPC back to the shelf of unfulfilled hopes." He descried the fact that NIPC was still "passing the tin cup" after twenty years, often to ungrateful communities, including one that was even then withholding a customary $50,000 payment "pending NIPC action which might be detrimental to the contributor's best interest." Rockwell found it "unbelievable" that NIPC was being "held captive to such caveman-like tactics."[48]

He could take solace in the fact that planning agencies across the country were in similar predicaments. The second *Regional Plan for New York and its Environs*, published in 1968, shared much the same fate of the Finger Plan. Its calls for regional open space, increasing affordable housing, and job training programs for minorities, were largely ignored.

In one regional goal, however, the New York plan did see some success. It promoted the development of "two dozen partially self-contained metropolitan communities," which laid groundwork for transit-oriented developments around several commuter-rail stations, including New Brunswick, New Jersey; New Rochelle, New York; and Stamford, Connecticut. This suggests that NIPC may have seen more success with its Multi-Town Cluster Design, which Larry Christmas and other insiders had preferred. The principle lesson from other cities, however, was that the ambitious plans of the late 1960s were destined to be largely ignored by local governments, which had little incentive to implement them.

Rockwell returned to private practice, joining a planning firm with his daughter, Ellen, and dabbling in architectural pursuits at his Winnetka home. He embraced projects he could see through to completion, perhaps to compensate for the memory of his years at NIPC. He designed and installed solar panels to heat the family home, which were among the first residential solar panels in the region. He pursued such projects until his death in 1994 at the age of 79. Meanwhile, Save Our Suburbs, his old nemesis, faded away.[49] Dropka and McIntosh found no younger leaders to take up their cause. Their organization shut down, and its records—boxes stacked in McIntosh's basement a few blocks from Rockwell's home—were thrown away.

This portrait of a residential subdivision in west suburban Hoffman Estates shows the curvilinear configuration of streets that became popular in developments of the 1970s and 1980s. Hoffman Estates grew from 2.1 square miles in 1960 to 15.8 in 1980, a seven-fold increase. *(Charles Hanlon, Land Planning Services)*

11

IN THIS CHAPTER

The Northeastern Illinois Planning Commission tries to be more responsive to local governments as federal funding for regional planning dries up. The agency places greater emphasis on encouraging communities to enter intergovernmental agreements, even while gently pushing them to deal with environmental issues and "urban sprawl." Meanwhile, pressure builds to overhaul the regional planning institutions due to rising concern for their perceived weaknesses.

"LIKE THE UNITED NATIONS":
NIPC And Regional Diplomacy, 1979 – 2004

I n the late 1970s, continuing resistance to regional planning coupled with rising financial difficulties cast a pall over the work of regional planners. With a conservative tide sweeping the country, the federal government's gradual withdrawal of regional planning support for planning became a rapid retreat. Local governments continued to voice their distrust of centralized authorities. All in all, it seemed that the planning model was broken, and no one was quite sure how to fix it.

Matthew Rockwell, a long-time leader on the planning stage, retired in 1979 as director of Northeastern Illinois Planning Commission (NIPC). The at-large committee appointed to recommend his replacement made no secret that it wanted the agency to move in a new direction. Developer Lew Manilow and planner Robert Teska questioned whether NIPC's mission was still relevant. Stephen Friedman, a planning consultant, insisted that "political astuteness" should be a major requirement for the agency's new leader.[1]

Lawrence Christmas, NIPC's executive director from 1980 to 1992, moved quickly to rework the organization's image and expand support for local governments. *(Northeastern Illinois Planning Commission)*

Some of the best advice, however, came from an insider, Larry Christmas, executive director of the Metropolitan Housing and Planning Council (MHPC). Christmas, previously NIPC's director of planning, wanted to transform the agency into a "forum" to help communities address local problems.[2] He also wanted to repair the relationships with member communities and make NIPC more client-driven. His priorities underscored the opinions of the community leaders who were asked about changes they wanted to see at NIPC.

NIPC needed someone who could build good will and end perceptions that the agency aspired to become a full-fledged metropolitan government. The best person to accomplish this, the committee felt, was Christmas, who as a young planner honed his skills as a consultant preparing plans for Evanston and Winnetka, an experience that gave him a distinctly local perspective on regional issues.

Christmas moved quickly to rework NIPC's image and reputation—using both frankness and willingness to listen. He openly acknowledged the organization's limitations. "We're like the United Nations, except that we have no army—and more governments," he once quipped to a reporter.[3] The differences between Rockwell and Christmas were readily apparent to the agency's staff. Rockwell looked for symmetry and structure grounded in architectural principles. Christmas, a student of sociology and economics, saw the dynamics of social forces that drove change. "Matt Rockwell tended to approach regional issues as problems to be solved through regional design," recalled Christmas years later. "We learned from each other."[4]

Regardless of methodology, NIPC's survival in the early 1980s meant enduring the worst budget crisis in its history. Direct federal support for regional planning was already falling off when Christmas assumed leadership, and Ronald Reagan's victory in 1980 made it clear that more federal cutbacks were coming. "We're faced with cutbacks leading toward abandonment of area-wide planning," Christmas warned in 1981. "There are communities who will say, 'Why are we supporting regional planning if the state and federal governments are walking away from it?'"[5]

The agency's revenue peaked at $5.4 million in 1977; by 1980, it had fallen to less than half that, a downward trend made worse by skyrocketing inflation. Christmas held strong views about what NIPC should do and understood that he had to avoid skirmishes of the kind that had plagued Rockwell. Revenue from local governments had never been so important to NIPC's future, even as the overall budgetary picture rapidly deteriorated.

Focusing on technical planning rather than comprehensive visions helped NIPC mend local relationships. It launched a program to promote and assist intergovernmental planning as well as a "fellowship program" that sent young planning professionals into the field. As staff numbers dwindled, Christmas assigned senior managers to the Local Service Officer program, making the agency's veterans available to counties and villages for planning assistance. In addition, Christmas pushed the NIPC board to focus on areas that lent themselves to general agreement, even while reassuring the commissioners that he was "not about to … abandon principle."[6]

The formula worked for NIPC commissioner Florence Boone, Glencoe village president, who commented, "As [NIPC's] federal funding has gone down, [its] responsiveness to local government has increased considerably." The consensus-driven approach was manifest in NIPC's regional land-use plans of the early 1980s. Ruth Kretschmer, chair of NIPC's planning and policy development committee, noted: "We are trying to be less specific and rely more on existing plans of counties and municipalities. We want to use standards, rather than lines."[7]

The new approach did not please everyone, especially those who still wanted more aggressive management of regional development. "They're giving the store away," complained Don Klein, executive director of Barrington Area Council of Governments. "We don't think that's planning at all," said Lane Kendig, director of the Lake County Planning Department.[8]

But Christmas felt he had little choice in the matter. In 1982, Governor Jim Thompson cut off the annual

Mathew Rockwell *(far left, in front of map)* attends a NIPC meeting shortly before his retirement, circa 1979. Jim McClure, NIPC president and president of the village of Oak Park *(center; leaning forward)* is apparently making a comment, with W. Rakow, member of Kane County Board, to his immediate right. Staffer John Swanson is seated to the left of Rockwell. *(Northeastern Illinois Planning Commission)*

appropriation that state government had long provided to NIPC.[9] Declining "A-95" funding, the demise of the HUD 701 program, the loss of NIPC's state appropriation,

along with the discovery of an auditor's error (which incorrectly showed a positive fund balance when Christmas arrived) made for a dire budgetary situation. Regional planning agencies around the country were dealing with comparable circumstances. Most cut staff drastically. "Many similar agencies are hunkering down and folding their tents," warned George Hemmens, planning professor at the University of Illinois at Chicago.[10] NIPC was not folding its tent, but its staff headcount plummeted, from a high of more than 150 in the 1970s to just 30 by the early 1980s.[11] As a result many staff duties and operations were curtailed. Christmas even took a voluntary pay cut. [12]

The agency coped with the financial losses by concentrating on several narrowly defined tasks where it could still make a difference. Senior staff, including Max Dieber, Jim Ford, and John Swanson, focused on forecasts, "functional plans," planning skills training, and technical advising. They brought local governments together in sub-regional areas to wrestle with issues ranging from affordable housing to solid waste disposal. As evidence of its respect for locally generated plans, NIPC prepared an elaborate regional map as part of its 1984 plan that was, in effect, an agglomeration of the plans of several hundred individual communities and agencies.[13]

A padlock and chain block entry to the U.S. Steel Works in the South Chicago neighborhood, which closed in 1992. South Works was one of several major steel plants shuttered since 1980, resulting in double-digit unemployment in some South Side neighborhoods. *(American Planning Association)*

The lack of geographic specificity in its recommendations, however, meant that NIPC essentially retreated from its attempt to create a distict regional "armature," a comprehensive plan to guide local plans. This encouraged sub-regional entities, such as county governments, municipal leagues, and councils of government, to fill the void, becoming alternate forums for discussion of sub-regional issues. As the prestige of NIPC waned, the agency found itself competing for the attention of local officials and community leaders.

By the late 1980s, federal support accounted for less than a third of the commission's budget, with deeper cuts yet to come.[14] Christmas chastised the state for failing to provide a consistent income stream—a challenge that NIPC had wrestled with from its inception. Following the path of his predecessor, he proposed legislation that would allow NIPC to levy a small property tax, as planning agencies were doing in Milwaukee, San Diego, and the Twin Cities. Short of that, he wanted a state-mandated requirement that local governments pay for NIPC programs.[15] "I'm not ruling anything out," he warned the agency's board members.

Plight of the Inner City

Meanwhile, planners and policymakers turned their attention from regions to what seemed more urgent—inner-city job loss and neighborhood decay. Chicago and its historic satellite cities—Aurora, Elgin, Joliet, and Waukegan—as well as the steel towns of northwest Indiana, reeled socially and financially from falling industrial employment. The city of Chicago's population dipped below three million in the 1980 census, and its decline showed no sign of stopping.

Rising interest rates and inflation raised questions about the future of cities in the Midwestern "Rust Belt," especially in their aging inner cores. The prognosis was most bleak in urban neighborhoods with large African-American populations, due to rising unemployment, high crime rates, and discriminatory lending practices. As "white flight" continued to distant suburbs, some urbanologists and planners warned that metropolitan areas around the country would soon be hollowed out, giving rise to the "doughnut hypothesis," the idea that regions would have empty central cities surrounded by concentric rings of thriving suburbs.

To keep regional planning relevant in an era of intense urban challenges, Larry Christmas cultivated NIPC's strength as convener and mediator, helping to resolve turf battles among suburban governments. County officials were seeing much of their-long range planning undone by aggressive municipal governments, who ignored county plans and often annexed large swaths of land merely to preempt other towns from doing so. Communities were compelled to protect and expand their tax bases, making coordinated sub-regional and regional planning nearly impossible.

Indeed, throughout its history, NIPC actively promoted intergovernmental agreements to help solve "greater than local" problems. With Christmas at the helm, the agency made important strides in creating new types of "interjurisdictional solutions."[16] NIPC created a "Corridor Council"—the first of its kind in the country—to address the impacts of a North-South Toll Road extension (I-355) into central Lake County. Local communities and transportation officials in Springfield supported this, and NIPC went on to staff four more such forums, each focusing on different corridors. NIPC helped to broker agreements on preferred road alignments and intersections, aesthetics, conservation, and related issues. In some cases, communities negotiated boundary and land-use agreements through the newly formed councils.

Christmas also steered NIPC to a leadership role in conservation debates, turning the agency's attention to loss of natural habitat, farmland conservation, and biodiversity. He had served briefly as the acting director of the Open Lands Project, where he had recruited Judith Stockdale and Gerald Adelman to that organization. Now at NIPC, he made them partners on a new regional "greenways" plan. The agency also promoted transit-oriented design and the revitalization of historic town centers.

While pleased with this progress, Christmas strongly believed that the state government, through its taxation and school funding policies, gave municipalities far too much incentive to compete among themselves to annex land and to pursue low density development contrary to sound planning principles. With the problem in mind, NIPC launched a two-year effort in early 1990 to address rising concerns over suburban sprawl.[17]

This product of this effort, the Strategic Plan for Land Resource Management, was adopted by the commission on June 18, 1992. In the spirit of the Finger Plan, it called for slowing the population movement into low-density patterns on the region's periphery, which threatened open space and prime

Cartoon lampooning the strategies that planners use to promote public participation. *(Reprinted from* Stop Me Before I Plan Again, *by Richard Hedman, copyright 1977 by the American Society of Planning Officials, now known as the American Planning Association)*

farmland. However, as journalist Harold Henderson noted, the plan did not try to create "a beautiful utopia, as NIPC's previous efforts did in 1968." Rather, it sought to "get rid of the incentives to foster sprawl."[18] The plan recommended giving priority to new state planning laws that promoted cooperation among communities. In sharp contrast to earlier plans, roughly half of its recommendations were addressed at least partially to the state government.

Larry Christmas retired in June 1992 and the board promoted Phil Peters, NIPC's planning director, to the executive director's office. Peters, who had joined the organization only a few weeks after Christmas had in 1963, was held in high esteem by many municipal and county officials as a patient planner who focused on incremental rather than wholesale change. As the successor of Larry Christmas, he continued his predecessor's direction for NIPC while refraining from calls for more-aggressive regional planning. "We don't think Oregon-style statewide land planning is doable," he told the *Chicago Reader.* "The people of Illinois aren't ready for it."[19]

Under Peters, the agency's staff pursued functional plans and strategies identified in the 1992 Strategic Plan, with its Greenways Plan—produced jointly with Openlands Project—proving particularly influential. NIPC also made progress in its efforts to push the state to strengthen support for intergovernmental agreements.[20] But old problems often reappeared. One proposal of the 1992 plan, concerning "diversified regional centers" (DRCs) i.e., high-density hubs for public transportation and other infrastructure, became particularly contentious. Communities voiced concern about NIPC identifying areas for high-density development. Local officials feared that some "regional centers" would receive favored status. An old adversary, the Village of Oak Brook, made clear that it did not want to be identified as a DRC in NIPC's plan. Recognizing the sensitivity of the issue, NIPC backed away from the entire concept.

From retirement, Larry Christmas shot back, calling Oak Brook the "ultimate product of tax-based planning" to the detriment of regional planning goals. "It's like Monopoly—a wonderful board game, but all but one player loses," he said, referring to the village's ability to achieve huge property tax and sales tax growth while struggling communities got little or nothing from all the development. "I have no objection to some local governments winning more than others, but I do object to having the losers lose so dramatically," he told the *Chicago Reader*'s Harold Henderson.[21]

Restlessness among Civic Leaders

By the mid-1990s, growing numbers in the region's civic community were restless over what they perceived as NIPC's "too passive" approach to regional planning. In the San Francisco Bay Area, momentum was building to create a vast greenbelt around the suburban periphery. In New York, the Regional Plan Association was producing its third plan, far more ambitious than anything contemplated in Chicago. When completed in 1996, *A Region at Risk: The Third Regional Plan for the New York–New Jersey–Connecticut Metropolitan Region*, was held up as a model for other metropolitan areas. State governments, particularly on the east and west coasts, were preparing to adopt statewide growth-management policies.

MarySue Barrett, executive director of the Metropolitan Planning Council, speaks to the press, with MPC vice-president Peter Skosey. *(Metropolitan Planning Council)*

In Chicago, there were no such milestones to celebrate. Instead, the region carried on with the nearly fifty-year separation of its land-use and transportation planning agencies. Many felt that the absence of an ambitious regional agenda left the Chicago region less competitive in the emerging global economy. The Metropolitan Planning Council and the Commercial Club of Chicago joined forces to map out a new strategy for regional development, culminating, as discussed in the next chapter, in the Commercial Club's Metropolis Project.

To be sure, NIPC was pushing hard to expand its agenda. With the Metropolitan Planning Council, it co-chaired the Campaign for Sensible Growth, a consortium of towns and civic groups promoting "smart growth" strategies. NIPC strengthened ties with other organizations and with university researchers to gain their expertise in its functional plans. And NIPC strongly supported Chicago Wilderness, a new, powerful consortium committed to conservation planning.

Nevertheless, the agency increasingly looked over its shoulder toward a restless and revived civic sector. Many local officials who were active on the commission grew apprehensive for its future. In some respects, NIPC was powerless to answer its critics. Lacking federal designation as the region's official metropolitan planning organization, it could not by itself take steps to more clearly align land-use and transportation planning. In 1997, the agency again petitioned the state to have itself designated the region's official MPO, replacing CATS. Once again, it was denied.

Phil Peters felt pressure from the civic groups, but he remained pragmatic about his agency. As he told the *Chicago Tribune*: "I've heard concerns expressed that the commission is not being a leader and that we haven't been out in front on certain issues ... I think the commission has to identify what it can do and then do that."[23] Suffering from a debilitating illness, Peters retired in December 1998, after six years as executive director of NIPC.

Recognizing the need for a fresh start, the NIPC board went outside the agency for a new executive director and hired Ron Thomas, a Seattle-based consultant who had recently headed a civic-based planning effort for Racine, Wisconsin. Thomas took the reins at NIPC in early 2000.

Thomas scored some early victories, as NIPC adopted a biodiversity recovery plan prepared by Chicago Wilderness and another important plan for water resource management (see Appendix E). But despite the obstacles his agency faced, he sought nonetheless to rally the region around an ambitious "growth management framework" with an elaborate set of goals to give new direction to regional policy and development.

To lay a foundation for this, he negotiated a new interagency agreement with CATS, the state transportation department, and the Regional Transportation Authority to more closely integrate NIPC's land-use schemes into regional transportation planning. NIPC conducted this work under the moniker Common Ground, espousing "community-based regionalism"—the idea that people should participate directly in the plan-making process. It was hoped that this process would build a new constituency for regional planning, which would in turn encourage local governments to support regional policies. The Common Ground planning process looked toward the horizon year 2040.[24] After two years of public meetings to refine regional goals, and another two years of geographic analysis and mapmaking, NIPC's finished product, the 2040 Regional Framework Plan (see sidebar, opposite) received board approval on June 29, 2005.

Nevertheless, NIPC was losing its fight to remain politically viable. CATS prepared its 2030 Regional

Daniel Lauber, an advocate for "open communities," makes a presentation, circa 1985. The attorney became widely known for his efforts to push suburban villages to increase their supply of affordable housing. *(American Planning Association)*

NIPC's Final Act: The 2040 Framework Plan

Envisioning a massive regional "conversation" to identify goals for the region starting in 2001, the Northeastern Illinois Planning Commission turned to state-of-the-art participation technologies and innovative communications strategies to hear from everyday citizens.[24] Although funding was tight, forcing it to scale back plans for multi-site videoconferencing, the effort—conducted under the moniker "Common Ground"—remained ambitious in scope. At a "regional town meeting" in October 2001, with nearly a thousand participants, the agency used electronic "shareware" to identify fifty-six regional issues that would be addressed in a new regional plan.

The culmination of these efforts and supporting analysis was the 2040 Framework Plan. In addition to offering strategies to protect natural lands and water resources, it sought to direct regional development into urban centers and transportation corridors, building upon an earlier proposal in the organization's 1993 strategic plan that called for the creation of diversified regional centers. NIPC went to great lengths to build consensus around this "centers" concept, meeting with communities in clusters and assembling their ideas into a geographic information system. Reaching out to the "cluster groups" and local advisors allowed them to identify and categorize centers in accordance with their different urban functions.

Such analysis allowed for a hierarchy of centers that ranged from complex metropolitan centers (such as Evanston) to village centers (smaller suburbs such as Mount Prospect) and tiny hamlets as well as "neighborhood centers" in Chicago. Planners applied this concept across the entire region, including dense inner-city neighborhoods and sprawling suburban areas. As with the armature of NIPC's 1968 Finger Plan, the framework provided a "regional architecture" for local area planning, helping to steer communities toward regional goals. It was also intended to guide the agency's forecasting and the transportation plans produced by CATS. The board approved the plan in June 2005.

As Matthew Rockwell faced resistance to his effort to make the Finger Plan relevant, so Ron Thomas struggled to make his Common Ground project a factor in the regional-growth equation. Local communities had little incentive to embrace the plan. For its part, CATS showed little willingness to loosen its hold on transportation planning. In fact, as NIPC was conducting its work, CATS persuaded it to not display a detailed transportation system. The resulting plan map showed just general travel flow lines, rather than the detailed multi-modal system that NIPC derived from its research and community meetings.

Despite the obstacles, Common Ground did receive accolades, winning the "national plan of the year" award from the American Planning Association for innovative public participation and mapmaking. But the effort did little to forestall the political forces slowly pushing NIPC toward dissolution. It would be the last major planning document the agency produced.

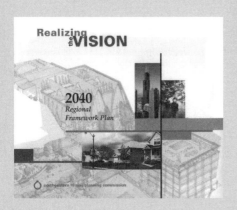

NIPC's *2040 Regional Framework Plan*, the culmination of a four-year effort ending in 2005.

Transportation Plan only nominally in compliance with the interagency agreement Thomas had negotiated. NIPC also found itself vying for the public's attention with a variety of civic organizations that had created their own plans. The nonprofit Center for Neighborhood Technology pursued a regional plan that offered an alternative to the transportation agency's officially-sanctioned plan. As discussed in the next chapter, the civic group Metropolis 2020 was working on a full-blown regional land-use and transportation plan.

At this late point in the organization's history, it was perhaps too much to expect that NIPC's planning framework would gain widespread support. By the early 2000s, NIPC faced relentless criticism and was hard-pressed to create any comprehensive plan that would have favorable prospects of implementation. The chasm between the region's transportation and land-use planning seemed as wide as ever, fueling criticism of both agencies.

Thomas, in some respects, won the battle but lost the war. He completed Common Ground in the face of serious financial constraints and scant political and civic support. Less than two years after the framework plan was released, the agency was merged with CATS, its longtime counterpart and occasional rival, to create the Chicago Metropolitan Agency for Planning. As discussed at length in Chapter 12, regional planning would again start anew.

Ultimately, NIPC followed the path of the Chicago Plan Commission and the Chicago Regional Plan Association (RPA), relinquishing its role on the regional stage after more than four decades of service. The RPA had been absorbed into NIPC almost a half-century before. Now NIPC would be absorbed. In both instances, a restless civic sector facilitated the change.

By late 2007, NIPC's name and identity had vanished. But the regional problems it had struggled with would continue to dominate and shape its successor.

BRINGING LAND USE AND TRANSPORTATION TOGETHER

Elmer W. Johnson *(left)* talks with then State Senator Barack Obama; Father Raymond Baumhart *(second from right)*, former president of Loyola University of Chicago; and Charles H. Shaw *(right)*, chairman of The Shaw Company, circa 1999. *(Chicago Metropolis 2020)*

12

IN THIS CHAPTER

Civic interest in planning for the Chicago region experiences a renaissance during the 1980s and 1990s. The Metropolitan Planning Council and the Commercial Club spearhead the Regional Agenda Project, followed a decade later by the creation of the non-profit Chicago Metropolis 2020. The organization brings new energy to regional analysis and planning while pushing to reform the official planning agencies. A half-century after the creation of NIPC and CATS, the two are merged into the newly created Chicago Metropolitan Agency for Planning (CMAP).

A CIVIC RENAISSANCE IN A GLOBAL CITY

The Commercial Club of Chicago had gradually surrendered its role as an agent of regional change after completing the *Plan of Chicago* and helping create the Chicago Plan Commission. In the early 1980s, Donald S. Perkins, chairman of the executive committee of Jewel Food Stores and past president of the club, criticized his organization for having, as he put it, a "Rip Van Winkle history."[1] The membership, comprised heavily of senior business executives, looked to find a way to strengthen its voice on issues facing the region.

In the spring of 1983, the club created the Civic Committee with its own office, budget, and full-time staff to serve as such a voice. This committee was smaller than the club as a whole but enjoyed significant financial support from the corporate sector. Perkins was named chairman and Lawrence Howe, vice chairman of the Jewel grocery store chain, was named executive director.

Rust Belt and Regional Partnership

The success of the new endeavor was anything but guaranteed. The Club had tried to revive its metropolitan agenda several times before. In 1963, its leaders set out to "make practical proposals on all major sectors of Chicago's life" with hopes that "the result would be a new Burnham Plan."[2] In 1971, Thomas Ayers of Commonwealth Edison began work on a similar initiative. After making little progress, Ayers turned to club president Perkins for assistance, but even then, as Perkin's later conceded, "nothing happened."

A sign erected by a local resident in protest of a proposed landfill in Barlett, circa 1979. The western part of DuPage County was experiencing dramatic population growth at the time. *(American Planning Association)*

This latest move, however, seemed different. Not only was the Civic Committee seen as an integral part of the Club's future, but its creation came amid an economic downturn that left the region searching for leadership and direction. The country entered a deep recession in 1980, shutting hundreds of factories and leaving tens of thousands without work. Big steel mills closed in southeast Chicago, with the demise of Wisconsin Steel alone costing 3,500 jobs. Other stalwarts of local industry, like the Schwinn Bicycle Company, moved out of town, pushing the state's unemployment rate to 12.8 percent in early 1983—the highest since the Great Depression.

There was such widespread sentiment that inept governance deserved much of the blame that the Task Force on the Future of Illinois, which the state legislature created in 1979, called for fundamental change in the state's "investment policy." Task Force leader George A. Ranney, Jr., drew on his experience as the state's deputy budget director to call for a new agency to assess the implications of rising taxation and to "examine the relationships between government programs."[3] If the state was to return to prosperity, the group concluded, it had to move beyond its simplistic one-year-at-a-time approach to budgeting and policymaking.

Much of the pessimism among government agencies was driven by recognition that the region would receive little help from Washington. The Reagan administration's "New Federalism" dimmed hopes that a downward trend in federal aid would be reversed. Nor was the private sector bullish about the future. A study of the regional job market, sponsored by the Commercial Club in 1983, warned that more devastating employment losses would affect middle-income workers.[4]

Such concerns led the Commercial Club to pursue goals markedly different from those pursued by Daniel H. Burnham and Edward H. Bennett seventy-five years earlier. The 1909 *Plan of Chicago* sought to prepare a bustling industrial city for more robust growth. Now, the Civic Committee would try to help the region navigate a treacherous "Rust Belt" economy. With further job losses in manufacturing inevitable, the region needed to find a way to revive its economic engines. Many displaced workers had already left for the West Coast and Sun Belt, where a high-tech boom was underway.

The situation was hardly helped by Chicago's "Council Wars" that raged through the early 1980s, pitting Mayor Harold Washington against a group of disenchanted aldermen. These controversies, and the almost continual strife over the city's public schools, offered sobering reminders of how the central city and the region remained divided along racial and ethnic lines. Such strife later spurred *The Wall Street Journal* to famously call Chicago "Beirut on the Lake," and U.S. education secretary William Bennett, never one for subtlety, to pronounce its public schools "the worst in the country."[5]

A notable bright spot for planners, however, was the renewed vibrancy of downtown Chicago. Remarkable things were happening in and around the Loop, with an office-construction boom underway. As construction cranes reappeared in the mid-1980s, the strength of the Central Area came to be seen as a springboard for regional improvement, just as it had decades before in the *Plan of Chicago*.

The downtown renaissance was fueled by the expansion of specialized professional services, including advertising, financial, and legal services, which drew Chicago into the ranks of emerging "global cities."[6] Tax increment financing and a growing residential market contributed to the rejuvenation of the Central Area. Dearborn Park, built by a public-private venture on old rail yards just south of the Loop, proved that a large middle-class population would live within walking distance of downtown

The Deep Tunnel Project, shown here in May 1983, offers a dramatic example of major public works achievement coordinated by a regional agency. Commissioned by the Metropolitan Water Reclamation District of Greater Chicago in the mid-1970s to deal with stormwater and sewage problems, this system of tunnels and reservoirs is one of the largest projects of its kind ever undertaken in the United States. *(American Planning Association)*

South Michigan Avenue's "street wall" appears through the lens of an artist photographer. The thirty-eight-story Willoughby Tower *(left)* and other historic buildings reflect from the metallic Cloud Gate sculpture in Millennium Park, more commonly known as the Bean. *(Kelsie Kilner Collection)*

jobs.[7] Championed during the 1970s by Thomas Ayers, Sears chairman; Gordon M. Metcalf; and Donald M. Graham, chief executive officer of Continental Bank, it was the largest residential planned development in the city's history at the time. Dearborn Park revitalized part of the inner city while capturing the imagination of civic leadership.

Hoping to push policy in new directions, the Civic Committee in 1984 joined with the Metropolitan Planning Council and the University of Chicago to launch the Regional Partnership. To set the partnership in motion, the committee joined with University of Chicago's Larry Lynn and MPC's George A. Ranney, Jr., an active board member, and Executive Director Mary Decker to assemble an expert panel to evaluate the metropolitan area's ills.[8]

Ranney harnessed his network of business partners, civic leaders, and influential friends for the benefit of the new initiative. Much of the partnership's day-to-day leadership, however, came from MPC's Mary Decker and Deborah Stone. In 1985, the partnership officially launched the Regional Agenda Project, with teams of experts assembled to study metropolitan issues, culminating in a series of recommendations for state and local governments. A report released the following year demanded that elected officials become more assertive in dealing with metropolitan planning issues and that they quit blaming Washington for the region's problems. "Whether we support New Federalism or not, we must accept the fact that it has been instituted at a national level and has resulted in the transfer of numerous programs to state governments," noted Decker. "The state has not picked up its piece of the equation."[9]

Despite an improving national economy in the mid-1980s, the Chicago metropolitan area still stood at an economic crossroads. Many spoke of a "jobless recovery" that was forcing displaced factory workers to relocate to the Sun Belt. Several large national corporations moved their headquarters out of the region, a problem particularly acute in the transportation sector. Once the home of a dozen large railroads, the region could now claim just three, the Chicago & North Western, Illinois Central, and Santa Fe, all of which would eventually be swallowed up by larger carriers based elsewhere.

When a turnaround finally occurred, consequently, its intensity took many by surprise. In the late 1980s, large suburban office parks, massive subdivisions, and huge downtown office towers signaled improved consumer confidence–the region as a whole was faring somewhat better than other aging cities on the Great Lakes. The city's politics, meanwhile, settled down. In 1989, three years after Mayor Washington's unexpected death, and twelve years after the passing of his father, Richard M. Daley was elected mayor of Chicago. Daley made further investment in the Central Area a key part of his agenda, although not without criticism from neighborhood activists.

The uneven pace of employment growth, however, made suburban politics more vexing than ever. A particularly striking imbalance occurred in the creation of high-paying corporate jobs throughout the region, with affluent DuPage County experiencing spectacular growth in white-collar, professional services jobs, while southern Cook and Will County saw little such development. The complete absence of major corporate headquarters in the southern part of the metropolitan area suggested an emerging division of suburban communities into the "haves" and "have nots," a problem with distinct racial overtones.

This cartoon humorously depicts some of the tradeoffs in promoting development and preserving natural areas. (Reprinted from Stop Me Before I Plan Again, by Richard Hedman, copyright 1977 by the American Society of Planning Officials, now known as the American Planning Association)

Circumstances seemed particularly bleak in older industrial areas south of the city. Ford Heights earned notoriety for being one of the poorest and most crime-ridden suburbs in the country. Proposals to build a major airport to stimulate job creation in this part of the region bogged down. In 1991, Sears, Roebuck & Company moved its headquarters from downtown Chicago to north suburban Hoffman Estates, forcing many employees living south of the Loop to relocate or accept long commutes. This fostered

Elmer W. Johnson and Corinne G. Wood, Illinois Lieutenant Governor, share the podium at a March 1, 1999, press conference at the Inland Steel Building announcing the establishment of Chicago Metropolis 2020. *(Chicago Metropolis 2020)*

resentment and raised questions about the state's motives in subsidizing the company's move.

Civic leaders challenged this imbalance, blaming regional planning and the fragmented process in which major decisions were made. The region had more local governments, authorities, and districts—1,250 by one count—than any other urbanized area of the country. NIPC, while positioning itself as a leader of environmental planning and a facilitator of intergovernmental agreements, was criticized as a "toothless tiger," unable to elicit large-scale change.[10] In 1995, a white paper by MPC's Deborah Stone became something of a manifesto, calling for a plan and process to bring order to the uncoordinated actions of hundreds of local governments.[11]

Elmer W. Johnson and the Metropolis Project

The Commercial Club, still eager to build upon the legacy of Burnham's 1909 *Plan*, embarked on a strategic planning effort to determine what initiatives they would undertake with the coming of the new century. This effort, led by Richard L. Thomas, chairman and CEO of the First National Bank of Chicago and chairman of the club, and Arnold R. Weber, retired president of Northwestern University and president of the club, enjoyed the backing of many prominent Chicago executives within the club.

One member of the strategic planning committee was Elmer W. Johnson, an attorney and former General Motors executive who was simultaneously building his own coalition of individuals and organizations. Born to Scandinavian immigrant parents, Johnson was described by David Roeder of the *Sun-Times* as a "free thinker" who cared deeply about how "urban life could be modified to relieve such problems as poor schools and a lack of affordable housing."[12] Johnson had deep civic roots, being a partner at the Chicago law firm Kirkland & Ellis and active in MPC and various charities.

Nevertheless, the entrepreneurial Johnson initially pursued his advocacy agenda independently, covering his costs partially from external grant funding. Disgruntled about the direction of the U.S. auto industry, and the implications of continuing automobile dominance of metropolitan life, Johnson sought to set transportation and land-use planning in new directions, making his opinions known in a provocative 1993 essay, *Avoiding the Collision of Cities and Cars*. His strident views put him at odds with many of his former colleagues in Detroit, a tension that he seemed to relish.

As a result of the strategic planning effort, the Commercial Club launched the Metropolis Project in 1996, which would in some ways echo its effort to create the 1909 *Plan* while having a less-architecturally and more-socially and economically oriented focus. Soon, more than two-hundred Club members were participating in six committees organized to study regional problems. Each committee prepared a report of its findings and recommendations, running the gambit from educational improvements to environmental initiatives. Johnson, project director, then drafted chapters based on these reports and turned them over to the club to review in a series of forums.

Awareness of the effort grew as the club reached out to leaders and interest groups to broaden its perspective on the region's problems. At a weekend retreat, seventy leaders joined committee members to discuss the findings of the Metropolis Project and review draft recommendations. Most were warmly received, but a few proved controversial, such as the idea of creating a "regional coordinating council" that would administer regional revenue sharing, i.e. a system of earmarking a portion of local property tax revenues for projects of regional importance, as done in the Minneapolis-St. Paul area. This notion, and a related proposal to merge planning institutions, including NIPC, CATS, and the RTA into a new, muscular regional agency, were strongly opposed by many local governments.

The Metropolis Project culminated in *Chicago Metropolis 2020: The Chicago Plan for the 21st Century*, published by the Commercial Club. In late 1998, the Commercial Club released a summary report and announced the establishment of a new entity, Chicago Metropolis 2020, followed by the full *Chicago Metropolis 2020* report in January 1999. An extended essay on the region's interrelated problems, *Chicago Metropolis 2020* was "driven by a dream" of what metropolitan Chicago could become, envisioning the region as "an incubator of enterprise" that finds "nourishment in diversity."[13]

Initially published as a soft-cover report, *Chicago Metropolis 2020* was later republished as a handsomely illustrated book. "This is one report you won't find simply sitting on the shelf," Ranney, Jr., assured readers.[14] Historian Carl Smith later described it as one of the most significant planning documents in the region's history. To some observers, however, it was all too much. Edwin Mills, an economist, called the effort "too much like a speech from a politician who thinks he can save the world" in a report for he wrote for the Heartland Institute,

Chicago Metropolis 2020 by Elmer W. Johnson.

a free-market think tank based in Chicago. David Roeder of the *Sun-Times* criticized *Chicago Metropolis 2020* for proposing "an overarching, non-elected metro government that would add to costs and bureaucracies."[15]

The targeted agencies did not respond warmly to any proposed merger and municipal officials remained downright hostile to the revenues-sharing proposal, regarding it as one more attempt to reduce their authority and autonomy.[16] Some characterized the proposals as a threat to the independence of all communities, echoing the accusations of "socialism" against the NIPC thirty years earlier. Tom Marcucucci, mayor of Elmhurst and NIPC board member, held nothing back in a *Chicago Tribune* interview, declaring: "The guy who wrote this must be from Moscow." He added, "These people are centralized planners and they are not on our side."[17]

A New Organization: Chicago Metropolis 2020

Chicago Metropolis 2020 called for the creation of a permanent organization that would advocate for its ideas, much as the Chicago Plan Commission once did for proposals of the *Plan of Chicago*. In keeping with its recommendation to create this organization, the Commercial Club in 1999 founded the nonprofit Chicago Metropolis 2020 with a governing executive council composed of Commercial Club members and other prominent business, labor, and civic leaders. Andrew J. McKenna was named the founding chairman.

George A. Ranney, Jr., speaks to members of the press about the "Revealing Chicago" photography exhibit by Terry Evans at Millennium Park, June 10, 2005. (Chicago Metropolis 2020)

Frank H. Beal, a professional planner and longtime associate of George A. Ranney, Jr., became executive director. Beal had worked at the state's energy and natural resources office and later served as president and CEO of Ryerson International, a unit of Inland Steel. Ranney was named the organization's president. He considered Beal an "equal partner" in shaping its agenda.[18] Together they made a highly effective civic planning team—one that echoed the effectiveness of the Burnham, Jr., and Kingery partnership years before.

The John D. and Catherine T. MacArthur Foundation, headed by Adele Simmons, offered financial support for a new regional plan.[19] Simmons had a longstanding interest in the region due to both the influences of her family (her widowed grandmother married John V. Farwell, president of the Commercial Club prior to the release of the *Plan of Chicago*) and her work at the foundation. Familiar with the many groups engaged in metropolitan affairs, Simmons believed that if the Commercial Club wanted to produce plans that had impact, it needed to aggressively reach out beyond its membership to include other organizations and tap into the diversity of the region.[20]

Metropolis 2020 set up office, appropriately enough, in the landmark Inland Steel building downtown, assembling an executive team that included King Harris, Paula Wolff, James LaBelle, and other experienced executives from the public and private sectors. Simmons, formerly of MacArthur, joined the team as well. Beal opted not to put heavy emphasis on coalition building, leaving that to MPC and other organizations. Nor did he attempt to curry favor with the official planning agencies. Rather, Metropolis 2020 came at the old problem of regional planning in a fresh way, as a spirited and independent actor, willing to take a more confrontational approach while producing fresh analysis to support its metropolitan agenda. The organization's reluctance to compromise impressed private foundations and corporate donors.

Metropolis Plan

Metropolis 2020 laid groundwork for a regional plan by gathering stakeholders to identify goals and undertaking studies of the region's economic and social conditions.

Mixed-used development around the Arlington Heights commuter rail station *(note condominium tower at rear)* offers a vivid illustration of the reemerging market for new residential units along suburban rail lines in the 1990s. Such development, encouraged in the Metropolis 2020 plan, echoed the goals of the 1968 Finger Plan. *(Cyrus Khazai Collection)*

Free of state and federal mandates and the local politics that bound the agencies CATS and NIPC, Metropolis 2020 could move quickly to lay out a contemporary regional plan based on complex modeling, statistical analysis, and workshops to solicit public opinion.

In spite of the organization's wealth of executive experience, finding a way through the technical thickets of regional planning required outside expertise. The group retained consultant John Fregonese, former director of the Metro Council in Portland, Oregon, to prepare future regional scenarios that would be the focal point for public discussions. At "community leaders workshops," attendees gathered around table-size maps, using paper "chips" to mark out potential transportation corridors, land use and densities in the future— "input" allowing for computer-based geographic analysis. Critical land use and forecast data came from NIPC.

The resulting Metropolis Plan, released in the spring of 2003 and looking toward the horizon year 2030, concentrated new development near urban and suburban centers oriented to public transit. The plan called for revitalizing the historic satellite cities and retrofitting newer suburban office centers to support transit, including the so-called "edge cities" of suburban office development. Around rail stations, the plan foresaw clusters of dense development, linked by arterial roads retrofitted with "bus rapid transit" service. The finished product resembled in some ways the Finger Plan of 1968, with its emphasis on suburban nodes oriented to transit corridors. Yet it also devoted a great deal of attention to improving freight corridors.

The Metropolis Plan scenario envisioned, by the year 2030, three-hundred fewer square miles of urbanized land than what would be developed if contemporary growth patterns continued. The plan sought to ease traffic congestion and promote more efficient energy consumption and community revitalization through "infill" development. The Metropolis Plan complemented a series of "regional indexes" measuring progress toward the plan's goals.

Toward Regional Reform

Metropolis 2020 and its ambitious agenda created some awkward moments for NIPC, which, as noted in Chapter 11, was conducting its own "Common Ground" planning project. NIPC staff looked with some skepticism on the Metropolis Plan; its promised reduction of development along the suburban fringe seemed unrealistic given current trends. Furthermore, the plan's total implementation would require sweeping statewide legislation, which again seemed unrealistic considering that the Illinois General Assembly had made only modest changes to planning-related laws during the past forty-five years.

Skepticism was directed at the so-called "superagency" proposed by Metropolis 2020. Encompassing not only CATS, NIPC, and the RTA, but the Illinois State Toll Highway Authority (ISTHA) as well, this "regional commission" would require a seemingly impossible political breakthrough in Springfield. Municipal officials, who were overwhelmingly opposed to the idea, voiced the familiar criticism that too much power would become concentrated in the hands of one entity, possibly trampling over local prerogatives and autonomy. They feared the merger would disrupt long-accepted ways of distributing federal and state transportation dollars. Such concerns over "the loss of local control" would need to be resolved before any significant reform of regional planning could occur.

Resistance came as no surprise to Metropolis 2020, which remained committed to demonstrating what it believed could be achieved with stronger regional planning. New opportunities appeared in 2003 when the Democrats took control of the state legislature, Rod Blagojevich became governor, and metropolitan reform legislation gradually began to appear. The state passed a technical-planning assistance act, although it left the measure unfunded. The legislature also passed an affordable-housing law requiring Illinois communities to plan for housing for low-to-middle-income households.[21]

A Breakthrough of Sorts

In early 2004, a special legislative panel chaired by U.S. Rep. William Lipinski was convened to make recommendations to the governor and General Assembly about improving regional planning for metropolitan Chicago.[22] At public hearings, the panel immediately felt the strength of local officials' opposition to a merger of regional agencies. In response, the panel modified its proposal, limiting the combination to CATS and NIPC. The new entity, called the "regional planning board," rather than the more official-sounding "commission," was dedicated to integrating regional land-use and transportation planning. The RTA would be strengthened but dealt with through separate legislation. Another accommodation was to preserve the identity of the two merged organizations as well as the structure of their boards while still putting them under the new planning board.

State Representative Julie Hamos (D-Evanston). *(Julie Hamos District Office)*

The Lipinski panel prepared the ground for ongoing merger discussions that continued into 2005. NIPC and CATS officials met in ad hoc committees to devise a counterproposal, one that would maintain the two agencies but create a "land use/transportation coordinating committee" to oversee their planning work. Civic reformers saw this as foot-dragging, and a merger initiative moved forward in the General Assembly. In early 2005, Julie Hamos (D-Evanston) and Suzanne Bassi (R-Palatine), members of the House Mass Transit Committee, produced legislation for a streamlined regional planning agency, with a new board that would replace CATS as the designated Metropolitan Planning Organization.

When officials at CATS and NIPC—organizations that would be dissolved by the legislation—were informed of the bill, they sought a compromise. Through the spring of 2005, a dialogue of sorts took place among the legislative leaders and local officials in the Metropolitan Mayors Caucus. The Mayors Caucus, founded by Mayor Richard M. Daley and suburban mayors in the late 1990s was becoming a forum for high-level discussion of shared city-suburban concerns. As Hamos drafted legislation for the new regional planning board, she asked for its input, particularly when it came to the composition of the Board. After a provision was made assuring direct mayoral involvement in the selection of the board, the caucus felt comfortable with the legislation and worked vigorously to allay fears among local officials that it would threaten long-accustomed means of distributing federal transportation funds to local governments. Local officials gradually gained confidence that their sovereignty would be respected.

Mayor Richard M. Daley *(center)* meets with his suburban counterparts at a Metropolitan Mayors Caucus event, circa 2008. The Caucus, a forum for high-level responses to shared city-suburban concerns, had worked to allay fears among local officials several years earlier that a new regional planning board would threaten local sovereignty. *(Metropolitan Mayors Caucus)*

The proposed legislation gradually took its final form. The sponsors, relying upon behind-the-scenes guidance from Metropolis 2020, sought to craft a new agency that would effectively coordinate regional transportation and land-use planning, while remaining responsive to local prerogatives. The arguments from both sides nonetheless became heated. NIPC Executive Director Ron Thomas joined with many of his commissioners in openly criticizing the proposed merger. Thomas believed that a combined agency would favor transportation planning, over the more nuanced requirements of land-use planning. Nevertheless, momentum behind the merger proposal grew stronger, Thomas was informed that Metropolis 2020 was not about to "let this issue die."[23]

Genesis of CMAP

On May 19, 2005, the Regional Planning Act passed unanimously in the General Assembly. Signed by the governor a few months later, the act created a new Regional Planning Board (RPB) to not only advocate generally for metropolitan Chicago, but to take responsibility for producing the regional transportation plans required by the federal government and to attend to comprehensive planning. Over a three-year period, the staffs of CATS and NIPC would "transition" into the new unified agency. This marked the most significant change in the state's planning landscape since the creation of the RTA in 1974. George A. Ranney, Jr., expressed hope that, at the very least, the long-running confusion over the division of responsibilities in regional planning had at last been resolved.

As with most other regional entities created by the state, debate quickly arose over who would be appointed to the board and control the agenda. The RPB would be roughly apportioned according to the regional population distribution and limited to fifteen people. The mayor of Chicago and the Cook County Board would each appoint five, while the boards of the five collar counties would appoint one each (with newly added Kendall County appointing its member jointly with Kane County).[24] Nonetheless, all county board appointments would be made with the "advice" of suburban mayors, virtually assuring that these elected officials would enjoy heavy representation. In June

2006, with an ambitious new regional plan already on its agenda, the board renamed the new organization the Chicago Metropolitan Agency for Planning (CMAP).

A New Era Begins

Despite the groundbreaking change, doubts remained about the prospects for CMAP. Some questioned whether the agency really had the powers it needed to affect change. The new agency had no more authority than its predecessors, its role being largely advisory. The fifteen-member board also would be constrained by a supermajority rule to affirm any initiative, allowing a relatively small group of members to block the will of the majority. In addition, the new agency faced the same funding problems that long hampered NIPC, with no dedicated, independent funding stream and a continued reliance on local contributions.

The legislative breakthrough was nonetheless good news for the civic leaders who had launched a movement more than twenty years before to reshape planning for the region. In some respects, Metropolis 2020 enjoyed the success that had eluded Daniel Burnham, Jr.'s Regional Planning Association a half-century before. Whereas Burnham, Jr., opposed the creation of NIPC on the grounds that it would create "duplicative" agencies, Metropolis had orchestrated a merger to overcome such duplication. One of the agency's first initiatives was to launch the creation of a new comprehensive plan.

Many of the key civic figures stayed on the scene after the new agency's creation. Ranney continued with Metropolis 2020 to push a reform agenda while tending to his personal passion, the Prairie Crossing Conservation Community in north suburban Grayslake. In 2006, he accepted, with John Bryan, the position of co-chair, with Adele Simmons the vice chair, of the 2009 Burnham Plan Centennial celebration. The centennial commemoration would encourage diverse constituencies to honor the region's rich heritage while calling attention to the continuing need to plan for its future.

Elmer W. Johnson spent three years in quiet research and writing at the Aspen Institute, living just long enough to see the "superagency" he espoused gain life. He died in the midst of another book project on February 19, 2008. Commercial Club member and *Chicago Sun-Times* publisher Cyrus Freidheim, Jr, remembered him as "giant intellectual" who gave "service to service like nobody else I've ever met."[25]

Air-traffic controllers at Municipal (Midway) Airport look over a crowded tarmac outside the American Airlines concourse, circa 1958. By the early 1960s, virtually all airline operations had been transferred to O'Hare. *(Robert F. Soraparu Collection; Christopher Lynch Collection)*

13

IN THIS CHAPTER

The city of Chicago and opposing suburban interests produce competing plans to add capacity to the region's airport system. As conflicts intensify, agencies devoted to regional planning are compelled to adopt neutral positions. Separate proposals for the expansion of O'Hare and the construction of a new south suburban airport move forward simultaneously. The city eventually gains the upper hand and launches the massive O'Hare Modernization Program.

THE PROBLEM OF AIRPORTS:

A Metropolitan Case Study

S ince the advent of scheduled passenger flight, the City of Chicago has enjoyed dominance of the region's commercial airports. Intergovernmental cooperation for financing and operation of major airports has been largely nonexistent. Both O'Hare and Midway (formerly Municipal) are controlled and operated by the city.

Circumstances are much different in other major metropolitan areas. In New York, an intergovernmental port authority represents three states and operates four major airports. A variety of different government entities operate the airports of Los Angeles. Detroit's airport system is run by a county government. In the San Francisco Bay Area, each of three major airports is operated by a different governmental entity. In Boston, the region's primary airport is run by a state-managed port authority.

The situation in metropolitan Chicago, however, is not entirely unique. In four other of the twelve most-populous urbanized regions in the country—Atlanta, Houston, Phoenix, and Philadelphia—the entire commercial airport system is run by the largest city in the region. Nevertheless, among the eight metropolitan areas that have *more than one* major commercial airport, Chicago has select company. Only Houston's airport system is also run entirely by the municipal government of the region's largest city.

The growth of the suburban population in metropolitan Chicago has virtually guaranteed that airports would become a source of intergovernmental friction. The Chicago region has more than four times the suburban population of other U.S. metropolitan areas where commercial airports are run exclusively by the region's largest city. More than four-million people and 225 village governments in metropolitan Chicago have no direct input into the region's commercial airport affairs.

Dominance by the City

The legacy of the City of Chicago's dominance is partially due to the historic distribution of the region's population. No suburban community or "satellite city" in the metropolitan area had even 3 percent of Chicago's population seventy years ago, when commercial air service was taking root in American cities. With such a large share of the regional population within the city limits of Chicago, airport development in outlying areas was less viable than in other metropolitan areas.

Another factor was the Chicago Plan Commission's role in planning for airports. With its early airport studies financed primarily by the city of Chicago, the Plan Commission conducted its evaluations with an eye toward the needs of the city. Although the Chicago Regional Planning Association (RPA) was also active in airport planning, that body lacked the ability to mobilize resources in the same way that the Plan Commission could.

Midway Airport appears saturated with traffic in this 1950s view. Cicero Avenue runs across the bottom of the photograph. Demand had grown to the point that parking spilled over to the east side of street. *(Robert F. Soraparu Collection, Christopher Lynch Collection)*

Airports outside the city's boundaries, as a result, played only fleeting roles in the region's commercial aviation. Maywood Airport and Checkerboard Field, pioneers of the development of air mail service, lost their scheduled flights by the early 1930s. For a brief time in the 1940s, Glenview Naval Air Station (formerly Curtiss Wright Field) had flights to New York operated by United Airlines. An airport in Lansing (Illinois) had extensive mail operations but no dedicated passenger service. Palwaukee Field in suburban Wheeling has never offered scheduled passenger service. Gary, Indiana has suffered off-and-on service for many years, with never more than a few flights daily—despite having viable runways and terminal facilities. No suburban airport offers significant commercial passenger service today.

A hanger at Midway Airport sits deserted, circa 1970, several years after being abandoned by United Airlines. *(Robert F. Soraparu Collection)*

The Chicago Plan Commission and the RPA surrendered their leadership of aviation planning in the 1950s, leaving metropolitan Chicago without a regional planning organization able to press for thoughtful, measured growth of the airport system. Although the Northeastern Illinois Planning Commission (NIPC) long supported airport planning, it cautiously adopted neutral stances on critical issues related to airport expansion. The Metropolitan Mayors Caucus has also opted to steer clear of controversies, apparently recognizing that reaching consensus would be all but impossible.

The Search for Airports

The policy debate about Chicago's commercial airports prior to 1945 centered on the need to relieve pressure on Municipal (Midway) Airport and to provide a facility capable of handling new and ever larger planes. As described in Chapter 4, the Chicago Plan Commission worked with the Chicago RPA and other organizations to identify prospective sites for major commercial airports. The organizations gave serious consideration to a variety of sites outside the city's boundaries, including existing airports near south suburban Harvey and Lansing.

It is unlikely that the Harvey or Lansing sites, well south of the city, would have been operated by the City of Chicago had they been selected to become major airports. Both were established airports located a considerable distance from the city limits.[1] In 1943 the Plan Commission chose to transform the site of Orchard Place Airport/Douglas Field, a military facility just a few miles northwest of the city, into a major commercial facility.

O'Hare Field's innovative two-level roadway system, with separate levels for motorists to reach arrivals and departures, remains uncongested in this 1963 photo. The surface parking lot at left would soon give way to the Hilton Hotel and main parking garage. *(Bill Engdahl photo, Hedrich-Blessing, Chicago History Museum)*

After World War II, the RPA drafted legislation for the General Assembly that allowed the city to acquire the site. Initially, however, it was not clear that this purchase would be possible. The Village of Bensenville objected vigorously to the city acquiring the land, which straddled the Cook-DuPage county line. After a great deal of negotiation, a court ruled in favor of the city, clearing the way for construction of O'Hare International Airport. A year after the first commercial flights departed from the partially completed facility in 1955, the city struck a deal with neighboring towns allowing it to annex a thin strip of land (along the present-day Kennedy Expressway), connecting the airport to the city and thus bringing it within legal city limits.

After O'Hare's formal dedication in 1963, there was periodic discussion of replacing the now-underutilized Midway Airport with a new airport within city limits, possibly on landfill in Lake Michigan or near Lake Calumet on the city's south side. Instead of these, however, the city focused on expanding O'Hare, building a new runway in 1969 that expanded capacity but also prompted some suburban governments, particularly those on the west side of the airport, to organize around noise concerns. City-suburb relations on O'Hare issues took a turn for the worse.

O'Hare, which replaced Midway as the busiest airport in the world, began to suffer from congestion in the early 1970s. By 1979, congestion on its runways had grown to

A model of the O'Hare grounds prepared in the 1960s shows the enormous dimensions of this city-owned facility. O'Hare earned the title of World's Busiest Airport, previously held by Midway Airport, within a decade after its first commercial flight departure in 1955. *(Chicago History Museum)*

such an extent that the federal government imposed "slot" controls at peak times, limiting the number of takeoffs and landings. Consequently, airlines began eying the languishing Midway, whose little-used runways were now partially covered by clumps of grass. Midway Airlines commenced operations there in 1979, but it was not until Southwest Airlines launched service at the facility in 1984 that a great revival appeared to be in the offing. While not eliminating the long-term need for airport system expansion, Midway's renaissance allowed the policymakers to postpone critical decisions without significant political consequences.

By the late 1980s, Midway's capacity was approaching saturation. For the first time since the late 1940s, there was serious debate about building another airport in the region. The Northeastern Illinois Planning Commission (NIPC), however, chose to distance itself from potential political conflict, recognizing that the "airport issue" was one of great sensitivity to its board members, who represented both the city and suburbs. Another problem was that certain alternative sites proposed for the third airport, including Gary, Milwaukee, and Rockford, were located outside NIPC's planning area, which complicated the agency's ability to take a position.

Nevertheless, NIPC did join an alliance of state governments including Illinois, Indiana, and Wisconsin to help launch the Chicago Airport Capacity Study in 1988.

The airport study group considered a variety of locations in the southern part of the region, including rural sites near Kankakee and Peotone. In 1992, however, the group's newly completed study recommended building a new airport at Lake Calumet, on the city's far southeast side, at a location that Chicago aviation planners were already considering. The prospective site, situated on wetlands, trash landfills, and a nearby neighborhood, lay in the midst of old industrial districts and blue collar neighborhoods. Partly because the Lake Calumet site was relatively close to downtown Chicago (fifteen miles away), the city publicly endorsed the site.

This aerial view of O'Hare International Airport shows the density of commercial and residential development surrounding the airport's perimeter as well the airport's new north runway *(extending left to right in this photo, just above the diagonal runways)* under construction at the time. Other runway projects on the opposite end of the complex to be completed by 2016 involves substantial commercial displacement and the relocation of lengthy stretches of Irving Park Road on its southern edge. *(City of Chicago)*

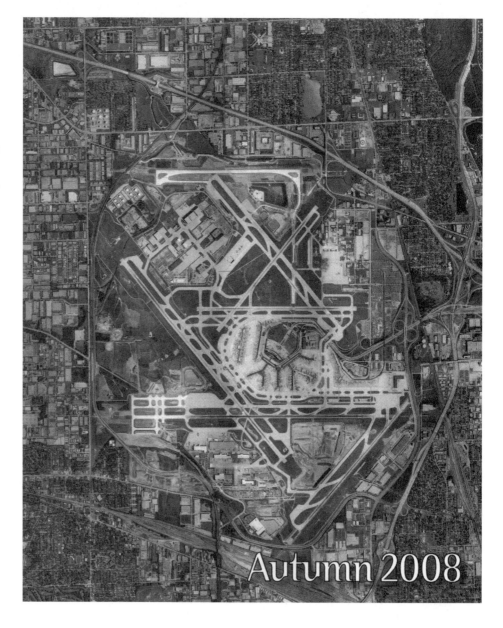

The Lake Calumet Airport may have been built had issues over its control been resolved. Two downstate Republicans, Governor Jim Edgar and Secretary of State George Ryan, who later succeeded Edgar as governor, supported the proposal, but other state officials reamined opposed. The state made its involvement in the airport's construction conditional on the city's willingness to share control and revenues with other governmental units, presumably through the creation of a regional airport authority. When the Illinois legislature failed to approve a regional airport authority, as the Airport Capacity Study had recommended, the effort hit a roadblock.

Then came a political bombshell—recently elected mayor Richard M. Daley announced his decision in July 1992 to walk away from the project. "Sometimes in life you have to face reality," he said in a news conference. "We're facing reality," he added, leaving no doubt that his decision was final.[2] The mayor also made it clear that the city wasn't interested in assisting efforts to identify a new airport site outside city limits.

The mayor's decision apparently stemmed not only from his concerns over control, but also from consideration of the complexity of the Lake Calumet proposal, which required destruction of wetlands and threatened surrounding neighborhoods with a great deal of noise. In addition, the Lake Calumet proposal limited the growth potential of Midway. Resolving these issues would have required the mayor to navigate treacherous political waters.

The demise of the Lake Calumet proposal set the city and suburbs on divergent paths. Mayor Daley showed no interest in cooperating with plans for a new airport on a "green grass" (i.e., rural) site, possibly near south suburban Peotone or in northwest Indiana. Neighboring states distanced themselves from the Chicago airport problem, while the state of Illinois seemed content to let the city shape its own aviation future.

City–Suburb Conflict Intensifies

For the next decade, the City of Chicago and various suburban organizations advanced competing agendas for expansion of airport capacity. The city reaffirmed its determination to expand O'Hare, enjoying support from local business and civic organizations, including the Chicagoland Chamber of Commerce. Strong support also came from Business Leaders for Transportation, an advocacy group co-sponsored by the Commercial Club and the Metropolitan Planning Council. Through public advocacy and publicity, these civic groups pushed hard for expansion at O'Hare.

Opposing these groups was an alliance of stakeholders, essentially divided into two camps. The first was led by the Suburban O'Hare Commission (SOC), whose most active members included the suburbs of Bensenville, Elk Grove Village, and Park Ridge. The SOC spared no expense to block the city's intentions for O'Hare. It felt strongly that expansion would worsen congestion and land-use problems and ultimately undermine the economy of adjacent communities. The organization rallied the opposition behind the idea that airport noise and roadway traffic would be intolerable if O'Hare was significantly expanded. The SOC also generated a great deal of animosity over the city's plans to relocate many homes and business in neighboring communities as part of proposed runway expansions.

A second camp opposing O'Hare's expansion was led by U.S. Representative Jesse Jackson, Jr., whose congressional district included a large swath of the south suburbs. Jackson's camp favored a

A sign on U.S. Route 66, at the site of the proposed South Suburban (Peotone) Airport, tells the distance to downtown Chicago. Most of the proposed area remains in agricultural use. *(Chaddick Collection)*

Airports of Metropolitan Chicago (opposite page).

This map shows the region's airport system, including existing airports, abandoned airfields, and new facilities proposed to relieve Midway and O'Hare. The large footprint of the proposed Peotone (South Suburban) airport depicts that facility at full "build-out," a scenario rarely contemplated today. No airport outside of Chicago's city limits has sustained large-scale commercial passenger operations for extended periods. As noted, various scenarios for an airport in Lake Michigan have also been proposed.

new airport at the south suburban Peotone site, some thirty-five miles south of the city, one of the sites considered by the Airport Capacity Study years earlier. Jackson believed the airport would become a major jobs generator for the southern part of the region. The Will County board formed another faction favoring the Peotone site. This site's supporters gained the endorsement of most communities near the proposed airport, although resistance in the Peotone area arose through a citizen-led group called Shut This Airport Nightmare Down (STAND). STAND enjoyed great popular support, especially among rural residents in and around the proposed airport's footprint.

The disagreements among these groups became awkward for NIPC. Struggling to find middle ground, the agency expressed its support in 1990 for a third airport but was careful to avoid naming a particular site. When it became clear after the demise of the Lake Calumet proposal that the likely alternative was Peotone, this position became untenable among some NIPC board members. Therefore, the agency withdrew its support for a new airport in 1993, citing concerns that it would promote sprawl. The NIPC board wanted the state to continue exploring site options, but it retreated to the less-controversial stance of anticipating two different airport scenarios in its forecasts and plans. Its year 2020 population and jobs forecasts, produced in the late 1990s, included scenarios for both a Peotone airport and an expansion of O'Hare.

Looking to bridge the gap between the city and suburbs, some expressed interest in creating a new airport authority to serve the entire region. The city of Chicago, however, staunchly opposed any proposal that involved tapping into existing airport revenues, including the lucrative revenues from passenger facility charges on travelers at Midway and O'Hare. Apparently to safeguard funds generated at its airports and forestall discussion about creating a truly regional authority, the city made a

Airports of Metropolitan Chicago

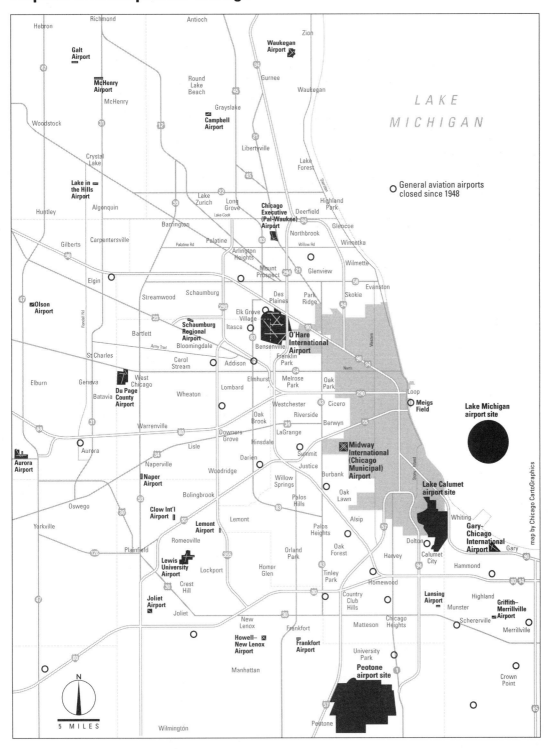

Richmond Antioch
Hebron Zion
Galt Airport
Waukegan Airport
Round Lake Beach Gurnee
McHenry Airport
McHenry Grayslake Waukegan
Woodstock **Campbell Airport**
Libertyville
Crystal Lake Lake Forest
Lake in the Hills Airport
Huntley Algonquin Lake Zurich Long Grove **Chicago Executive (Pal-Waukee) Airport** Highland Park
Gilberts Carpentersville Barrington Palatine Deerfield Glencoe
Olson Airport Elgin Streamwood Schaumburg Arlington Heights Northbrook Winnetka
Bartlett **Schaumburg Regional Airport** Itasca Des Plaines Mount Prospect Park Ridge Wilmette
St Charles Bloomingdale Bensenville **O'Hare International Airport** Skokie Evanston
Elburn Geneva Carol Stream Addison Franklin Park
Batavia **Du Page County Airport** Wheaton Lombard Elmhurst Melrose Park Oak Park Loop
Warrenville Oak Brook Westchester Cicero **Meigs Field**
Aurora Lisle Downers Grove Riverside Berwyn **Lake Michigan airport site**
Aurora Airport Naperville Darien LaGrange
Naper Airport Woodridge Willow Springs Summit **Midway International (Chicago Municipal) Airport**
Bolingbrook Justice Burbank
Oswego **Clow Int'l Airport** Lemont Palos Hills Oak Lawn **Lake Calumet airport site**
Yorkville **Lemont Airport** Palos Heights Alsip Whiting
Plainfield Romeoville Orland Park Oak Forest Harvey **Gary-Chicago International Airport** Gary
Lewis University Airport Lockport Homer Glen Tinley Park Dolton Calumet City Hammond
Joliet Airport Crest Hill Homewood **Lansing Airport** Highland **Griffith-Merrillville Airport**
Joliet New Lenox Frankfort Country Club Hills Munster Schererville Merrillville
Howell-New Lenox Airport **Frankfort Airport** Matteson Chicago Heights
Manhattan University Park **Peotone airport site** Crown Point
Wilmington Peotone

General aviation airports closed since 1948

LAKE MICHIGAN

N
5 MILES

map by Chicago CartoGraphics

DC-9 jets operated by Midway Metrolink line up at the gates of Midway Airlines in the mid-1980s. Traffic at the airport was growing sharply at the time, helping to relieve pressure on overburdened O'Hare.
(Robert F. Sorparu Collection)

preemptive move, creating the Chicago–Gary Regional Airport Authority in 1995. This authority, firmly controlled by city government, enjoyed some oversight of operations at O'Hare, Midway, and the newly renamed Gary–Chicago Airport. If the suburbs wanted an airport, they would have to move forward independently of the city and northwest Indiana.

The NIPC board also remained neutral toward the proposed expansion of O'Hare. Merely describing that airport's possible expansion, as NIPC did in 1997, generated a furious response, with Elk Grove Village and Park Ridge—both SOC communities—accusing NIPC of a pro-O'Hare bias. NIPC's executive director, Phil Peters, tried to reassure anxious suburbs, telling them, "We have not taken a position."[3]

SOC attorney Joseph Karaganis found this unacceptable, accusing NIPC of failing to "bite the bullet" by making a decision about "the biggest economic issue facing the region."[4] NIPC refused to take the bait, steering clear of all positions that could be construed as endorsement of any proposal. The absence of a strong regional institution helping to guide the debate left a void that subregional groups were eager to fill.

Opposition Takes Root

All parties, city and suburban, recognized that enlisting the support of state government and the airlines would bring momentum to their side. Backers of the Peotone site successfully pushed the state to conduct an initial engineering study for this proposed facility, although they had no success with the airlines. The largest carriers at O'Hare, American and United, showed little interest in financing any form of airport expansion. Nevertheless, both companies understood that a wholly uncooperative stance on their part could deny them a place at the table when key decisions were made. While insisting that they were not willing to pay substantially higher airport fees, the carriers aligned themselves tenuously with the pro-O'Hare camp.[5]

Meanwhile, the mayor kept mum about his specific plans for O'Hare. At the same time, however, he made known his interest in using the airport in Gary to expand the region's aviation capacity. The Gary-Chicago Airport was part of the city-controlled authority and less threatening to the airlines. Over the next several years, however, commercial air service at Gary performed poorly, as one airline after another came and went. The facility suffered through spotty, irregular service.

Finally, in the summer of 2001, Mayor Daley did what many expected from him years earlier: he announced a massive expansion plan for O'Hare. The city's $12 billion plan included reconfiguration of existing runways and construction of several new ones on annexed land. The airport would receive major transit and highway improvements, including a new road for western access from DuPage County.

The timing of Daley's announcement was unfortunate. Air travel dropped dramatically after the terrorist attacks of September 11, 2001, precipitating a crisis in the industry. The 9/11 tragedy raised fears that demand was far too soft to justify both expanding O'Hare and building a new airport. Certain members of the pro-O'Hare coalition, meanwhile, expressed readiness to jump ship as concern grew that the city was too inflexible in its approach. On March 30, 2003, Mayor Daley weakened this coalition by closing and tearing up the runway at Meigs Field, a small-but-useful downtown airport that occupied land he envisioned for lakefront parkland. This surprise move generated outrage and raised questions about the mayor's ability to cultivate the relationships necessary to bring the complex O'Hare expansion project to completion.

Gradually, however, public and political opinion turned in Daley's favor. In 2003, Democrat Rod Blagojevich succeeded George Ryan as governor. The Chicagoan soon took executive action allowing the city to continue expanding O'Hare without risk of state interference. The governor gave Chicago the authority to more easily condemn land needed for the project, both within city limits and in neighboring suburbs. The state also continued to buy land for a Peotone airport, although recurrent budget crises in the early 2000s forced it to scale back.

When federal approval finally came for the first phase of the city's O'Hare modernization program, in late 2005, the debate over the region's airport problems effectively ended. The city entered into agreements with American, United, and other airlines to help finance the program and invested heavily in the necessary land for the expansion, including considerable acreage within the village limits of Bensenville.

Despite the momentum on its side, the city had to overcome stiff opposition. Efforts to expand O'Hare and in the process relocate more than 2,000 residents and 280 businesses in neighboring communities fueled resentment and more legal battles. Proponents of the south suburban site led by Rep. Jackson refused to surrender, giving their favored project the compelling name Abraham Lincoln International Airport.[46] They sought private capital to begin its construction and made inroads in Washington to have federal funding considered for the project. Nevertheless, the south suburban cause suffered from a continuing rift between Rep. Jackson and the Will County board over the form of the proposed airport authority.

The city's efforts at O'Hare reached a milestone in late 2008 with the opening of a new runway in the airport's northern section. This accomplishment, and the state's ongoing lack of strong support for the Peotone site, suggested that the south suburban airport proposal would be tabled indefinitely. By early 2009, the city embarked on the O'Hare modernization program's "completion phase," a much more costly endeavor on the airport's south end, scheduled for completion by 2016.

Closing Review: Regionalism's Failure

The dominance that the City of Chicago enjoyed, both before and after abandoning the Lake Calumet Airport proposal in 1993, has long been a source of political contention, even intrigue, in the metropolitan region. Battles for new airports and runways have damaged the delicate fabric of intergovernmental relations. But the city's long insistence on retaining control of these facilities has perhaps proven prescient. Efforts underway to lease Midway Airport to a private consortium, for example, could generate a large sum of money to pay down the city's debt.

The airport problem differs from most contentious regional issues, insofar as suburban interests tend to oppose regional revenue sharing schemes. The airport debate is framed in the opposite way, with the city of Chicago resisting moves to create a truly regional authority. Indeed, the city apparently established its aviation partnership with Gary to ensure its dominant position. This has certainly made the south suburban airport proposal much more difficult to realize.

The neutrality of regional planning organizations on pivotal airport issues—due to their limited powers to affect key decisions and to their planning-area limitations—came at a heavy price. The lack of unity among NIPC commissioners left the agency unable to play a key role as convenor and facilitator of this critical regional discussion. Without a credible regional organization bringing together the different interests, factions could operate largely without fear of political consequences.

One such faction, the Suburban O'Hare Commission, shows how "institutionalized opposition" can emerge to hamper projects that otherwise enjoy a great deal

Mayor Richard J. Daley (*second from right*), O'Hare modernization manager Rosemarie Andolino (*second from left*), and other officials symbolically lift the first shovel of dirt at the groundbreaking for the airport's new North Runway, September 30, 2005. *(City of Chicago)*

The Gary-Chicago airport has seen on-and-off commercial airline service for many years. When this photo was taken in March 2009, there had been no scheduled commercial flight since the demise of Skybus Airlines the previous summer—despite continual improvements to runways and aggressive marketing programs to raise public awareness of the facility. *(Cyrus Khazai Collection)*

of regional support. With deep coffers and an experienced legal team, the SOC long pursued its goals with great sophistication. Its professionalism sets it apart from earlier groups that opposed regional initiatives, such as Save Our Suburbs, or the "kNOwRTA" coalition that opposed the Regional Transportation Authority. For its sheer persistence and aptitude, the SOC has few peers among groups formed by municipal governments to fight policies of a neighboring government.

Another consequence of the absence of decisive regional leadership is the fragmentation of efforts to expand the ground transportation system required for O'Hare's expansion. Although the airport's runway and terminal expansions are managed by the city, responsibility for improving roads and suburban transit services around the airport rests largely with counties, the state, and the Chicago Metropolitan Agency for Planning. For its part, CMAP has avoided making decisive statements on airport issues in much the same way that NIPC did.

"For the foreseeable future," writes David M. Young, in the close to his definitive *Chicago Aviation: An Illustrated History*, "O'Hare and Midway will continue to dominate Chicago aviation."[7] Advocates and students of regional planning will find this belief is as true today as it was when Young's book was published in 2003—with consequences for the region far beyond investment in commercial airports.

Navy Pier's Ferris Wheel rekindles the legacy of the featured attraction of the 1893 World's Columbian Exposition. The pier today serves a recreational role as envisioned in the *Plan of Chicago*. (Grace Anderson and Kimberly Deng Collection)

In this volume, we have retraced a 100-year journey from the creation of the *Plan of Chicago* to today and recounted how planners and institutions sought to create bold visions for the future of the metropolitan area. Throughout this journey, we found an almost insatiable "will to plan," even when the resources for such planning were distressingly thin. Citizen-advocates played an indispensable role keeping the agenda fresh and vibrant, forming civic associations of regional concern that engaged the public sector. For their part, professional planners worked with great technical acuity to create official plans for the region. Together, their work forms a tapestry of inspiration, achievement, and disappointment.

CONCLUSION:
LOOKING TO THE FUTURE

Looking at the many people behind these ambitious efforts, we discern some remarkable partnerships. Daniel H. Burnham and Edward H. Bennett's fruitful partnership in the early 1900s was echoed later in the four-decade working relationship of Daniel Burnham, Jr., and Robert Kingery. Matthew Rockwell, the insightful urban planner and architect at the helm of NIPC, assembled a dynamic team in the 1960s that produced the influential, if not implemented, Finger Plan. His successor Larry Christmas, a key member of Rockwell's team, learned from Rockwell's architectural approach while applying his own knowledge of urban forces to steer NIPC in new directions during the 1980s. More recently, the collaboration between George A. Ranney, Jr., and Frank E. Beal proved instrumental to the achievements of Chicago Metropolis 2020.

The civic sector gave forth remarkable leaders, including some women who left their mark on a male-dominated field. Dorothy Rubel, director of the Metropolitan Housing Council (predecessor to today's Metropolitan Planning Council, or MPC), clearly shaped the regional agenda during her tenure beginning in the 1940s. MPC long cultivated effective female leaders, including more recent directors Mary Decker and MarySue Barrett. During the early 2000s, State Representative Julie Hamos demonstrated critical leadership as a reform-minded legislator. Even dissenters added important voices to the regional conversation, as shown by the many women leading the Save Our Suburbs movement that burst on the scene in the 1960s.

THE BURNHAM PLAN
CENTENNIAL

Logo for the centennial
commemoration of the 1909
Plan of Chicago.

Given the 1909 *Plan's* persistent role as a guiding force, the past one hundred years may be remembered as "the Burnham Century." Leaders looked back to it as a gold standard, capable of inspiring and educating. The plan guided the Chicago Plan Commission's initiatives for public works and conservation through the 1930s. Daniel Burnham, Jr., revered and often referred to his father's work, even as his RPA shifted attention to suburban infrastructure on a scale far beyond what his father's plan conceived. Matthew Rockwell also became an important link in this chain of connection, as a planner-architect greatly influenced by the Burnhams. Years later, during the 1990s, the Commercial Club of Chicago turned again to its heritage as sponsor of the 1909 *Plan*, launching the Metropolis Project that echoed the organization's historic role of cultivating civic involvement in planning.

Burnham and Bennett's enormous undertaking and monumental vision bequeathed a great tradition in regional planning. The leadership emanating from the civic sector set the stage for a century of dynamic public-private interaction in the quest to create visions for metropolitan change. Citizen advocates continually provoked public officials, creating a dialectic that engendered the rise and fall of organizations and an ebb and flow of citizen participation.

The Two Threads

The first half of "Burnham's Century" was dominated by individuals working in civic organizations, often as volunteers. The *Plan of Chicago* was a distinctively civic-led undertaking, and the Chicago Plan Commission, while established by the city of Chicago, was civic in both composition and outlook. Later, in the 1920s, the Chicago Regional Planning Association was formed as a non-profit organization. The Metropolitan Housing Council assumed its important role as voice and advocate for regional planning during the 1930s.

The second half of the century was dominated by public organizations chartered by the state. Two new institutions—the Chicago Area Transportation Study (CATS) and the Northeastern Illinois Planning Commission (NIPC)—were created in the mid-1950s. Both publicly funded, these agencies took more bureaucratic and technical approaches to transportation and land-use planning than their predecessors. In the process, the Plan Commission and the RPA gradually exited the regional planning stage, as did the Cook County Board.

As the Chicago region claims its place among a select group of "global cities," however, its future still rests heavily on its non-governmental leaders. Powerful civic forces instigated the creation of the Chicago Metropolitan Agency for Planning (CMAP) in 2005, as an attempt to finally integrate transportation and land-use planning into a single comprehensive plan. Nonprofit groups such as Center for Neighborhood Technology, Chicago Council on Global Affairs, Metropolis 2020, MPC, and Openlands continue to be influential players on the regional scene, often serving as watchdogs of public action.

Chicago and its great metropolitan counterpart, New York, have arrived at something of a mirror image of one another in efforts to plan for their respective regions. While Chicago streamlined and (at least in a limited way) strengthened its regional planning apparatus with CMAP, New York did away with its region-wide agency years ago. The state government of New York broke up the old Tri-State Regional Commission into smaller, more geographically focused councils of government. In both regions, powerful civic forces were the impetus for the changes. In the case of New York, the influential Regional Plan Association was behind both the Tri-State Commission's creation in 1962 as well as its dissolution in the early 1980s. The New York RPA continues to have sucess in implementing its most recent plan, completed in 1996, but it faces challenges harnessing the necessary civic energy to move ambitious planning ideas forward.[1]

Although Chicago now has a single agency to plan comprehensively for the region, it lacks a major civic body of such continuity as the New York RPA, one ready to prepare and implement regional plans. The Chicago RPA, which disappeared more than fifty years ago, might have become such a body, although Daniel Burnham, Jr., chose not to pursue a regional plan to update the 1909 *Plan*. For now, it seems, a public agency, CMAP, will dominate Chicago area planning (see later in this chapter).

The Forces in Play

The two threads—civic energy and public commitment—at times have spun into a great converging force that draws the Chicago region together. This force of convergence, however, is by no means irresistible and, in fact, is often quite weak in a region as complex and highly diverse as Chicago. It may be that it was easier to devise and implement a regional plan in Daniel H. Burnham's time, when the metropolitan region essentially consisted of the city of Chicago and no large suburbs. Most outlying communities possessed little capacity or wherewithal to pursue ambitious planning efforts of their own. Unlike today's planners, Burnham did not face some 275 strong-willed municipal boards, most of them backed by technically trained staff. Be that as it may, today's regional planners must now accept the challenge of working in a highly fragmented environment, where initiatives will be challenged by divergent political and economic interests.

In the last 100 years, at least three "diverging forces" have appeared to thwart efforts to create a consensus vision for the region. Regional agencies may ignore them or evade them for a time, but eventually these forces must be confronted in one way or another. We discuss them only briefly here.

The first is the division between the city of Chicago and the hundreds of suburban governments surrounding it. This tension was clearly understood by Burnham and Bennett as a potential political barrier to their regional goals. In the *Plan of Chicago*, they urged that the city annex land on its periphery in a rational fashion, so as to help manage growth patterns going outward. That occurred only to a limited extent. For many years, this problem was reflected in the often uncoordinated agendas of regional planning institutions, with the Chicago Plan Commission increasingly focused on planning

An Analysis Of

METROPOLITAN GOVERNMENT

And Its Effects On

YOUR HOME

YOUR SCHOOLS

YOUR VILLAGE

YOUR CITY

YOUR TOWNSHIP

YOUR COUNTY

YOUR STATE

YOUR COUNTRY

This graphic, prepared in 1979 by Save Our Suburbs (SOS), illustrates the group's strident view of the potential implications of "metropolitan government." "SOS" used such materials in its campaigns to mobilize people in opposition to regional agencies seeking to exert influence over local planning.

within the city while the Chicago RPA directed most of its attention to the expanding suburban areas. The city and suburbs did come together in the 1940s and 1950s to push for massive public works projects. In more recent years, however, such displays of cooperation are often lacking, as demonstrated in the disputes surrounding the expansion of O'Hare Airport. The official regional agencies have shown time and again that they were unwilling or unable to deal with this and other volatile issues.

City-suburban cooperation took an important step forward when Chicago's mayor Richard M. Daley reached out to suburban mayors to form the Metropolitan Mayors Caucus in 1997. This dialogue suggested that the region's mayors were eager to both discuss regional problems and to find practical ways to cooperate to solve them. Today the conclave creates a kind of "standing alliance" that gives the metropolitan area one voice on legislative matters in Springfield and Washington. That the mayors should meet directly, independently of the official agencies, is undoubtedly necessary at times. However, it also points to the difficulties that the regional agencies have in sponsoring meaningful discussions and in reconciling opposing views.

The second diverging force appears in the deep-seated skepticism of the populace, including municipal and county officials, toward the intentions of regional agencies. This skepticism came to a head in the 1960s, as heated debates about the rise of "metro government" made the powers of regional agencies an explosive issue. Anti-regional forces spread fear of super governments limiting local independence and bringing big city problems to suburban doorsteps. Such grievances arose once more in the 1970s when battle lines were drawn between the city and the suburbs over the creation of the RTA.

Such distrust may be inevitable due to statewide policies that have encouraged the creation of so many municipal governments, while putting them in competition to expand their tax bases and gain public amenities. Regional agencies, unlike local governments, have no clear constituencies behind them. Not being elected by the people, they are unable to speak with the same sort of authority as officials who have electorates behind them.

Regional agencies are nonetheless well-positioned to promote and implement plans in some areas, such as roadbuilding and road improvements, investment in transit lines, and the protection of natural resources. Such initiatives usually offer benefits of immediate value to local governments. But attempts by regional agencies to move aggressively into other areas, such as promoting affordable housing, tend to be met with resentment. For this reason, NIPC saw much more success over the years in its work on natural resource conservation and "greenways" plans than in its attempts to create housing plans.

The third divergence stems from uncoordinated regional planning for transportation and land use. The 1909 *Plan*, which sought to integrate these in and around downtown Chicago, remains a persuasive argument for some form of coordinated approach to help people move through the region's space. It was not until the rapid spread of auto-oriented development after World War II that policymakers felt an urgency to become more systematic in coordinating plans for land-use and transportation systems. It was just then, however, that the state created two separate agencies—CATS and NIPC—to plan for these functions. These agencies never coordinated their work to a high degree, tending rather to treat their respective areas of planning as distinct functions.[2] Their separateness and sometime rivalry finally ended in 2005 with the creation of CMAP. As we note in the sidebar, however, a great deal more work needs to be done to bring these two functions together.

Looking Forward

In the early 1900s, concerns over rapid and seemingly chaotic growth encouraged the city's civic elite to enlist Daniel Burnham to create a regional plan. Today, civic leaders keep that debate going, constantly provoking dialogue on ways to keep the region competitive in the emerging global scene. Some have suggested the region should be defined as a "Crescent Corridor" reaching from South Bend to Milwaukee. Other advocates and planners increasingly consider Chicago to be the hub of a vast region encompassing virtually all of the Midwest, a point emphasized in the research of Richard Longworth. This view has fueled interest in adopting policies that transcend not just municipal but state boundaries.

For regional planning agencies, which for now must focus on the more traditionally defined regional area of a few counties, cultivating greater support for their plans will likely require cooperation among local, state, and federal government. Advocates of regional planning will look for the kind of state intervention that has strengthened regional planning in other metropolitan areas.[4] Planning advocates might push for a Portland-style arrangement, a strong, elected metropolitan authority to control regional growth boundaries.[5] Other possibilities, such as the regional tax base sharing strategy of the Minneapolis–St. Paul area, may also be on the agenda.

For now, these types of arrangements probably remain beyond the possible in Illinois. In addition, they probably will not in themselves be sufficient to overcome the great forces of divergence that we describe above. CMAP and its civic partners will need to balance all-encompassing comprehensive plans with more-targeted efforts. Initiatives to improve the flow of freight, to alleviate traffic congestion, and to assemble community councils for affordable housing will probably gain little publicity but can achieve much good. The patient pursuit of solutions to these problems will likely constitute the heart of the profession of regional planning.

Social and political forces originating outside the region, meanwhile, will push the planning agenda in new directions. The demand for greater accountability and openness in state government, the election of Barack

The Chicago Metropolitan Agency for Planning

The Regional Planning Act of 2005 marked the beginning of what might be described as a fourth era in planning for the metropolitan region. A major landmark, it follows upon the creation of the Chicago Plan Commission in 1909, the organization of the Chicago Regional Planning Association in 1923, and the post-war formation of public planning agencies such as NIPC, CATS, and RTA. The Act established the Regional Planning Board, soon after renamed the Chicago Metropolitan Agency for Planning (CMAP), with responsibility for creating comprehensive regional plans.

In early 2006, the CMAP board appointed Randall Blankenhorn, formerly with the state's transportation department, as the agency's first executive director. Blankenhorn assembled an energetic and youthful staff, giving CMAP more visibility than its predecessor organizations had enjoyed in recent years. In early 2008, he and the board led the agency into an ambitious effort to create a comprehensive plan under the banner "Go To 2040." Using sophisticated scenario-building and modeling processes, the agency began to identify strategies to guide growth and capital investment throughout the region. CMAP hopes to build on publicity generated by the centennial of the 1909 *Plan of Chicago*, restarting a dialogue about "thinking big." The scale of this effort fulfilled and perhaps even exceeded the mandate of the legislative act creating the agency.

The energy behind the creation of CMAP and continued civic concern for its work raises hope that the agency can bring renewed respect and relevance to regional planning. A streamlined board of fifteen, together with a combined staff gives it strengths that NIPC and CATS did not enjoy in their final years. The agency is already demonstrating a strong capacity for regional research and data gathering. For CMAP to achieve its goals, however, it must now couple its role as researcher and information provider with that of planner and promoter of plans. And it must try to accomplish this with no more power to implement its plans than its predecessors had.

With its role being primarily advisory, the agency's challenge is to channel transportation funding according to a clear set of priorities outlined in a comprehensive regional plan. Although this is no small task, optimism remains that the agency can succeed, in part due to renewed national interest in providing federal support to regional agencies. The possibility is even held out that the federal government will disperse infrastructure funds directly to these agencies, rather than having all transportation dollars pass through state governments.

Whether or not this occurs, however, the CMAP board must contend with the fact it is not the officially designated metropolitan planning organization for the region. That role remains with the successor to the CATS Policy Committee, now CMAP's Policy Committee. The two entities presently coordinate transportation planning through a "special memorandum of understanding." In the long term, however, this arrangement may prove inadequate, if the CMAP board is to effectively integrate the region's transportation plan into its broader agenda for regional development.

If its comprehensive plans are to achieve success, CMAP will need to tap into the energy of the civic sector and capture the general public's imagination with innovative planning schemes. The experiences of earlier generations of regional planners remain relevant. After all, the *Plan of Chicago* succeeded in part because of the salesmanship of the architects and citizen-planners who created it. The civic sector's regional vision remained indispensable throughout the succeeding decades.

A "visioning session" held by the Chicago Metropolitan Agency for Planning in the city's Hyde Park neighborhood in May, 2007. CMAP launched an ambitious new regional plan effort shortly after the agency's creation in 2005. *(Chicago Metropolitan Agency for Planning)*

Since the 1960s, however, planners at public agencies have enjoyed far less support from civic actors, a problem that CMAP will need to reverse. The agency's Citizens' Advisory Committee, an entity mandated by the act creating CMAP, should help to deepen its links to communities and civic groups. Yet it is fair to assume that the general public still remains largely unfamiliar with the organization and its regional mission. Gaining the support of the civic community and tapping its energy—something that CMAP's predecessor agencies had difficulty doing—will require years of relationship building and public education. Striving for greater civic sector representation on the board could help to accelerate this process.

Meanwhile, the agency must continue to build durable relationships with municipalities and counties. As part of its work to create regional forecasts and plans, CMAP will need to seek consensus while promoting a free flow of information between itself and local governments. By patiently working with municipal planners, planners at CMAP can encourage communities to adopt strategies that gradually bring local intentions into an overarching regional vision.

Even then, the diverging forces described in this chapter will be difficult to overcome. As Joseph Schofer of Northwestern University has noted, there is hope, nonetheless, that CMAP might rekindle the Chicago region's reputation for innovation, making it, once again, a leader in creating "great plans and the tools to accomplish them."[3]

Obama to the presidency, the fluctuating price of fossil fuels, and an increasingly powerful environmental movement, are several of the factors promising to shape the work of regional planners. The profession will no doubt see exciting times in the years ahead.

Some observers believe that there is much about regional planning that is essentially impossible, that it is a well-intended but often misguided activity that generally does not meet the needs of the people. Noted scholar Robert Bruggeman casts doubt on the benefits of policies to discourage the outward migration of the population, arguing that we should be "wary of making any sweeping generalizations about the so-called problems of sprawl, let alone remedies for them."[6] Much of the disappointment—and futility—felt by planners over the past century lends support to these views.

Yet others are much more sanguine on the possibilities of regional planning institutions to shape the development of metropolitan regions. Scholar and urban planning professor George Hemmens wrote in 1993 that Chicago is a "sleeping giant" on the regional planning scene. His observation remains apt today, as many await its awakening in another great plan for the Chicago region, a vision that long inspires people as Burnham and Bennett's *Plan of Chicago* did a century ago.

The Burnham-Bennett Legacy in Metropolitan Chicago — A Postscript

People living in densely populated areas require a degree of knowledge and control over their surroundings. Whether it's Chicago, Tokyo, Moscow, Johannesburg, or Istanbul, urban residents need to understand and anticipate changes in their community if they are to avoid feeling overwhelmed by the chaos that seems to lurk just at the edge of urban living. Urban dwellers seek to affect the powers of government, to nurture the development of local educational and cultural institutions to meet social needs, and to constantly monitor changes in housing, transport, and health care.

One might call their ability to navigate and manipulate urban environments a form of literacy, a social comprehension that enables individuals to understand and interpret the environment surrounding them. Such literacy also empowers individuals to create and communicate ideas about how to improve this environment. A subset of this comprehension, urban planning literacy, involves organized attempts to foster both directed and spontaneous decisions in order to shape the growth of a metropolitan region. This deliberative kind of planning sets out to achieve goals and cultivate knowledge about the community while giving individuals a chance to participate fully in a debate about how a region is organized.

The 1909 *Plan of Chicago* remains a singular artifact of this kind of literacy—it is a potent testament of a region's commitment to comprehensive improvement even after 100 years. Its longevity stems not so much from the technical skills of Burnham and Bennett in showing how the region could prepare for the future, but rather from their collaborative efforts to create and sustain a "narrative" of urban living that appeals to the greatest number of people throughout a region. Their vision knits a pragmatic tapestry about resolving the aesthetic problems that occur when humans live in close proximity to each other and the organizational problems that occur when they choose to live in such density. The "Burnham Plan" represents one of the earliest twentieth century arguments about how the "life and death" of great cities can be best understood using modern concepts of sociology, economics, political science, and rational management.

Burnham and Bennett's call for heightened public expectations and organized planning in the 1909 *Plan*, together with the efforts of the Chicago Plan Commission to achieve these goals, cultivated a shared literacy that has been passed down through generations. This literacy was imbued by their adept use of recognizable themes—images, history, and vivid comparisons—from the 3,000-year-old record of a civilized urban society. In their plan, Burnham and Bennett consistently refer to the wellspring of familiar cultural markers embedded in late nineteenth and early twentieth century America to paint a portrait of what aesthetically pleasing urban life might look like when managed

John A. Shuler is an Associate Professor and Bibliographer of Urban Planning/Government Information at University of Illinois Chicago Library. Since receiving his MLS from the University of California, Los Angeles in 1983, Prof.Shuler writes, teaches, and lectures extensively on government information policy and urban planning issues.

by the promise of modern technology and management. The plan makes references to ancient Greece and Rome, to the grand architectural vistas of Europe's royal cities, and to the socially enlightened techniques of managing the industrial cities of England. They educate readers about the classical heritage of modern comprehensive planning.

The plan draws inspiration from the City Beautiful Movement that grew out of the technologies and consequences—and horrors—that followed the American Civil War. For nearly fifty years after the defeat of the rural South, sweeping reforms in many of the country's urban centers shaped social and political landscapes at all levels of society—sharpened further by the thinking and organizing of dozens of social movements that led to the end of slavery, struggled to give women the right to vote, promoted new faiths and religious practices, and deepened individual spiritual improvement through new communes and communities. National mobilization to wage the Civil War demonstrated a clear need for large-scale rational planning and recovery—especially with respect to resettlement, health improvement, rebuilding, and economic recovery. Such social movements and actions accelerated efforts to take on corruption and incompetence in urban government by reforming civil service. These movements also promoted land-use planning, as well as efforts to improve public education; further, such movements pushed locally elected officials to become more accountable to voters rather than answering only to political parties.

Other reforms pulled at the linkages between social issues, whether it was between disease, substandard housing, and water and sewage treatment or between well-ordered streets, public right of ways, and mobility. Reformers studied the cultural and physical aspects of play, organized sport, and other forms of adult education and self-improvement. There was a revolution in critical thinking about how people live and work in cities—thinking that tapped into popular religious beliefs about enlightened spiritual life that embraced "good works" through participation in settlement homes, slum clearance, housing reform, and education. On the social and economic side, there was a growing acceptance of the idea that a happy worker is a productive one—and that "labor benefits capital" if the workers are protected from exploitation and have access to healthful open spaces, good education, democratic governance, and a predictable structure of reward for their efforts.

Burnham and Bennett practiced urban planning within this larger national "literacy" of civic reform while recasting the story from one determined by fate, social status, or some other destiny that individuals could not control to a vision of urban life as safe, intellectually engaging, and profitable for all inhabitants. Planning for cities seemed a logical extension of the planning that was already underway at the hundreds of national and regional private corporations growing out of the ashes of the Civil War. This type of planning was only beginning to affect the evolution of urban public corporations and governments at the time. When the *Plan of Chicago* was released in 1909, the city's success was directly linked to the fate of powerful private corporations, including railroads, iron and steel producers, meat packers, financial institutions, and wholesale and retail trade companies. Indeed, Chicago was considered by some to be the first "modern" city, having grown at an extraordinary rate between 1830 and 1909 and, due to the great fire of 1871, having a rare chance to rebuild itself with new technologies and relationships.

Changing Times

The 1909 *Plan*'s narrative, while remaining powerful for the first two decades after its approval, gradually lost its sway over the rapidly growing professional planning community. The *Plan*'s supporters began to seek support outside Chicago's city limits in the late 1920s in order to implement some of its regional aspects—transportation, parks, and coordinated economic development. Even with the direct involvement of the sons of Bennett and Burnham through the 1950s, the Burnham-Bennett narrative began to lose its power—a fact evident as economic and political events roiled the region for the next seventy-five years. Economic depression, global war, and economic recovery mixed with extensive social and political dislocation created by racial segregation—all would work against the rather simplistic idea that enlightened and engaged individuals could overcome these obstacles. But the failure to fully implement the plan's vision came from one critical source—local government laws in Illinois that essentially limited the financial and political viability of institutions pursuing regional goals.

Local governments could pursue only modest urban planning agendas and, like regional institutions, lacked financial authority necessary for ambitious metropolitan-wide planning. This created a series of what we now call private/public partnerships to sustain cooperation among the different governments. Early examples include building the canal systems between Lake Michigan and the Mississippi River, which were federal, state, and regional efforts. Nevertheless, these efforts only resolved narrowly defined economic or environmental challenges. Local government in Illinois achieved "home rule" after the 1970 constitutional convention. But the fiscal and political fragmentation of local governance continued—and continues—to frustrate efforts to bring the same comprehensive approach to the regions planning.

Today, there are more than 6,900 Illinois local governments, about a third of them in the six counties surrounding Chicago. This remains one of the principal reasons the 1909 *Plan*'s narrative remains so powerful, yet so far from fulfillment. The hundreds of local governments in the region can only influence and/or plan for their own distinct institutional destinies, leaving many of the 1909 *Plan*'s ideals of comprehensive planning to private initiatives and special state-mandated districts with specialized regional goals (such as efficient public transportation and water reclamation) as well as to technical applications of federal law (such as in certain areas of environmental protection).

A Wellspring of Urban Literacy

As various organizations and individuals throughout metropolitan Chicago attempt to resolve difficult regional problems, they must struggle to "work around" these institutional failures. Nevertheless, it is fascinating to note that planners still tap into the same wellspring of urban "literacy" imbued by Burnham and Bennett's plan. We see this in gradual improvements to the lakefront, the recent effort to prepare a bid for the 2016 Summer Olympics, and gradual expansions to the region's system of forest preserves and parklands. The urban literacy of 2009 draws upon the same syntax of hope and aesthetics that Burnham and Bennett did to "tell the story" of urban living that is both satisfying and productive.

Nevertheless, the methods used to build support for planning must constantly change to remain relevant. Residents are more involved in the economic, technologic, political, and social fate of their neighborhoods. Many individuals vigorously resist efforts to have critical decisions about their neighborhoods determined by remote or elite organizations. Burnham and Bennett would applaud the cooperation evident in many of these planning efforts, but they would deplore the lost opportunities to cultivate large-scale planning for the region. This perhaps speaks to the Plan's enduring draw on Chicago's popular imagination—it remains the single eloquent testament on a future metropolitan community that reflects what might be the best of our urban nature.

APPENDICES

Resources for Historians

This resources section draws attention to notable works that explore the rich tapestry of Chicago regional planning. We mention only a small portion of the available literature while making a special effort to include the writings of practicing planners. The resources appear under five general headings below. Full citations for all scholarly works mentioned here can be found in the references section.

A. Regional Plans of the Early Twentieth Century

As we note throughout this volume, Chicago regional planning remains deeply rooted in the legacy of Daniel H. Burnham and Edward H. Bennett's 1909 *Plan of Chicago*. As the first comprehensive attempt to create a regional vision for Chicago, the 1909 *Plan* has inspired a great deal of interpretive literature.

Historical volumes by Charles Moore (1921), Carl Condit (1964), and Thomas Hines (1974) have long been standard references on Burnham and the *Plan of Chicago*. Scholarly works by Kristen Schaffer (2003) of the University of North Carolina, and Carl Smith (2007) of Northwestern University, stand out as valuable recent contributions. Hugh Bartling (2006) of DePaul University published research on the team of planners (including Daniel Burnham, Jr.,) that prepared the Plan of Evanston, and on Edward Bennett's Plan of Winnetka.

Useful perspectives on Burnham and Bennett are by no means limited to academic researchers. The Ely Chapter of Lambda Alpha International, an honorary society devoted to real estate economics, published *The Plan of Chicago @ 100: 15 Views of Burnham's Legacy for the New Century* (2009). The volume consists of contributions by the club's members, who offer many insights into the contemporary relevance of the 1909 *Plan*. *The Encyclopedia of Chicago* (2004), edited by James R. Grossman, Ann Durkin Keating, and Janice L. Reiff, offers rich perspective on the region's planning heritage. Cinematographer Judith Paine McBrien of The Archimedia Workshop has also done extensive research on the Daniel Burnham legacy for a documentary film.

The most extensive collection of archival materials on the work of Daniel Burnham and Edward Bennett is housed in the Ryerson and Burnham Archives at the Art Institute of Chicago. Another important repository is the Newberry Library in Chicago, while Lake Forest College in Lake Forest, Illinois, holds an extensive collection of materials on the life of Edward H. Bennett. Lake Forest College has prepared virtual, three-dimensional models of selected structures from the *Plan of Chicago* through its Virtual Burnham Initiative (vbi.lakeforest.edu).

The records of the Chicago Plan Commission are located in the Municipal Reference section of the Harold Washington Library in Chicago. These are unfortunately incomplete. Several of the Commission's annual reports, for example, are unavailable. However, a relatively comprehensive synopsis of the commission's first half-century of work is available in Helen Whitehead's *History of the Chicago Plan Commission*. This volume was published by the Chicago Plan Commission in 1960.

The papers of the Chicago Regional Planning Association are part of the NIPC Archives at the Chicago History Museum. The business journals of Daniel Burnham, Jr., as well as other Burnham family documents, are held in the archives at the Art Institute of Chicago.

PLAN
OF
EVANSTON

PRINTED BY
BOWMAN PUBLISHING COMPANY
EVANSTON, ILLINOIS

ILLUSTRATIONS BY THE
AMERICAN COLORTYPE COMPANY

B. Northeastern Illinois Planning Commission

The Northeastern Illinois Planning Commission (NIPC) stood at the center of regional planning activity for fifty years from 1957 to 2007. Until recently, however, there has been relatively little interpretive literature devoted to its work. Archival material on the organization is held in the NIPC Archives collection at the Chicago History Museum as well as the library of the University of Illinois at Chicago. These collections include documents concerning the organization's creation, drafts of NIPC plans, and official correspondence.

A remarkable record of the agency's work is contained in *Fifty Years of Regional Planning: 1957–2007 by the Northeastern Illinois Planning Commission.* This volume by NIPC veterans promises to become a standard reference on Chicago regional planning history. It offers comprehensive discussions of the entire array of the agency's work over five decades, in chapters authored by former senior staff members. The book provides researchers with unique perspectives into the life and thinking of a major metropolitan planning organization. Many of the original documents used by the contributors may be found in the NIPC archives mentioned above.

Fifty Years of Regional Planning
By the Northeastern Illinois
Planning Commission

1957-2007

Completed in 2008, the volume takes a frank look at the organization's many political and technical challenges. It points out the agency's many innovations as well, including its sustained efforts to integrate authentic public participation into the regional planning agenda. The various chapters also discuss the evolution of the agency's forecasting activity and its continual efforts to integrate regional transportation schemes into its plans. What emerges is the story of an organization navigating a difficult political climate, one that often did not appreciate NIPC's genuine regional approach to problem solving.

The volume consists of nine chapters: NIPC Antecedents (by Robert Ducharme); History, Organization (Jim Ford); Local Planning Assistance (John Paige); Research, Data Services, and Forecasting (Max Dieber, Suhail al Chalabi, Charles Metalitz, and Mary Cele Smith); Public Participation Program (Lorenz Aggens); Comprehensive Land Use Planning (Lawrence Christmas); Water Resources Planning (Ducharme); Open Space Planning (Richard Mariner); and Housing Planning Program (Ducharme).

Robert Ducharme, editor of the volume, served as NIPC's deputy director from 1967 to 1979. He opens the volume with a chronology of significant regional planning and infrastructure accomplishments that preceded NIPC, including the major works of the Chicago Regional Planning Association. The Appendices include lists of the organization's commissioners and staff (by Alexandra Radtke), a summary of the agency's funding sources and budget fluctuations over the years, and a list of agency's plans and publications.

C. Superhighways and the Chicago Areas Transportation Study

The Chicago Area Transportation Study (CATS) has been a focus of research by scholars and planning practitioners for several decades. The organization's analytical methods and technical innovations, particularly those conveyed in its 1962 plan, are considered important in the history of transportation planning for U.S. metropolitan areas.

The achievements of CATS during its formative years are chronicled in Andrew Plummer's *The Chicago Area Transportation Study: Creating the First Plan (1955–1962)*. Plummer, who began work at CATS in 1967 and served as the organization's associate executive director from 1991 to 1999, recounts the path-breaking efforts to compile data on regional travel patterns, as well as the political circumstances affecting the agency in the lead up to its 1962 plan. This document is available on the web site of the Chicago Metropolitan Agency for Planning.

Plummer also maintains an Internet site, cookcountyexpressways.com, which explores the history of Cook County expressways, giving particular attention to the political issues surrounding their construction. His findings are based on his own archival research as well as his recollections of the career of his father, Andrew V. Plummer, Sr., who worked for the Cook County Highway Department for most of his professional life and served as its superintendent from 1961 until his death in 1967.

The technical innovation behind the CATS plan has also generated a great deal of scholarly literature, including works by John McDonald (1988), Andrew Boyce (1980, 2007), and Alan Black (1990). Roger Creighton (1970), who served as the agency's assistant director, also authored a notable reference work on transportation planning. Dennis McClendon (2004) has written extensively on the history of the region's highways in the *Encyclopedia of Chicago* and other publications.

There is no centralized archive for the Chicago Area Transportation Study. The papers of the agency's first director, Douglas Carroll, are held at the Cornell University Library in New York. Many original documents related to expressway planning and construction, including those produced in the late 1930s and 1940s and described in this volume, are located in the Municipal Reference section of the Harold Washington Library in Chicago.

METROPOLITAN GOVERNMENT
AND THE REAL WORLD:
THE CASE OF CHICAGO

by Gilbert Y. Steiner

CENTER FOR RESEARCH IN URBAN GOVERNMENT
LOYOLA UNIVERSITY, CHICAGO
JANUARY, 196

D. Race and Ethnicity

Race and ethnicity have long been part of the debate over metropolitan planning and governance in the Chicago region. While an extensive literature exists on racial issues specific to the inner city (see Grimshaw, 1992), a few writings discuss their *regional* dimensions.

Some of the most notable early analysis of race and ethnicity came from the University of Chicago's School of Sociology in the 1910s and 1920s. Louis Wirth (1938) of the so-called Chicago School broke new ground with his evaluations of racial patterns throughout the region. For a summary of this research, see Abbot (1999) and Bulmer (1984). Generally, however, racial analysis received only passing reference in regional plans and planning studies prior to the 1950s.

Concern with the racial implications of regional planning grew sharply after race riots in Cicero in 1951. When funds began flowing into urban renewal and superhighway construction later that decade, the social strife generated by the dislocation of urban population and black migration to suburbs grew in intensity. Discussion of the racial implications of metropolitan planning and regional governance were forcefully articulated in Gilbert Steiner's 1966 book, *Metropolitan Government and the Real World: The Case of Chicago*. Steiner, a professor at Loyola University, argued that regional government would set back the political aspirations of urban blacks by diluting their political power base.

The Northeastern Illinois Planning Commission (NIPC) tried to assimilate much of the ongoing debate about race in the metropolitan region as it prepared its first comprehensive regional plan. In a 1966 report, NIPC reviewed the opinions of several noted planners with respect to its three regional scenarios. The report stated that, "the multi-town plan will have the tendency to segregate as much as possible, especially where it counts most," but also that "… the Finger Plan might offer the best hope" with respect to extending the black population into the suburbs. Clearly, the Commission was concerned with its plan's potential impact on regional population distribution by race.

Other notable planning-related publications of the era included the Kerner Commission Report of 1968, which described the need to open up the suburbs to black residents. As the regional housing question entered federal court in the *Gautreaux v. Chicago Housing Authority* case, it generated a great deal of literature (see Polikoff, 2006). The *Gautreaux* ruling required the Chicago Housing Authority to offer housing vouchers to public housing residents, in a relocation program that was eventually managed by the nonprofit Leadership Council for Metropolitan Open Communities.

In more recent decades, the confluence of race and regional concerns has generated a wide body of research, with resulting literature coming under such headings as environmental justice, metropolitan "open housing," and exclusionary zoning. NIPC and CATS brought these concerns directly into their planning processes, as their plans and reports of the past forty years amply show. Nevertheless, activists such as Jacky Grimshaw, with the Center for Neighborhood Technology, often criticized the agencies, and the regional planning system in general, for their inability to compel suburban communities to address these issues.

E. Civic-Sponsored Planning Initiatives

Civic organizations have been agents of change on the regional scene since before the publication of the *Plan of Chicago* a century ago. Beginning with just a few elite groups, such as the Commercial Club of Chicago, the number of organizations directly or indirectly concerned with metropolitan affairs has expanded considerably. Many of these have produced pertinent literature and even their own regional plans.

The past two decades have seen a particularly large number of attempts by non-governmental organizations to create plans with detailed, highly articulated spatial schemes. Their maps and related analyses have been coupled with full-blown public participation strategies. This book has discussed at length the work of the Metropolis 2020 organization during the 1990s and early 2000s (Chapter 12). Metropolis 2020's key regional plan is called *The Metropolis Plan: Choices for the Chicago Region* (2003). The group has expanded upon this with important functional plans including a freight plan (2004) and *Homes for a Changing Region* (2005, updated 2009).

Another important contributor has been the Center for Neighborhood Technology (CNT), a Chicago-based nonprofit group founded in 1978, which has acquired sophisticated mapping and data production capabilities. CNT has advocated especially for expanded public transit access that maximizes employment accessibility for lower income workers in the city and suburbs. CNT created the Chicagoland Transportation and Air Quality Commission, which issued its Citizen Transportation Plan in 1995, based upon input from citizen task forces. The group followed this in 2002 with *Changing Direction: Transportation Choices for 2030*, a regional plan that offered an alternative to the Regional Transportation Plan produced by CATS.

Another landmark document comes from the Chicago Wilderness consortium, founded in 1996 by thirty-four public and private organizations. The consortium's membership now includes 230 organizations and entities including many local governments. The *Biodiversity Recovery Plan* (1999), adopted by NIPC, laid a policy foundation for subsequent mapping efforts to identify high-value resource areas. These efforts resulted in the *Green Infrastructure Vision: Bringing Nature to People*, a plan that has been continually refined over the years, identifying millions of acres for protection across an expansive metropolitan region. The consortium's *Atlas of Biodiversity* serves as a companion to the recovery plan.

Openlands, formerly known as Openlands Project, has produced numerous regional plans and maps over the years, often working in conjunction with other nonprofit and public agencies. It joined with NIPC to produce the *Northeastern Illinois Regional Greenways and Trails Implementation Program* (1997). Openlands also worked with NIPC on the *Northeastern Illinois Regional Water Trails Map and Plan* (2002) and joined with CNT to produce *Natural Connections: Green Infrastructure in Wisconsin, Illinois, and Indiana* (2004), which includes an inventory of natural lands. In the 1990s, Openlands applied computer-based spatial analysis to predict a loss of farmland and natural lands through suburban expansion. Earlier, it played a key role in establishing the Canal Corridor Association to manage the Illinois & Michigan Canal National Heritage Corridor. This latter conservation initiative, launched in the 1970s, was spearheaded by Gerald Adelman, who later became Openlands' executive director.

Appendix F: Chicago History Museum Illustrations and Credits

We extend our gratitude to the staff of the Chicago History Museum for their assistance in providing maps, photographs and illustrations for this volume. We provide below negative numbers and other pertinent information that could not be included in the photo captions.

Page 15: ICHi-39070

Page 18: Artist: Navigato; ICHi-24225

Page 19: ICHi-25717

Page 20: ICHi-31929

Page 36: HB-01564

Page 39: ICHi-59904

Page 40: Printer: unknown; ICHi-17446

Page 58: Photographer: Hedrich-Blessing; HB-10976

Page 62: ICHi-25709

Page 63: Photographer: unknown; ICHi-24726

Page 70: Photographer: J. McCarthy; ICHi-59893

Page 72: Photographer: Robert Metz; ICHi-59898

Page 73: ICHi-59894

Page 74: Photographer: Alison Lighthall; ICHi-59892

Page 78: ICHi-23437

Page 80: ICHi-32484

Page 82: ICHi-59897

Page 92: Photographer unknown; ICHi-59895

Page 98: ICHi-59899

Page 100: ICHi-59896

Page 122: Photographer Hedrich-Blessing; HB-32695-C

Page 184: Photographer: Bill Engdahl; HB-25500-B2

Page 185: Photograph: Hedrich-Blessing; HB-25500-P

REFERENCES

Abbott, Andrew. 1999. *Department and Discipline: Chicago Sociology at One Hundred.* Chicago: University of Chicago Press.

Abbott, Carl. 2007. *Urban American in the Modern Age: 1920 to the Present.* Wheeling, IL: Harlan Davidson.

Allen, John G. 1996. *From Centralization to Decentralization: The Politics of Transit in Chicagoland.* Ph.D. thesis, MIT Department of Urban Studies and Planning, 1996.

Bartling, Hugh. 2008, Burnham's Suburban Legacy: The 1917 Plan of Evanston, Illinois, Presented at the International Planning History Society, 13th Biennial Conference, Chicago.

Black, Alan. 1990. The Chicago Area Transportation Study: A Case Study of Rational Planning. *Journal of Planning Education and Research* 10 (Fall): 27–37.

Black, Russell Van Nest. 1967. *Planning and the Planning Profession: The Past Fifty Years, 1917–1967.* Washington, DC: American Institute of Planners.

Bosselman, Fred P. 1992. The Commodification of "Nature's Metropolis": The Historical Context of Illinois' Unique Zoning Standards. *Northern Illinois University Law Review* 12 (Summer): 527–84.

Boyce, David E., Norman D. Day, and Chris McDonald. 1970. *Metropolitan Plan Making: An Analysis of Experience with the Preparation and Evaluation of Alternative Land Use and Transportation Plans.* Philadelphia: Regional Science Research Institute.

Boyce, David. 2007. "An Account of a Road Network Design Method: Expressway Spacing, System Configuration and Economic Evaluation." In *Infrastrukturprobleme bei Bevölkerungsrückgang* (Infrastructure Problems under Population Decline), X. Feng and A. M. Popescu, eds. Schriften zur öffentlichen Verwaltung und öffentlichen Wirtschaft, Bd. 202, Berliner Wissenschafts-Verlag, Berlin, 131–159.

Boyce, David. 1980. A Silver Jubilee for Urban Transportation Planning, *Environment and Planning* 12: 267–8.

Boyer, M. Christine. 1983. *Dreaming the Rational City: The Myth of American City Planning.* Cambridge, MA: MIT Press.

Bulmer, Martin. 1984. *The Chicago School of Sociology: Institutionalization, Diversity, and the Rise of Sociological Research.* Chicago: University of Chicago Press.

Bruegmann, Robert. 2005. *Sprawl: A Compact History.* Chicago: University of Chicago Press.

Burnham, Daniel H., and Edward H. Bennett. 1993. *Plan of Chicago.* Edited by Charles Moore, with an introduction by Kristen Schaffer. New York: Princeton Architectural Press. First published 1909 by the Commercial Club of Chicago.

Center for Neighborhood Technology. 2002. *Changing Direction: Transportation Choices for 2030.*

Chaddick, Harry F. 1990. *Chaddick! Success Against All Odds.* Chicago: Harry F. Chaddick Associates.

Chicago Home Rule Commission. 1954. *Chicago's Government: Its Structural Modernization and Home Rule Problems.* Chicago: University of Chicago Press.

Chicago Metropolis 2020. 2003. *Metropolis Plan: Choices for the Chicago Region.*

Chicago Metropolitan Agency for Planning. 2008. *Fifty Years of Regional Planning by the Northeastern Illinois Planning Commission.*

Chicago Plan Commission. 1943. *Master Plan of Residential Land Use of Chicago.* Municipal Reference Collection, Harold Washington Library Center, Chicago Public Library.

Chicago Real Estate Board. 1923. *Final Report of the Library, City Planning and Zoning Committee of the Chicago Real Estate Board on Zoning in Chicago.* Municipal Reference Collection, Harold Washington Library Center, Chicago Public Library.

Condit, Carl W. 1964. *The Chicago School of Architecture: A History of Commercial and Public Building in the Chicago Area, 1875–1925.* Chicago: University of Chicago Press.

Cohen, Adam, and Elizabeth Taylor. 2000. *American Pharaoh: Mayor Richard J. Daley: His Battle for Chicago and the Nation.* Boston: Little, Brown and Company.

Creighton, Roger L. 1970. *Urban Transportation Planning.* Urbana, IL: University of Illinois Press.

Cronon, William. 1991. *Nature's Metropolis: Chicago and the Great West.* New York: W.W. Norton.

DiJohn, Joseph. 2009 The Burnham Transportation Plan of Chicago: 100 Years Later. Paper presented at the Transportation Research Forum Annual Meeting.

Draper, John E. 1982. *Edward H. Bennett, Architect and City Planner, 1874–1954.* Chicago: Art Institute of Chicago.

Ebner, Michael H. 1989. *Chicago's North Shore: A Suburban History.* Chicago: University of Chicago Press.

Hoch, Charles. 1994 *What Planners Do: Power, Politics, and Persuasion* Chicago: Planners Press, American Planning Association.

Grossman, James R., Ann Durkin Keating, and Janice L. Reiff, editors. 2004. *Encyclopedia of Chicago.* Chicago: University of Chicago Press.

Grimshaw, William J. 1992. *Bitter Fruit: Black Politics and the Chicago Machine: 1931–1991.* Chicago: University of Chicago Press.

Hall, Peter. 2002. *Cities of Tomorrow: An Intellectual History of Urban Planning and Design in the Twentieth Century,* 3rd ed. Malden, MA: Blackwell Publishing.

Hines, Thomas S. 1979. *Burnham of Chicago: Architect and Planner.* Chicago: University of Chicago Press.

Johnson, D.A 1995. *Planning the Great Metropolis: The 1929 Regional Plan of New York and Its Environs.* New York: Routledge.

Johnson, Elmer. 2001. *Metropolis 2020: The Chicago Plan for the Twenty-First Century.* Chicago: University of Chicago Press.

Johnson, Elmer W. 1993. *Avoiding the Collision of Cities and Cars.* Cambridge, MA: American Academy of Arts and Sciences.

Johnson, Vilas. 1977. *A History of the Commercial Club of Chicago.* Chicago: The Commercial Club of Chicago.

Kamin, Blair. 2001. *Why Architecture Matters: Lessons from Chicago.* Chicago: University of Chicago Press.

Karlen, Harvey M. 1958. *The Governments of Chicago.* Chicago: Courier Publishing.

Keating, Ann Durkin. 2002. *Building Chicago: Suburban Developers and the Creation of a Divided Metropolis.* Urbana, IL: University of Illinois Press.

Keating, Ann Durkin. 2005. *Chicagoland: City and Suburbs in the Railroad Age.* Chicago: University of Chicago Press.

Koval, John P., Larry Bennett, Michael I. J. Bennett, Fassil Demissie, Roberta Garner, and Kiljoong Kim, editors. 2006. *The New Chicago: A Social and Cultural Analysis.* Philadelphia: Temple University Press.

Krueckeberg, Donald A., ed. 1983. *Introduction to Planning History in the United States.* New Brunswick, NJ: Center for Urban Policy Research, Rutgers University.

Levy, John M. 2005. *Contemporary Urban Planning,* Upper Saddle River, NJ: Prentice Hall.

Lewis, Arnold. 1997. *An Early Encounter with Tomorrow: Europeans, Chicago's Loop, and the World's Columbian Exposition.* Urbana: University of Illinois Press.

Luccarelli, Mark. 1997. *Lewis Mumford and the Ecological Region: The Politics of Planning.* New York: Guilford Press.

Mammoser, Alan. 2006 "The Hitch in the Plan: A New Chicago Metropolitan Planning Agency is Advisory Only, Making It No More Powerful than Its Predecessors." *Illinois Issues* (November): 25–26.

Mammoser, Alan. 2002 "Stretching the Boundaries: With a Region that Takes in Part of Three State, the Chicago Area is Ready for Some Serious Planning." *Planning* (January): 22–24.

Mayer, Harold M., and Richard C. Wade. 1969. *Chicago: Growth of a Metropolis.* Chicago: University of Chicago Press.

McCarthy, Kathleen D. 1982. *Noblesse Oblige: Charity and Philanthropy in Chicago: 1849–1929.* Chicago: University of Chicago Press.

Miller, Donald L. 1996. *City of the Century: The Epic of Chicago and the Making of America.* New York: Simon & Schuster.

Mills, Edwin S. 2002. *Dreams, Plans, and Reality: A Critique of Chicago Metropolis 2020,* No. 92. Chicago: Heartland Institute.

Monroe, Harriet. 1962. *John Wellborn Root: A Study of His Life and Work.* Park Forest, IL: Prairie School Press.

Moody, Walter Dwight. 1911. *Wacker's Manual of the Plan of Chicago: Municipal Economy.* Chicago: Sherman and Co.

Moore, Charles. 1921. *Daniel H. Burnham: Architect and Planner of Cities.* New York: Houghton Mifflin.

Northeastern Illinois Planning Commission. 1958–1995. *Annual Report.* (various issues)

Northeastern Illinois Planning Commission. 1966. "The Alternative Plans for the Metropolitan Region for the Next Twenty Five Years and How They are Viewed by the City Planners," Document in Northeastern Illinois Planning Commission Archives at the Chicago History Museum.

Northeastern Illinois Planning Commission.1968. Comprehensive General Plan

Open Lands Project. 2004. *Natural Connections: Green Infrastructure in Wisconsin, Illinois, and Indiana.*

Orfield, Myron. 1997. *Metropolitics: A Regional Agenda for Community and Stability.* Washington, DC: Brookings Institution; Cambridge, MA: Lincoln Institute of Land Policy.

Park, Robert E., Ernest Burgess, and Roderic McKenzie. 1925. *The City.* Chicago: University of Chicago Press.

Peterson, Jon A. 2003. *The Birth of City Planning in the United States: 1840–1917.* Baltimore: The John Hopkins University Press.

Polikoff, Alexander. 2006. *Waiting for Gautreaux: A Story of Segregation, Housing, and the Black Ghetto.* Evanston, IL: Northwestern University Press.

Rast, Joel. 1999. *Remaking Chicago: The Political Origins of Urban Industrial Change.* DeKalb: Northern Illinois University Press.

Rusk, David. 1993. *Cities Without Suburbs.* Washington, DC: Woodrow Wilson Center Press.

Sassen, Saskia. 1991. *The Global City: New York, London, Tokyo.* Princeton, NJ: Princeton University Press.

Schaffer, Kristen. 2003. *Daniel H. Burnham: Visionary Architect and Planner.* New York: Rizzoli.

Schlereth, Thomas J. 1981. "Burnham's Plan and Moody's Manual: City Planning as Progressive Reform." *Journal of the American Planning Association* 47:1, 70–82.

Schrenk, Lisa D. 2007. *Building a Century of Progress: The Architecture of Chicago's 1933–34 World's Fair.* Minneapolis: University of Minnesota Press.

Schwieterman, Joseph P., and Martin E. Toth. 2001. *Shaping Contemporary Suburbia: Perspectives on Development Control in Metropolitan Chicago.* Chicago: Law Bulletin Publishing.

Schwieterman, Joseph P., and Dana M. Caspall. 2006. *The Politics of Place: A History of Zoning in Chicago.* Chicago: Lake Claremont Press.

Smith, Carl. 2007. *The Plan of Chicago: Daniel Burnham and the Remaking of the American City.* Chicago: University of Chicago Press.

Solof, Mark. 1998. *History of Metropolitan Planning Organizations.* Newark: New Jersey Transportation Planning Authority.

Stone, Deborah C. 1995. Creating a Regional Community: The Case for Regional Cooperation. A report of the Metropolitan Planning Council's Regional Cooperation Initiative, Chicago, Illinois.

Thomas, June Manning, and Marsha Ritzdorf, eds. 997. *Urban Planning and the African-American Community: In the Shadows* Thousand Oaks, CA: Sage.

Village of Euclid v. Ambler Realty Corp., 272 U.S. 365 (1926).

2009. *Virtual Burnham Initiative.* Lake Forest College. vbi.lakeforest.edu. June 15, 2009.

Wille, Lois. 1997. *At Home in the Loop: How Clout and Community Built Chicago's Dearborn Park.* Carbondale: Southern Illinois University Press.

Wilson, William H. 1989. *The City Beautiful Movement.* Baltimore, MD: The John Hopkins University Press.

Wirth, Louis. 1937. Urbanism as a Way of Life: The City and Contemporary Civilization. *American Journal of Sociology* 44: 1-24.

Wrigley, Robert L. 1960. The Plan of Chicago: Its Fiftieth Anniversary. *Journal of the American Planning Association* 26: 1, 31–38.

Wrigley, Robert L., Jr., 1983. *Introduction to Planning History in the United States.* Edited by Donald A. Kruekeberg. New Brunswick, NJ: Center for Urban Policy Research, Rutgers University.

Young, David M. 2003. *Chicago Aviation: An Illustrated History.* DeKalb: Northern Illinois University Press.

Zukowsky, John. 1979. *The Plan of Chicago: 1909–1979.* Chicago: Art Institute of Chicago.

Zukowsky, John, ed. 1987. *Chicago Architecture. Birth of a Metropolis: 1872–1922; Reconfiguration of an American Metropolis: 1923–1993* (2 vols).

NOTES

INTRODUCTION

1   Thomas Hines, "Cities need U.S. Air' Daley: Planners Mark 50th Anniversary," *Chicago Daily Tribune*, December 19, 1959, p. 8.

2   Northeastern Illinois Planning Commission, *Annual Report,* 1970 2.

3   Mayo Fesler, statement to committee, City Club of Chicago, April 25, 1923, NIPC papers, Chicago Historical Society.

CHAPTER 1

1   Charles Moore, *Daniel H. Burnham, Architect, Planner of Cities,* (Boston: Houghton Mifflin, 1921), 147.

2   Thomas S. Hines, *Burnham of Chicago: Architect and Planner* (Chicago: University of Chicago Press, 1979), 265.

3   Perkin's commission produced a highly influential proposal for an "outer belt" of forest preserves in 1904 entitled "The Outer Belt of Forest Preserves and Parkways for Chicago and Cook County."

4   Charles H. Thorne, *The Merchants Club of Chicago* (Chicago: Commercial Club of Chicago, 1922), 7.

5   Joan E. Draper, *Edward H. Bennett: Architect and City Planner* 1874–1954. (Chicago: The Art Institute of Chicago, 1982), 11. Draper found this quote in a letter from Burnham to James Phelan, dated November 20, 1905, and in a letter from Burnham to William Greer Harrison, dated September 15, 1905.

6   Thomas S. Hines, *Burnham of Chicago* (Chicago: University of Chicago Press, 1979), 180.

7   Kristen Schaffer, "Fabric of City Life: The Social Agenda in Burnham's Draft of the Plan of Chicago," introduction to Daniel H. Burnham and Edward H. Bennett, *Plan of Chicago*, ed. Charles Moore, (Princeton, N.J.: Princeton University Press, 1993), v–xiv.

8   Hines, *Burnham of Chicago*, 180.

9   Ibid, 325.

10 Ibid, 314.

11 "Daniel Burnham, Architect, Dead; Designer of 'Chicago Plan' Succumbs at Heidelberg While on Tour; Planned Big Buildings; New Field Museum One of Pet Schemes; Beautifying Work Elsewhere Unfinished." *Chicago Daily Tribune*, June 2, 1912, 2.

12 DePaul University professor Hugh Bartling has explored the Plan of Evanston in detail. A summary is available at urbanresearchlab.com/evanston.aspx. Lauren Fischer of DePaul University is a co-author of this section of Chapter 1.

13 William P. Hayes, "Development of the Forest Preserve District of Cook County" (master's thesis, DePaul University, 1949).

14 Robert F. Wrigley, *Introduction of Planning History in the United States*, ed. Donald A. Kruekeberg (New Brunswick, N.J., Center for Urban Policy Research, Rutgers University, 1983), 59.

15 See discussion in Carl Smith, *Plan of Chicago: Daniel Burnham and the Remaking of the American City* (Chicago: University of Chicago Press, 2006), 125–128, 155–159.

16 Schaffer, "Fabric of City Life," v–xiv.

17 Smith, *Plan of Chicago*, 125–128, 155–159.

CHAPTER 2

1   D.H. Burnham, "Two Major Policies of the Chicago Regional Planning Association," undated document, circa 1926, in Chicago Regional Planning Association archives, Chicago History Museum.

2   For a discussion of this, see Helen Whitehead, *History of the Chicago Plan Commission* (Chicago: Chicago Plan Commission, 1960), 1–34, available in the Chicago Municipal Reference Library.

3   John M. Levy, *Contemporary Urban Planning* (Upper Saddle River, NJ: Prentice Hall, 2005), 44–45; and Russell Van Nest, *Planning and the Planning Profession: The Past Fifty Years, 1917–1967*, (Chicago: American Institute of Planners) 1967, 6–7.

4   For a discussion of the role of Delano and Norton in New York, see D.A. Johnson, *Planning the Great Metropolis: The 1929 Regional Plan of New York and Its Environs* (London: E&FN, 1995), 48–69.

5   Van Nest, *Planning and the Planning Profession*, 7.

6   Ibid.

7   *City Club Bulletin*, February 19, 1923, 29, Municipal Reference Collection, Harold Washington Library Center, Chicago Public Library.

8   Ibid.

9   Mayo Fesler statement to committee City Club of Chicago, April 25, 1923. NIPC papers, Chicago Historical Society.

10 "50 Mile Radius Chicago's Need in Growth Plan; Committee of 21 Files Regional Suggestions," *Chicago Daily Tribune*. July 15, 1923, 5.

11 Chicago Regional Plan Association, *Highways in the Region of Chicago: A Preliminary Study of the Highway Transportation System of the Chicago Region*, November 5, 1924, 4.

12 Ibid.

13 Comments about the Burnham Building are pervasive in Burnham, Jr.'s business journals during 1924 and 1925. Art Institute of Chicago Archives.

14 D.H. Burnham, "Two Major Policies of the Chicago Regional Planning Association," meeting minutes of the Chicago Regional Planning Association, April 27, 1932, NIPC papers, Chicago History Museum.

15 Daniel Burnham, Jr., business journal, July 15, 1923, Art Institute of Chicago Archives; and "50 Mile Radius Chicago's Need in Growth Plan; Committee of 21 Files Regional Suggestions," *Chicago Daily Tribune*. July 15, 1923, 5.

16 Daniel Burnham, Jr., business journal, August 5, 1925, Art Institute of Chicago Archives.

17 Meeting minutes of the Chicago Regional Planning Association, NIPC Papers, Chicago History Museum. Board meetings became more frequent and their agendas more complex. Charles Ball, who was still serving on Hoover's zoning commission, brought expertise about planning efforts underway in other metropolitan areas, while George A. Quinlan, Cook County superintendent of highways, lent his works on public-works initiatives.

18 Meeting minutes of the Chicago Regional Planning Association, NIPC Papers, Chicago History Museum. Burnham warned in 1925 that "ten thousand dollars more are desperately needed during 1925 to keep the movement alive, he worried greatly about its fiscal health."

19 D. H. Burnham, "Regional Plan Starts Cutting Traffic Knots." *Chicago Daily Tribune*. January 30, 1927, C1.

20 Daniel Burnham, Jr., business journal, September 25, 1925, Art Institute of Chicago Archives.

21 "Regional Highway Plan Boosted by Motor Industry," *Chicago Daily Tribune*, April 12, 1925, C9.

22 Vast Nast, *Planning and the Planning Profession*, 7.

23 Ibid.

24 Al Chase, "Chicagoland Suburbs Fight to Keep Apartments in Their Place: Burnham Tells of Steady Zoning Battle," *Chicago Daily Tribune*, August 7, 1932, 15. Burnham, Jr., had a particular disdain for the "spotty zoning of apartments in single family suburbs," which was seen as a particulary severe problem as landowners divided up homes into smaller units.

25 Ibid.

26 Daniel Burnham, Jr., business journal, July 17, 1933, Art Institute of Chicago Archives.

27 "Regional Planning Progress in the Region of Chicago", October 1927, Chicago Regional Planning Association, NIPC papers, Chicago History Museum.

28 Daniel Burnham, Jr., business journal, July 24, 1933, Art Institute of Chicago Archives.

29 There were 176 incorporated communities in this area and more than 30 others in Indiana. For a summary of the number of incorporated communities in the Illinois portion of the metropolitan area, see James Licklider and Bradley Roback, *A Compendium of Municipal Population and Land Area Information: The Chicago Metropolitan Area, 1950–2000* (Chicago: Chaddick Institute, 2001), 9.

30 "Sprague Tells First Aims of City Planners," *Chicago Daily Tribune*, February, 13, 1935.

31 Daniel Burnham, Jr., business journal, July 29, 1935, Art Institute of Chicago Archives.

32 Daniel Burnham, Jr., business journal, May 1, 1935, Art Institute of Chicago Archives.

33 Daniel Burnham, Jr., business journal, May 30, 1935, Art Institute of Chicago Archives.

CHAPTER 3

1   Such was the view of architect Raymond Hood, who was asked to submit a plan. "Architects Debate on Chicago's Fair," *New York Times*, February 27, 1931, 13.

2   Daniel Burnham, Jr., business journal, December 9, 1959, Art Institute of Chicago Archives.

3   Such concerns are expressed in Burnham, Jr.'s business journals throughout 1935.

4   Daniel Burnham, Jr., business journal, June 21, 1934, Art Institute of Chicago Archives.

5   "Foreign Villages to Dominate 1934 Fair," *Modern Mechanix*, April 1934. blog.modernmechanix.com/2008/03/01/foreign-villages-to-dominate-1934-worlds-fair. (accessed September 22, 2008).

6   "Topics of the Times - Well Done, Chicago," *New York Times*, November 2, 1934, 22.

7   Daniel Burnham, Jr., business journal, March 28, 1935, Art Institute of Chicago Archives.

CHAPTER 4

1   Quote from campus publication provided by research librarian at Wabash College library, April 2008.

2   "In Memoriam," *Journal of the American Institute of Planners*, Summer 1951, 129.

3   "Kingery Resigns," *Chicago Daily Tribune*, August 9, 1936, 4.

4   "Superhighway to Milwaukee is nearly finished," *Chicago Daily Tribune*, November 15, 1936.

5   Chicago Regional Planning Association, "Chicago-Milwaukee 'Super-Highway' Nears Completion," press release, January 1937, NIPC papers, Chicago History Museum.

6   "Winnetka Grade Separation Job Half finished," *Chicago Daily Tribune*, August 3, 1939.

7   "Mayor to Press Move to Legalize Planning Board," *Chicago Daily Tribune*, April 10, 1939, 3.

8   "Planning for Chicago," *Chicago Daily Tribune*, April 19, 1939, 14.

9   "180 Appointed as New Chicago Plan Advisers," *Chicago Daily Tribune*, November 5, 1939, SW2; "Mayor Is Urged to Revise City Planning Board," *Chicago Daily Tribune*, October 16, 1939, 7.

10 Daniel Burnham, Jr., business journal, January 17, 1939, Art Institute of Chicago Archives. Burnham first appears on the roster of Plan Commission members in the 1926 annual report and is listed as serving on the executive committee beginning in 1931, 1932 and through 1933. (Copies of the Plan Commission annual reports are missing from 1934–1938 in the Chicago Municipal Reference Library.) Burnham was dropped from the executive committee in 1935, according to his journal entry on June 21, 1935.

11 Daniel Burnham, Jr., business journal, July 20. 1939, Art Institute of Chicago Archives.

12 "George Horton New Chairman of Plan Group," *Chicago Daily Tribune*, June 16, 1940, S4.

13 "Planes to Roar Off Last Year's Fertile Acres," *Chicago Daily Tribune*, September 20, 1942, NW1.

14 Richard P. Doherty, "The Origin and Development of Chicago-O'Hare International Airport" (doctoral dissertation, Ball State University, 1970); see also "Orchard Place/Douglas Field: Its Early History" at Bensenville Public Library. ohare.bensenville.lib.il.us/orchard.html.

15 Chicago Association of Commerce, *Airport Program for Chicago and the Region of Chicago*, 1941, Municipal Reference Library, Harold Washington Library Center, Chicago Public Library.

16 Chicago Plan Commission, "Proposed Expressway Development Program (Initial Stage) for the City of Chicago," December 1943, Municipal Reference Library, Harold Washington Library Center, Chicago Public Library.

17 Chicago Regional Planning Association, meeting minutes, January 15, 1937, 2, NIPC papers, Chicago History Museum.

18 Daniel Burnham, Jr., business journal, July 15, 1935, Art Institute of Chicago Archives.

19 Lyn Messner, interview by Joseph P. Schwieterman, July 3, 2008, La Canada, California.

20 Daniel Burnham, Jr., business journal, March 22, 1944, Art Institute of Chicago Archives.

21 "Name 7 Men to New Port District Board," *Chicago Daily Tribune*, August 30, 1951, C5.

22 Daniel Burnham, Jr., business journal, October 22, 1951, Art Institute of Chicago Archives.

23 "Board Names Tri-State Rd. for Kingery," *Chicago Daily Tribune*, July 8, 1953.

CHAPTER 5

1   William Whyte, *The Organization Man*, (New York: Simon & Schuster, 1956), 209.

2   Ibid, 210.

3   Ed DeRouin, "Land of the Burlingtons," *First Fastest* 23, vol. 1, (Spring 2007), 5.

4   Ibid.

5   Thomas Buck, "Motors Traffic Highways; Speed of Cars in Rush Hours Cut to 4 M.P.H. Need Improved Rapid Transit Transportation," *Chicago Daily Tribune*, Feb 17, 1957, 35.

6   Mark Solof, *History of Metropolitan Planning Organizations* (New Jersey Transportation Planning Authority, 1977), 13, njtpa.org/Pub/Report/hist_mpo/default.aspx (accessed on March 1, 2008).

7   "Chicago and its Suburbs," *Chicago Daily Tribune*, July 4, 1955, 18.

8   Metropolitan Housing Council, *Annual Report*, 1934–1937.

9   Metropolitan Housing Council, *Annual Report*, 1940.

10   Metropolitan Housing Council, *Annual Report*, 1946–1947.

11   Metropolitan Housing Council, *Annual Report*, 1943–1944.

12   Metropolitan Housing and Planning Council, "Facts on the Metropolitan Housing and Planning Council of Chicago: A Citizen Crusade to Rebuild a City," January 1961, Municipal Reference Collection, Harold Washington Library Center, Chicago Public Library.

13   Metropolitan Housing Council, *Annual Report*, 1948–1949.

14   Daniel Burnham, Jr., business journal, February 2, 1949, Art Institute of Chicago Archives. Note also that in the following year, Norm Elkin and Robert Merriam (son of University of Chicago professor Charles Merriam) taught a course sponsored by MPHC on the implications of strengthening regional government.

15   Metropolitan Housing and Planning Council of Chicago, untitled document, June 1950, Special Collections Library, University of Illinois at Chicago.

16   Andrew V. Plummer, "The Chicago Area Transportation Study: Creating the First Plan (1955–1962)," 11, surveyarchive.org/Chicago/cats_1954-62.pdf (accessed on November 1, 2008).

17   The four organizations founding the Chicago Area Transportation Study were the City of Chicago, Cook County, the Illinois Department of Highways, and the Federal Highway Administration.

18   Andrew V. Plummer, "Building the Cook County Expressways," 2005, cookexpressways.com/PostOffice1955.html (accessed on July 1, 2008).

19   President Dwight D. Eisenhower, February 22, 1955, fhwa.dot.gov/interstate/quotable.htm (accessed on October 1, 2008).

20   Solof, *History of Metropolitan Planning Organizations*, 13.

21   "Save the Suburbs from Blunders," *Chicago Daily Tribune*, July 12, 1957, 8.

22   *Metropolitan Area Planning for Northeastern Illinois and Northwestern Indiana: A Report of the Committee on Metropolitan Area Planning.* (Chicago: Metropolitan Housing and Planning Council, October 15, 1956).

23   Leverett S. Lyon, ed., *Governmental Problems in the Chicago Metropolitan Area: A Report of the Northeastern Illinois Metropolitan Area Local Governmental Services Commission*, (1957).

24   There was growing sentiment that the region needed an organization that could encourage—and coerce when necessary—communities to develop polices that were in the best interest of the region. At the Chicago Regional Planning Association's annual conference at the La Salle Hotel in late 1957, the testimony from village managers and up-and-coming attorney Jack Siegel suggested that the need for this was most acute in the area of flood control.

25   "Metropolitan Area Planning," *Chicago Daily Tribune*. April 1, 1955, 12.

26   Daniel Burnham, Jr., business journal, May 21, 1957, Art Institute of Chicago Archives. "It now looks like the bill has been killed," he noted in that entry.

27   The NIPC board was gradually expanded over the years to 25 and eventually to 35 members. The NIPC planning area consisted of six counties, including Cook County and five "collar counties" around Cook: DuPage, Lake, Kane, McHenry, and Will. A seventh, Kendall County, began undergoing rapid suburban growth in the 2000s and joined the CATS policy committee in 2005. Kendall will probably come into the jurisdiction of the new Regional Planning Board as well.

28   Daniel Burnham, Jr., business journal, April 24, 1957, Art Institute of Chicago Archives.

29   Daniel Burnham, Jr., business journal, May 21, 1957, Art Institute of Chicago Archives.

30   Daniel Burnham, Jr., business journal, May 1, 1958, Art Institute of Chicago Archives.

31   Northeastern Illinois Metropolitan Area Planning Commission, press release, October 24, 1958, NIPC archives, Chicago History Museum.

32   Daniel Burnham, Jr., business journal, June 18, 1959, Art Institute of Chicago Archives.

33   Jim Ford, "History, Organization," in *Fifty Years of Regional Planning by the Northeastern Illinois Planning Commission* (Chicago: Chicago Metropolitan Agency for Planning, 2008), 33.

34   Northeastern Illinois Metropolitan Area Planning Commission, proceedings, 1960, N.D.

35   Ibid.

CHAPTER 6

1   "Eager Motorists Jam New Skyway," *Chicago Daily News*, April 16, 1958, 1.

2   Hal Foust, "A Great Day for Chicago! Skyway Open," *Chicago Daily Tribune*, April 17, 1958, 1. According to the article, some drivers had waited in line for 24 hours to use the bridge.

3   "Calumet Skyway Opens," *Chicago Daily News*, April 16, 1958, 1.

4   Hal Foust, "New West Side CTA Route to Open Sunday: First Rides Saturday Free to Public," *Chicago Daily Tribune*, Jun 19, 1958, C.

5   Hal Foust, "Tours New Congress Stretch West; Freeway to Link with Tollway Friday," *Chicago Daily Tribune*, November 17, 1958, 6; Hal Foust, "East and West Tollway will Open Friday; Link Provides 35 Miles of Expressways," *Chicago Daily Tribune*, November 21, 1958, A5.

6   "1959: Boom Year for Suburbs," *Chicago Daily News*, December 29, 1958, 8.

7   Robert Moses, December 1956," fhwa.dot.gov/interstate/quotable.htm (accessed March 1, 2008).

8   "C.&N.W. Has '54 Net. Loss of 4 1/2 Million," *Chicago Daily Tribune*, January 29, 1955, B5; "2 Dissidents Nominated for C. & N. W. Rail Board," *Chicago Daily Tribune*, April 13, 1955, C9.

9   "North Western Orders 16 More Suburban Cars; Similar to 16 Others in Last 3 Months," *Chicago Daily Tribune*, June 24, 1955, 3.

10   "C&NW Goes Diesel! 40,000 Riders Happy; Mayor Waves Off Last Steam Locomotive," *Chicago Daily Tribune*, May 11, 1956, 3.

11   David M. Young, Joseph DiJohn, and Norman Carlson, "Chicago Transit's Periodic Financial Woes," *First and Fastest, a Special Edition*, (Autumn 2007), 10.

12   "O'Hare-Loop Freeway Open," *Chicago Daily News*, November 5, 1960. 1.

13   Advertisement in *Chicago Daily News*, November. 7, 1960, 8.

14   "Daniel Ryan, 66, is Dead," *Chicago Daily Tribune*, April 9, 1961, 1.

15   "Dan Ryan Death has Real Impact," *Chicago Daily News*, April 10, 1961, 1.

16   "Dan Ryan Would Love It," *Chicago Sun-Times*, December 15, 1962, 1.

17   Fletcher Wilson, "Will Ryan Expressway add to Loop Jam," *Chicago Sun-Times*, December 14, 1962.

18   Hal Foust, "Southwest Expressway Opens, Called a 'Marvel'," *Chicago Tribune*, October 25, 1964, 1.

19   "Kennedy Sets Two Talks on O'Hare Visit; Daley Shares Stage at Airport," *Chicago Tribune*, March 19, 1963. A8.

20   Ibid.

CHAPTER 7

1   Chicago Area Transportation Study, *Chicago Area Transportation Study: Final Report, vol. 3* (Chicago: Chicago Area Transportation Study, 1962), 7.

2   Gladys Priddy, "Our Daily Trips in Counted Transportation Study: Survey Counts Trips to Find How We Travel," Chicago Daily Tribune, September 6, 1956, W1.

3   Plummer, "The Chicago Area Transportation Study: Creating the First Plan," 13.

4   Ibid, 11.

5   John F. McDonald, "The First Chicago Area Transportation Study Projects and Plans for Metropolitan Chicago in Retrospect," *Planning Perspectives* 3 (1988), 250, 253.

6   Thomas Buck, "Motors Traffic Highways; Speed of Cars in Rush Hours Cut to 4 M.P.H. Need Improved Rapid Transit Transportation. *Chicago Daily Tribune*, February 17, 1957, 35.

7   Priddy, "Our Daily Trips," S8.

8   Ibid.

9   Plummer, "The Chicago Area Transportation Study," 22–24.

10   Ibid, 15.

11   Lee Mertz, "Memories of 499," fhwa.dot.gov/infrastructure/memories.htm (accessed on November 1, 2009).

12   Plummer, "The Chicago Area Transportation Study," 18.

13   Hal Foust, "Tell Details of Vast, Road, Transit Plan: Engineers Put Cost at $2.2 Billion, "*Chicago Daily Tribune*, September 7, 1962, B8.

14   Chicago Area Transportation Study, *Final Report* (vol. 3), 7.

15   These CATS-affiliated mayors councils are distinct from the independent councils of government, although their responsibilities are often assumed by the COGs. The same mayors sit on both councils.

16   Plummer, "The Chicago Area Transportation Study," 30.

17   "Daley Accused of Bottling Up Travel Study," *Chicago Daily Tribune*, August 16, 1962; B2.

18   Ibid.

19   "20 Year Program for Chicago," *Chicago Daily Tribune,* September 20, 1962, 20.

20   Ibid.

21   "Mayor Daley speech to American Transit Association, October, 1923" Document in Northeastern Illinois Planning Commission archive, Chicago History Museum, Chicago, Ill.

22   Plummer, "The Chicago Area Transportation Study" 31.

23   Nationalmaster.com. "Crosstown Expressway," nationmaster.com/encyclopedia/Crosstown-Expressway (Interstate-494) (accessed September 13, 2008).

24   McDonald, "The First Chicago Area Transportation Study Projects and Plans for Metropolitan Chicago in Retrospect," 245–68.

25   David Boyce, "A Silver Jubilee for Urban Transportation Planning," *Environment and Planning* 12 (1980), 267–8. David Boyce has written, "If asked to designate a founding year for the field of urban transportation planning, I would expect many to name 1956, the year in which the Chicago Area Transportation Study (CATS) conducted its initial surveys."

26   David Boyce, interview by Joseph P. Schwieterman, December 22, 2009.

27   A bicycle and pedestrian task force, a community mobility task force, and many others met over the years, advising the policy committee on their areas of special concern. The role of citizen groups was purely advisory, with voting power to approve plans and the distribution of funds remaining solely in the hands of the policy committee.

28   Carroll died in 1986.

29   Creighton served as director of the Upstate New York Transportation Studies, 1961-1964, and later worked for the New York State Department of Public Works. One of the principal studies he undertook immediately after leaving CATS was the Niagara Frontier Transportation Study of the Buffalo, N.Y., region.

30   Plummer, "The Chicago Area Transportation Study," 32.

CHAPTER 8

1   Alan R. Lind, *Chicago Surface Lines* (Park Forest, IL: Transport History Press, 1979); Bruce G. Moffat, *The "L": The Development of Chicago's Rapid Transit System, 1888-1932* (Chicago: Central Electric Railfans' Association, 1995), 235-240, 260-261.

2   David Young, "Transit's Fiscal Fiasco: Looking for a Way Out," *Mass Transit*, July 1981, 8; also Forrest McDonald, *Insull* (Chicago: University of Chicago Press, 1962), 156-157.

3   McDonald, *Insull*, 156-57.

4   "Officials Help Observe Start of "L" Transfers; Street Car Ride Opens the Day's Celebration," *Chicago Daily Tribune*, September 23, 1935, 18.

5   "Order L-Surface Riders' Transfer System Today; Action by Commission to End Long Fight," *Chicago Daily Tribune*, June 7, 1935, 5; "Surface Lines Will Fight "L" Transfer Order; Plan Court Action to Block Ruling," *Chicago Daily Tribune*, June 8, 1935, 15.

6   "Joint Transfers Used at Rate of 25,000,000 a Year; Reports Show Steady Gain in Popularity," *Chicago Daily Tribune*, October 23, 1935, 10.

7   "'L' and Bus Lines Begin Swapping their Transfers," *Chicago Daily Tribune*, January 19, 1936. 5.

8   David Young, *Chicago Transit: An Illustrated History* (De Kalb: Northern Illinois University Press, 1998), 107-108.

9   Joseph A. Tecson, "The Regional Transportation Authority in Northeastern Illinois," *Chicago Bar Record*, Part 1, (May-June 1975; Part 2, July-August 1975), 7. Republished by the Regional Transportation Authority. rtachicago.com/aboutrta/history.asp (accessed October 1, 2008).

10   The idea of public ownership was a delicate matter, with investors challenging the sale price over several months in court. Through early 1945, Judge Igoe kept the private-ownership option on the table (and in fact favored it) in case public ownership did not work out.

11   George Krambles and Arthur H. Peterson, *CTA at 45* (Oak Park, IL: George Krambles Transit Scholarship Fund, 1993), 9, 30-35.

12   Cafferty's widow Pastora shared his interest in transit, and would subsequently serve on the Regional Transportation Authority's board during the 1970s, and again in the 1980s and 90s.

13   Constitution of the State of Illinois, Article XIII, General Provisions, Section 7.

14   George A. Ranney, Jr., interview by John Allen, September 14, 1993.

15   *Crisis and Solution: Public Transportation in Northeastern Illinois*. Report by the Governor's Transportation Task Force, January 1973, 83.

16   Tecson, "The Regional Transportation Authority in Northeastern Illinois," 13-18 .

17   Tom Buck, "Ogilvie task force reports; Chicago area transit needs $80-million subsidy," *Chicago Tribune*, January 6, 1973, 4.

18   Neil Mehler, "Regional unit pushed; Republicans in a corner on transit," *Chicago Tribune*, February 19, 1973, A12; Neil Mehler, "Hearing Saturday; Mayor to be first transit study witness," *Chicago Tribune*, April 3, 1973, 3; Edward Schreiber, "Daley pledges his help on transit bill," *Chicago Tribune*, June 29, 1973, 2.

19   "Blair's doublecross on RTA," *Chicago Tribune*, October 25, 1973, 20.

20   Ibid.

21   Alan Merridew, "Jackson hits black opposition to Daley," *Chicago Tribune*, March 21, 1974, 8.

22   Thomas Buck, "Rails Push 6-County Transit Unit," *Chicago Tribune*, July 11, 1972, B6.

23   Jack Houston, "Planner Attacks Planning," *Chicago Tribune*, December 13, 1970, S6.

24   "Everyone needs RTA," *Chicago Daily News*, March 18, 1974, C1.

25   Siim Sööt, James Kartheiser and Steven Wojtkiewicz, "The Chicago Area Regional Transportation Authority Referendum: Analysis of the Voter Support Demand Implications," *Traffic Quarterly*, July 1976, 341.

26   Edith Herman and David Gilbert, "Plan for Seceding from RTA is Told," *Chicago Tribune*, March 22, 1974, B15

27   "Brutus (Blair) stabs RTA," *Chicago Tribune*, April 20, 1974, S14.

28   Neil Mehler, "Argument on ERA; Stop RTA changes, group urges G.O.P.," *Chicago Tribune*, April 21, 1974, 24.

29   David Gilbert, "Blair RTA plan beaten in House," *Chicago Tribune*, May 30, 1974, 4.

30   Anton Tedesko, "Milton Pikarsky, 1924-1989," in *Memorial Tributes* vol. 4 (Washington, DC: National Academy of Engineering, 1991), 286-287.

31   Brian J. Cudahy, "The Universal Transfer: Getting Around the Chicago Area," *Transit Journal*, Summer 1977; David Young, "The Rock Island: Back From the Brink," *Mass Transit*, November 1978.

32   George A. Ranney, Jr., interview by John Allen, September 14, 1993.

33   Ian Savage, "Management objectives and the causes of mass transit deficits," *Transport Research Part A* 38 (March 2004), 81-99.

34   Pikarsky was by then already a figurehead, having earned suburban ire in various ways, including his going back on a promise to buy the ailing

Waukegan-North Bus Company after just a few months in office. This was in 1976, when the suburban members held up budget approval until Pikarsky was deprived of authority. This time they again refused budget approval.

35   David Young and Stanley Ziemba, "RTA chief had to quit—or be fired," *Chicago Tribune*, August 7, 1978, C1; David Young, "Pikarsky's successor; New RTA chief vows not to 'disown' Chicago," *Chicago Tribune*, August 16, 1978, A8.

36   Research by Ian Savage at Northwestern University shows that upwards of a third of the CTA's cost escalation during this period was attributable to higher wages and benefits and less demanding scheduling for its employers. See Savage (2004).

37   David Young, "Fares, Riders: Ups and Downs," *Mass Transit*, June 1983; Kenneth Cypra, "A Fare Demonstration in a Chicago Transit Corridor," RTA memorandum.

38   David Young, "Tired of RTA, private citizens run their own public transit," *Chicago Tribune*, August 2, 1982, 1; Nina C. Gitz, *Another Way to Go?* (Chicago: Metropolitan Housing and Planning Council, August 1982), 1 - 10; and Joseph P. Schwieterman, *Competition in Mass Transit: A Case Study of the Chicago Subscription Bus Phenomenon* (Evanston, IL: Northwestern University, Transportation Center, November 1983).

39   These ideas were generated by a transportation committee that included such notables as George A. Ranney, Jr. , former RTA board member Pastora Cafferty, and former RTA chairman Pikarsky. Instead of ascribing his downfall to his opponents, Pikarsky analyzed what had gone wrong and argued that what he identified as diseconomies of scale were intrinsic to large centralized transit authorities. He believed that the public might benefit if the RTA was replaced by smaller, more accountable units with more private sector participation.

40   Philip Lentz, "Plan to decentralize RTA wins Senate OK," *Chicago Tribune*, May 27, 1982. This bill competed with another bill supported by the Chicago Association of Commerce and Industry, and neither was enacted.

41   Julie Hamos, "Simplifying transit," Letters to the Editor, *Chicago Sun-Times*, November 12, 2001, 32; Julie Hamos, "Too many weak links in RTA transit plan," letter, *Chicago Sun-Times*, January 13, 2004, 32.

42   "Is The 1983 Transit Funding Formula Ready For Reform?" Initial Report to the Illinois House Committee on Mass Transit, April 13, 2005.

43   In February 2007, the state's auditor general found not only funding but also managerial inadequacies, which helped to diffuse tensions between those who said the CTA needed more money and those who said it needed better management. See William G. Holland, *Performance Audit, Mass Transit Agencies of Northeastern Illinois: RTA, CTA, Metra, and Pace*, Volume II (Springfield and Chicago: State of Illinois, Office of the Auditor General, March 2007).

CHAPTER 9

1   Betty J. Blim, interview by Matthew Laflin Rockwell, Art Institute of Chicago, 1983, artic.edu/aic/libraries/research/specialcollections/oralhistories/rockwell.html (accessed January 20, 2008).

2   John Baird, interview by Joseph P. Schwieterman and Joe Kearney, May 2007. Kearney is co-author of this portion of Chapter 9.

3   "Planners Name Urban Progress Committee; Leaders to Study Needs Cited in Tribune Series," *Chicago Tribune*. November 17, 1963,16.

4   Paul Oppermann, memo to Matthew Rockwell, dated November 22, 1963, NIPC papers, Chicago History Museum. The letter notes: "While you were gone, MHPC announced a new temporary organization known as the Council on Urban Progress [sic]. Newspaper reports indicated that they were going to inquire into Metropolitan Planning progress. This irritated Davis [Chester Davis, NIPC board president] who called to tell me this. He asked me to find out more about it, particularly through John Baird."

5   For a discussion of this issue, see Matthew Rockwell, "Speech given on April 15, 1964, Elk Grove Village, by Matthew L. Rockwell" Elk Grove Village, available in NIPC papers, Chicago History Museum, 1–7.

6   Committee on Urban Progress, *A Pattern for Greater Chicago*, July 1, 1965. Copy available in Illinois State University library.

7   "Urban Government Plan to be Discussed at N.U.," *Chicago Tribune*, December 12, 1965, W6.

8   Committee on Urban Progress, *A Pattern for Greater Chicago*, 5.

9   "Suburban Query Urban Plan," *Chicago Tribune*, September 5, 1965, NW1.

10   "Pay Close Attention at NIPC Hearing," *Hinsdale Doings*, October 7, 1965.

11   This scheme was formally called the Dispersed Regional City Composite Design.

12   Lawrence Christmas, "Comprehensive and Land Use Planning," in *Fifty Years of Regional Planning by the Northeastern Illinois Planning Commission* (Chicago: Chicago Metropolitan Agency for Planning, 2008), 165.

13   Robert L. Dishon, "3 Plans for Chicago's Future," *Chicago Daily News*, December 10, 1966, 1.

14   Lawrence Christmas, "Comprehensive and Land Use Planning," 165; and Robert Ducharme, "Housing Planning Program," in *Fifty Years of*

Regional Planning by the Northeastern Illinois Planning Commission (Chicago: Chicago Metropolitan Agency for Planning, 2008), 274–376.

15   Lawrence Christmas, interview by Joseph P. Schwieterman and Alan Mammoser, December 2008.

16   Lorenz W. Aggens, "Public Participation Program," in *Fifty Years of Regional Planning by the Northeastern Illinois Planning Commission* (Chicago: Chicago Metropolitan Agency for Planning, 2008), 80–84.

17   For an excellent discussion of the preparations for the Choice Train, see Aggens, "Public Participation Program," 81–83.

18   Matthew Rockwell, letter to Reuben Borsch, October 1, 1965, NIPC papers, Chicago History Museum.

CHAPTER 10

1   George Tagge, "G.O.P.'s Hopes Lie in Suburb Victory Punch," *Chicago Tribune*, November 3, 1958, 1.

2   Obituary of Eileen Sullivan McIntosh, *Chicago Tribune*, May 17, 1998, 124.

3   Eileen (McIntosh) Schaldenbrand, interview by Joseph P. Schwieterman and Joe Kearney, August 15, 2007.

4   Obituary of Adeline Dropka, *Chicago Tribune*, December 19, 2003, 22.

5   Alan Merridew, "Metropolitan Government Foes Fear Erosion of People's Rights," *Chicago Tribune*, February 5, 1976, W2.

6   Aggens, "Public Participation Program," 92.

7   Ibid, 88.

8   Ibid, 89.

9   Ibid, 88.

10   Ibid, 93.

11   "Anti-Plan Hecklers Force Meetings to End," *Chicago Tribune*, October 9, 1966, O5.

12   Ibid.

13   Dishon, "3 Plans for Chicago's Future," 1.

14   Lawrence Christmas, interview by Joseph P. Schwieterman and Alan Mammoser, December 2008.

15   The testing showed that the Finger Design's accessibility measures were comparable to the other scenarios in the inner urban core and, in some cases, better in the region's intermediate and outer areas.

16   Northeastern Illinois Planning Commission, *Diversity Within Order*, 1968, 91-93.

17   Planners also had concerns about the Finger Design. For example, its intensive development in the rail corridors would threaten high-value natural lands within these corridors. Regional planning often encounters such trade-offs.

18   Northeastern Illinois Planning Commission, *Annual Report*, 1967, 3.

19   Jim Ford, "History, Organization", in *Fifty Years of Regional Planning by the Northeastern Illinois Planning Commission* (Chicago: Chicago Metropolitan Agency for Planning, 2008), 38.

20   Northeastern Illinois Planning Commission, *Annual Report*, 1967, 3.

21   Michael Kilian, "NIPC Appointment Brings Sharp Remarks," *Chicago Tribune*, March 30, 1967, E11.

22   Thomas Buck, "Ogilvie Urges Panel of Local Governments," *Chicago Tribune*, June 29, 1967, A16.

23   "Group to Consider Regional Problems," *Chicago Tribune*, September 14, 1967, H1.

24   "NIPC to Consider Finger Plan," *Chicago Tribune*, March 17, 1968, N9, S11.

25   The full name of the plan was the Comprehensive General Plan for the Development of the Northeastern Illinois Counties.

26   Robert Ducharme, "Introduction," in *Fifty Years of Regional Planning by the Northeastern Illinois Planning Commission* (Chicago: Chicago Metropolitan Agency for Planning, 2008), 9.

27   John Paige, "Local Planning Assistance," in *Fifty Years of Regional Planning by the Northeastern Illinois Planning Commission* (Chicago: Chicago Metropolitan Agency for Planning, 2008), 52.

28   Rockwell uses these terms in a several documents appearing in the NIPC archives at the Chicago History Museum.

29   Barbara Amazaki, "Northeast Planning Commission Meets to Review Goals, Policies," *Chicago Tribune*, October 13, 1968, n.p.

30 Ibid.

31 Mark Solof, *History of Regional Planning Organizations*, 16

32 Christmas, "Comprehensive and Land Use Planning," 171–75

33 Ibid.

34 Ibid.

35 Lawrence Christmas, interview by Alan Mammoser and Joseph P. Schwieterman, December 2008.

36 Northeastern Illinois Planning Commission, *Annual Report*, 1970, 2.

37 Frank Maier, "Con-Con Delegates decide to oversee ruling drafting," *Chicago Daily News*, December 9, 1969, p. 1.

38 Commission on Urban Area Government, *Legislative Recommendations for Structural Modernization of Local Government*, January 1971.

39 Governor's Task Force on Regionalization, *A Regionalization Program for Illinois*, (Springfield, IL: Governor's Task for on Regionalization, January 7, 1971).

40 Norman Elkin, interview by Joseph P. Schwieterman, May 12, 2007. Elkin served as executive director of CUAG.

41 Ford, "History, Organization", 39.

42 Rockwell did succeed in passing legislation that gave NIPC the ability to borrow against expected revenues. See 77th *General Assembly Transcripts*, May 16, 1972, 21.

43 Ford, "History, Organization," 36.

44 For a discussion of this, see Lawrence Christmas, "Comprehensive and Land Use Planning," 165.

45 John McCarron, "Area Plan Agency in Fund Crises Too," *Chicago Tribune*, June 3, 1981, 15.

46 Du Page Mayors and Managers Conference, correspondence to Governor James Thompson, September 9, 1977, MPC Archives, University of Illinois-Chicago Library.

47 Illinois General Assembly, *Report on Joint Committee on Regional Government, Submitted to the Illinois General Assembly and Governor James R. Thompson, February 1979* (Springfield: Illinois General Assembly, 1979), 16.

48 Matthew Rockwell, "NIPC's Development Pays Off—For All But NIPC." *Chicago Tribune*, June 21, 1979, B2.

49 In 1972, it published a 71-page booklet, *USA or USSA*, calling for citizens to recognize the need to choose between the United States and the "United Socialist States of America." See *USA or USSA*, Save our Suburbs, Winnetka, 1972.

CHAPTER 11

1 Metropolitan Housing and Planning Council, untitled memo, July 31, 1979, detailing NIPC executive director search, MPC Archives, University of Illinois-Chicago Library.

2 Ibid.

3 Harold Henderson, "Cityscape: Who Planned this Mess," *Chicago Reader*, March 12, 1993, 1.

4 Lawrence Christmas, interview by Joseph P. Schwieterman and Alan Mammoser, December 2008.

5 McCarron, "Area plan agency in fund crises too," *Chicago Tribune*, 15.

6 James Kane, "Watchdog Lacks Bite, but Still Can Bark," *Chicago Tribune*, January 19, 1983, NW6.

7 "NIPC Alters Land Use Plan to Match Others," *Chicago Tribune*, September 16, 1982, B3.

8 James Kane, "Lake County, BACOG Rip Land Policy," *Chicago Tribune*, November 12, 1982, NW1.

9 Robert Ducharme, "Introduction," *Fifty Years of Regional Planning by the Northeastern Illinois Planning Commission* (Chicago: Chicago Metropolitan Agency for Planning, 2008), 7.

10 Kane, "Watchdog Lacks Bite, but Still Can Bark," NW6.

11 "The Region's Own Watchdog." *Chicago Tribune*, February 23, 1983, 18

12 Ducharme, "Introduction," 7.

13 *1984 Regional Land Use Plan.* Northeastern Illinois Planning Commission, 1984, C1.

14   Northeastern Illinois Planning Commission, *Fifty Years of Regional Planning by the Northeastern Illinois Planning Commission* (Chicago: Chicago Metropolitan Agency for Planning, 2008), viii.

15   Blair Kamin, "NIPC Seeks to Improve Its Funding," *Chicago Tribune*, May 11, 1989, 2.

16   Christmas, "Comprehensive and Land Use Planning," 22.

17   To raise awareness of the issue, NIPC touted its finding that, while the region saw a mere 4 percent population increase between 1970 and 1990, its developed land expanded by some 35 percent. The estimate on land development was believed to be in the 35 percent to 45 percent range

18   Henderson, "Cityscape: Who Planned this Mess," 1–5.

19   Ibid.

20   For example, the Report from the Blue Ribbon Panel on Intergovernmental Agreements and its legislative recommendations came out of the *Strategic Plan for Land Resource Management*.

21   Henderson, "Cityscape: Who Planned this Mess," 1–5.

22   Ray Quintanilla, "NIPC Looking to its Own Future with Leader Exiting, Agency at Crossroads," *Chicago Tribune*, December 9, 1998, 6.

23   The impact of the NIPC plan was felt most acutely in the development of the 2030 Regional Transportation Plan. Nevertheless, CATS opted not to use to use the newly created corridors map, preferring instead to use the travel corridors identified in the 2030 Regional Transportation Plan. This map appears in Chapter 4 of the plan document.

24   The agencies followed this agreement with a prospectus that laid out their timeline for planning, determining that a NIPC land-use plan would be in place to "guide" an update of the RTP in 2006. The document was called *Prospectus for Implementation*.

CHAPTER 12

1   Commercial Club of Chicago, *Together for Our City* (Chicago: Community Club of Chicago, 1996): 19.

2   Ibid.

3   "A Working Paper on the Future of Illinois," in *Task Force on the Future of Illinois*, 1979, Municipal Reference Collection, Harold Washington Library Center, Chicago Public Library.

4   Commercial Club of Chicago, *Jobs for Metropolitan Chicago* (Chicago: Commercial Club, 1983).

5   *The Wall Street Journal* called Chicago the "Beirut on the Lake" in the 1980s. Bennett made his comment in 1988.

6   Saskia Sassin, *The Global City* (Princeton, NJ: Princeton University Press, 2001).

7   Lois Willie, *At Home in the Loop: How Clout and Community Built Chicago's Dearborn Park* (Carbondale: Southern Illinois University Press, 1997).

8   John McCarron, "Report Sees Crises on the Horizon for Chicago Area," *Chicago Tribune*, January 25, 1987, 3.

9   Ibid.

10   George C. Hemmens and Janet McBride, "Planning and Development Decision Making in the Chicago Region," in *Metropolitan Governance Revisited: American/Canadian Intergovernmental Perspectives*, Donald Rothblatt and Andrew Sancton, ed (Berkeley, CA: Institute of Governmental Studies Press, 1998).

11   Metropolitan Planning Council, *Creating a Regional Community: The Case for Regional Cooperation*, (Chicago: Metropolitan Planning Council, 1995).

12   David Roeder, "Lawyer who led charge for Plan of Chicago dies," *Chicago Sun-Times*, February 20, 2008, 35.

13   Elmer Johnson, *Chicago Metropolis 2020: The Chicago Plan for the 21st Century* (Chicago: University of Chicago Press, 2001), xx.

14   David Roeder, "Tall Order for the Future," *Chicago Sun-Times*, March 2, 1999, 38.

15   This comment was based on an early draft released to the *Sun-Times* in November 2008. See David Roeder, "A Clumsy Approach to Regional Planning," *Chicago Sun-Times*, November 25, 1998, 70.

16   Ray Quintanilla, "NIPC Looking to its Own Future with Leader Exiting, Agency at Crossroads," *Chicago Tribune*, December 9, 1998, 6.

17   Gary Washburn and Ray Quintanilla, "Broad Civic 'Blueprint' Targets Sprawl, Education," *Chicago Tribune*, November 20, 1998, 1.

18   George A. Ranney, Jr., Interview by Joseph Schwieterman and Alan Mammoser, November 2008.

19 In 1998, with MacArthur's support, Myron Orfield worked to build support for the idea that metropolitan Chicago should develop systems to share property tax revenues.

20 Adele Simmons, interview by Joseph P. Schwieterman, December 2008.

21 The Illinois Affordable Housing Planning & Appeal Act, passed in 2003, requires communities to adopt housing plans to guide them toward creating homes affordable to those in low- and middle-income ranges.

22 The task force members, twenty-two in all, were appointed by the governor, the legislature, metropolitan mayors groups and the regional planning agencies. Just eleven members, those appointed by the governor and legislators, had the right to vote on the panel's resolutions (the other eleven were "nonvoting members"). Appointments of voting members followed party lines with the Democrats in control. The Democratic governor appointed Lipinski and two additional members. Four members came from the state assembly majority leadership and four from the minority leadership.

23 Northeastern Illinois Planning Commission, meeting minutes, June 26, 2004, NIPC papers, Chicago History Museum.

24 In addition to these fifteen, the CATS policy committee and the NIPC board each appoint one of their members to serve as non-voting members of the RPB.

25 David Roeder, "Lawyer Who Led Charge for Plan of Chicago Dies," *Chicago Sun-Times*, 35.

CHAPTER 13

1   Although each was on unincorporated land, the city would likely have been unable to bring these sites within its boundaries due to state law that precluded annexing noncontiguous land.

2   "Daley Dumps Airport: Mayor Says Lake Calumet Plan Dead; Foes Doubt," *Chicago Sun-Times*, July 2, 1992, 1.

3   Brad Webber, "O'Hare Suburbs Push NIPC on 'Neutrality'"; Commission Accused of Veiled Growth Bias," Chicago Tribune, November 5, 1998, 1.

4   Ibid.

5   Nonetheless, American's and United's support remained lukewarm. As many O'Hare expansion advocates rallied in the late 1990s to support the mayor's plans for a major redesign of that airport's terminal facilities (called "World Gateway"), these two airlines quietly voiced skepticism caused by fears of escalating costs.

6   There was an underlying weakness in the pro-Peotone coalition: the continuing distrust between the south-suburban faction and the SOC faction. South-suburban communities insisted that the municipalities affiliated with SOC, Bensenville, and Elk Grove Village, eventually withdraw from the consortium if the Peotone airport was built.

7   David Young, *Chicago Aviation: An Illustrated History* (DeKalb: Northern Illinois University Press, 2003), 214.

CHAPTER 14

1   Robert D. Yaro and Tony Hiss. "A Region at Risk: The Third Regional Plan For The New York-New Jersey-Connecticut Metropolitan Area." (Washington, D.C., Island press, 1996).

2   Coordinating land-use and transportation planning is a considerable challenge. Land-use concerns places and deals with what planners call "accessibility," requiring a careful positioning of features within places, in arrangements that result in the kinds of communities that people prefer. Long-range transportation planning concerns the connection of places to one another; it deals with what planners call "mobility". The two are not easily combined in a regional plan covering a large area. This is especially so when separate agencies are making regional land-use plans and regional transportation plans.

3   Richard Wronski, "Regional Board's 1st Boss is Veteran Planner from IDOT," *Chicago Tribune*, April 13, 2006, 6.

4   Among the most notable examples of this are Nashville, Tennessee, Salt Lake City, Utah, and Dade County in Florida.

5   In the 1970s, the Oregon governor laid the legislative groundwork that invited vigorous citizen-group advocacy on behalf of comprehensive planning. Since then, the high-profile group 1000 Friends of Oregon has deployed "big stick" enforcement by using legal action to force towns and counties to complete their comprehensive plans in coordination with broader regional plans.

INDEX